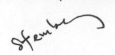

SYMBOLIC FUNCTIONING
IN CHILDHOOD

CHILD PSYCHOLOGY

A series of volumes edited by **David S. Palermo**

SYMBOLIC FUNCTIONING IN CHILDHOOD

edited by

NANCY R. SMITH
Boston University

MARGERY B. FRANKLIN
Sarah Lawrence College

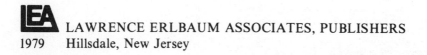 LAWRENCE ERLBAUM ASSOCIATES, PUBLISHERS
1979   Hillsdale, New Jersey

DISTRIBUTED BY THE HALSTED PRESS DIVISION OF
JOHN WILEY & SONS
New York   Toronto   London   Sydney

Lawrence Erlbaum Associates, Inc., Publishers
365 Broadway
Hillsdale, New Jersey 07642

Distributed solely by Halsted Press Division
John Wiley & Sons, Inc., New York

Library of Congress Cataloging in Publication Data

Main entry under title:

Symbolic functioning in childhood.

(Child psychology)
"Papers... originally presented at a conference,
'Symbolization and the Young Child,' held at Wheelock
College in October, 1975."
Includes bibliographies and indexes.
1. Symbolism (Psychology) in children—Congresses.
I. Smith, Nancy R.   II. Franklin, Margery B.
III. Series.
BF723.S94S9   155.4'13   79-17640
ISBN 0-470-26822-0

Printed in the United States of America

Contents

Preface

This volume presents current work of investigators involved in studying symbolic processes from a developmental perspective. It is intended to provide a selective view of the "state of the art" in a new and rapidly growing field, and to further the development of this specialized area of inquiry, which until recently has not laid claim to a distinctive identity.

In recent years, there has been a marked upsurge of interest in the study of symbolic phenomena—not only within psychology but in anthropology and philosophy, psychiatry and education. It would be difficult to trace the diverse sources of this interest and equally difficult, if challenging, to explicate relations among conceptualizations in different disciplines. That is beyond our present task, but a few remarks will elucidate the nature of the undertaking. Symbolic anthropologists have developed interpretations of cultural forms that have clear bearing on the psychological study of symbolization. Philosophers, particularly those concerned with aesthetics, have put forth schemes intended to encompass a range of symbolizing activity to display relations among different forms. Semioticians are concerned with developing conceptualizations that span disciplinary boundaries, interpreting symbolization in terms of a signification paradigm. Contemporary psychiatry draws on several different kinds of theoretical formulations in its probing discussions of symbolic phenomena. Transcending the wide-ranging and deep diversity of viewpoints and aims, there appears to be fundamental agreement that symbolizing processes—in one form or another—play a central role in myriad aspects of human functioning and in the development of a distinctively human consciousness. Thus, for scholars in many disciplines, the investigation of symbolic processes has become a primary concern. It can be argued that the study of the origins and development of symbolic functioning in childhood is central to all these inquiries.

The present volume is divided into four parts. The papers in the first section, *Nature and Determinants of Symbolic Functioning,* are concerned in part with basic questions of conceptualizing symbolic functioning and in part with specific symbolizing activities considered developmentally. In the second part, *Play, Gesture, and Graphic Representation,* fundamental issues are approached through inquiry into the ways in which tangible materials are structured and transformed in non-verbal symbolizing activity. The papers in the third section, *Language,* focus on aspects of symbolic functioning in the verbal domain—the child's early use of referential terms, and questions of relations among speaker, language, and context. The concluding section, *Symbolism and the Mythic World,* consists of a paper concerned with the classic question of how disparate domains are spanned in the process of symbolizing, in adults as well as children.

The papers in this volume are among those originally presented at a conference, "Symbolization and the Young Child," held at Wheelock College in October, 1975. Important contributions were made by conference presenters whose papers could not be included in the present volume: Judy Burton, Massachusetts College of Art; Courtney Cazden, Harvard University; Harriet Cuffaro, Bank Street College of Education; Sylvia Farnham-Diggory, University of Delaware; Dorothy Gross, Bank Street College of Education; Susan Kosoff, Wheelock College; Ilse Mattick, Wheelock College; Frances Minor, New York University; Florence Rossman, Wheelock College; Virginia Stern, Bank Street College of Education; Evelyn Weber, Wheelock College.

The conference was planned by Margery B. Franklin, Sarah Lawrence College; Susan Kosoff, Elizabeth Ann Liddle, Florence Rossman, Wheelock College; and Nancy R. Smith, Boston University. The editors of this volume take this occasion to acknowledge their appreciation of the contributions made by other members of the planning group and, in particular, the extremely thoughtful work of Elizabeth Ann Liddle, assisted by Sharon Bourke and Robin Beck. The conference was explicitly designed to provide an interchange of ideas among psychologists and educators concerned with various aspects of symbolization in childhood, and so to contribute to the development and dissemination of ideas in this field. We hope that the present volume will further contribute to the realization of this aim.

Nancy R. Smith

Margery B. Franklin

SYMBOLIC FUNCTIONING
IN CHILDHOOD

Introduction

Nancy R. Smith
School of Visual Arts, Boston University

Margery B. Franklin
Sarah Lawrence College

The papers in this volume reveal a range of approaches to the study of symbolic processes in childhood. The reader will discern that although contributors to this volume differ among themselves in specific areas of interest and to some degree in theoretical orientation, there is a certain family unity among them. Without attempting to identify this too closely, we would point out the common commitment to a developmental point of view and a shared conviction about the importance of symbolic processes in psychological functioning.

It must be recognized that symbolic functioning is not often delineated as a special field of inquiry within psychology, and that there is only a small literature directly addressed to psychological questions of symbolization. Now, the tide seems to be turning. In psychology, as in related disciplines, an increasing number of investigators are studying symbolic functioning and/or interpreting their previous works in such terms. Within developmental psychology, Bruner (Bruner, Olver, & Greenfield, 1969), Piaget (1951), and Werner and Kaplan (1963) have contributed most significantly to the current focus on representational-symbolic functioning. Werner and Kaplan, in particular, articulate the view that symbolization does not merely enter into the expression and communication of psychological content but plays a prime role in its formation. This general theoretical orientation informs many of the contributions to this volume; it will be seen that some contributors also draw on other major theoretical formulations—psychoanalytic conceptualizations and information theory.

The four papers in Part One, *Nature and Determinants of Symbolic Functioning*, address questions concerning basic processes and structures of

1

representational thinking and symbol formation. To some extent, these presentations use differing conceptual models and reflect different views of symbolizing. Nonetheless, it is clear that the authors share a developmental orientation, a focus on relations between a symbol's "external form" (or figurative aspect) and its "meaning"—and an interest in understanding the specific role of symbolizing in mental functioning.

In the first paper, "Developmental Origins of Structural Variation in Symbol Form," Smith proposes a model of structure and dynamics for all symbolic forms based on the developmental-organismic theory of Werner and Kaplan. The elements of signifier and referent are seen in interdependent relation to each other, and in a variety of structures which make possible a wide range of meaning relations. It appears that the foundations of these structures are established in early childhood through the perception of expressive properties or expressive attributes in the material form of both symbol and referent. Meanings are originally created by associations based on expressive properties. Such flexible links make possible the clustering of meanings around any one signifier. Another phenomenon of symbol structure is that of the layering or "stacking" of signifiers one upon the other. Within a complex symbol, each level of meaning is linked to a separate identifiable signifier. The whole symbol is conceptualized as a "stack" of signifiers with meanings fitted at each level. Symbols thus exhibit such nonlinear characteristics as multireferentiality and variation in referential connotation, and they may be linked in compound forms. This conceptualization of structure makes possible an analysis which aims at sytematization while remaining sensitive to the fundamentally flexible nature of the symbolic function.

The next paper, "The Affective Context and Psychodynamics of First Symbolization," is concerned with the emergence of symbolization in the context of the early mother-child relationship. Suggesting that the establishment of separate mental representations of self and other is essential for genuine symbolic functioning, Drucker draws on both psychoanalytic and cognitive theory to explore the conditions requisite for such representation and to identify the precursors of true symbols. In her discussion of the separation-individuation process, Drucker considers aspects of the young child's understanding of objects and events, his response to adults, and his play activities, in relation to the affective components of the mother-child interaction. She proposes that symbolization can be conceptualized in terms of two aspects or part processes—one having to do with the transmission of meaning, the re-presentation of content in new forms, and the other with a more primitive process of imbuing some aspect of experience with subjective "meaning." Calling the latter process "endowing," Drucker shows how this originates in the context of the early mother-infant relationship and how it is manifested in the infant's relation to objects. The formation of "transitional objects" exemplifies the process of endowing in which the affect of the mother-child relationship becomes invested in the object. In her discussion, Drucker provides an integrative formulation that draws on concepts of progressive differentiation in Werner and Kaplan, of object permanence and schemata in Piaget, and psychoanalytic conceptualizations.

In "Mundane Symbolism: The Relations among Objects, Names and Ideas," Potter examines the question of how symbols function in thought and memory. She is concerned with elucidating the contrast between two theories of mental representation in relation to symbol-recognition, and with examining implications for other aspects of symbolic functioning. The dual coding theory of mental representation posits separate systems for verbal and pictorial knowledge; in symbol-recognition, the stimulus (word or picture) evokes a medium specific representation (lexical entry *or* image) that is linked, through previous learning, to its counterpart. According to the conceptual coding model, recognition of words or pictures involves a route through medium-specific "way stations" to a conceptual system, in which knowledge is stored in abstract, amodal form. In this paper, Potter critically examines a wide range of experimental evidence bearing on each of these theories, and discusses her own recent research which was designed explicitly to investigate alternative implications of dual-coding theory and conceptual representation theory. Finally, Potter proposes that development of the ability to recognize pictures and words evolves from the child's ability to recognize and understand real objects, and suggests that perceptual recognition of objects is itself a form of symbolization since it involves abstraction away from the flux of sensory experience and reference to some type of conceptual representation.

"The Concept of Décalàge as It Applies to Representational Thinking," by Cocking and Sigel, centers on questions of interactions between forms of representation and operational level. It is proposed that the occurrence of horizontal décalàge may be related to variations in underlying representation; that is, temporal discrepancies in the application of operations to different situations may be due, in part, to the way in which the child mentally represents the task or situation. In order to investigate the way in which forms of representation (i.e., types of figurative knowledge) enter into problem solving, Cocking and Sigel tested preschool children on a range of tasks; these included tasks involving kinetic anticipatory imagery, static reproductive imagery, conservation of continuous quantity, specific aspects of language production and comprehension. They were particularly interested in distinguishing problem solutions (correct or otherwise) based on analogous versus homologous thinking. The tasks required operational thinking for correct solution. By testing preoperational children, Cocking and Sigel were able to examine the types of errors made and to use this analysis as a means of gaining insight into underlying structures and strategies. Their discussion is framed by consideration of a discrepancy model of development.

In Part II, *Play, Gesture and Graphic Representation*, various nonverbal modes of symbolization are discussed. The first three papers present research on young children's play and raise questions about the role of play in relation to developing cognitive abilities. The fourth paper proposes a taxonomy of forms of symbolic gesture and reports research on the child's development of mastery in this medium. Finally, the last paper in this section discusses the competencies required to copy graphic configurations.

In the first paper, "Some Preliminary Observations on Knowing and Pretending," Fein and Apfel report a longitudinal study in which significant shifts were observed in children's pretend feeding behaviors. A majority of the younger children (12 months) choose to pretend feed themselves with a spoon, while older children (18 months and above) choose to pretend feed a doll with a bottle. The children's choices were clearly purposeful and apparently not based on imitation of their own behavior, since the younger children select a bottle for pretend feeding less frequently than do the older children. An important factor to be taken into consideration is the increased "distance" between the symbolizer and the symbol indicated by the use of a doll, rather than the self, as recipient of the play action. Fein and Apfel suggest that the preferred form of pretending at each age indicates the frontier of the child's efforts for mastery. For the younger child, feeding the self with a spoon is an activity which has yet to be mastered. For the older child, feeding the doll is a rehearsal of the social roles of mother and child. In both instances, what is being played at is a developmentally salient issue. Interestingly, Fein and Apfel report that it is at this later stage that pretending exhibits more stereotyped forms as well as novel occurrences. It appears that as play becomes more socialized, stereotypic forms provide a common framework for cooperative play, while at the same time increased cognitive and symbolizing capacities make possible a wider variation on basic themes.

In her paper, "Pretense Play: A Cognitive Perspective," Golumb reports research in which she examined the logic of the fit between symbol and referent in progressively limited forced choice situations. The children, ranging in age from 2:8 to 5:9, chose, first, appropriate objects as signifiers, then neutral objects, and finally, rejected nonsuitable objects. Thus, the widespread belief that "any object will do" as a vehicle in young children's symbolic play appears to be erroneous. The transfer of operations from the domain of play to other cognitive tasks is at the base of a second study. Children of about four years of age were made aware of perspective-taking in role playing through discussions with the experimenters. These children improved significantly over the control group in Piagetian conservation tasks. Golumb proposes that the cognitive operations involved in perspective-taking are a form of proto-reversibility and thus contribute to greater ability in conservation tasks.

Wolf and Gardner, in "Style and Sequence in Early Symbolic Play," focus on questions of individual style in early play. They propose two main styles: "patterners" and "dramatists." One of these modes dominates an individual child's play but is accompanied by secondary use of the other. A longitudinal study including both naturalistic observation and test situations provided data on the early emergence of preferred styles and the course of development thereafter. For example, patterners often arrange the toys of pretend play into pleasing spatial arrangements while dramatists use them to role play and engage others. After a period of concentration on the preferred style, children go through a "balancing out" phase in which the rudiments of the other style are acquired. Remarking on the consistency of these findings with earlier reports of language/visual-spatial and person-centered/object-centered polarities, Wolf and Gardner note that the source of these widely-noted polarities remain unidentified

In the next paper, "Development of Gesture," Barten points out that there is increasing interest in gesture as a form of communication and symbolization but relatively little research on the gestural mode. With the explicit aim of facilitating such a study, Barten offers a taxonomy which identifies and describes the following forms of gesture: diectic, instrumental, expressive, enactive, and depictive. These distinctions reflect differences in both the intended function of the gesture, and the type of referent the symbolizer has in mind (i.e., feelings, actions or objects). The central question of development of mastery in the medium is considered in the context of research on depictive gesture. Here, Barten discusses her research on the development of depictive gesture, and some recent investigations of gesture in young deaf children. She provides an analysis of "mastery of the medium," showing that it has several interrelated components. Some of these have to do with "isolation" of the medium—the distinction between relevant and irrelevant aspects of gesture or body position, articulation of symbol-referent distinctions, and relative independence of medium from context; others are closely related to development of motor skill and organization; still others have to do with developing understanding of the requirements of successful communication.

In her paper, "Copying and Inventing: Similarities and Contrasts in Process and Performance," Shapiro undertakes a close analysis of copying activity. Drawing on a wide range of sources, including her own research on young children's copying of geometric forms, Shapiro elucidates the nature of the relations between perceptual and performatory activity. She emphasizes that several interrelated factors must be kept in mind when considering the nature of the links among discrimination, recognition, and copying. These are identified as follows: the child's ability to differentiate attributes of the stimulus; how and by whom the attributes are defined; the redefining of salient attributes during development; the status of the copier's developmental stage; the necessity for the copier to have experience in the medium and to have developed a system for representation. Lack of correspondence between perceptual and performatory activity is indicated in research showing, for example, that errors of discrimination do not necessarily lead to errors of production, and that accuracy of recognition does not by any means guarantee accuracy in performatory activity (copying); further, it is noted that the heightened perception of the connoisseur does not provide sufficient basis for successful performance. Shapiro points to the complex interplay between perceiving and performing, where each process may modify the other. In concluding, she suggests that insofar as copying involves invention of means to achieve an end, it may not be as far removed from creative activity as is often thought within Western culture.

It has been suggested by Werner and Kaplan (1963) that the use of language as a symbolic medium can be conceptualized in terms of relations among four components in the symbolizing situation—addressor, addressee, vehicle and referent. Without explicitly adopting this framework, each of the authors in Part III, *Language*, has focused on relations among at least two of these components and in this process has not only explored specific questions but contributed to the understanding of language qua symbolic medium, that is, a system which is fundamentally referential.

In "The Child's First Terms of Reference," Anglin begins by asking about the order of acquisition of category labels in the young child's lexicon: Do children first learn general terms (e.g., food) and then more specific terms (e.g., apple), or the reverse? In discussing this classic question, Anglin clarifies the theoretical issue of hierarchical ordering of terms and at the same time provides new data on empirical predictors of the order of acquisition of such terms. In this paper, Anglin examines a range of data—from diary studies to findings of his current research—to elucidate the nature of early developmental changes in the meanings of category labels. Here he takes issue with the widespread assumption that "overextension" is most characteristic of children's application of terms. Drawing on his own research, Anglin shows that the use of category labels varies as a function of several types of factors— the particular child, the specific terms, the nature of the instances and non-instances of the concept being tested. In addition, Anglin explores the discrepancy between children's responses on a definition task and their classification of concept instances. This leads directly to a concluding discussion on the nature of early concepts and alternative forms of concept storage (cf. Potter, this volume).

Britton's paper, "Learning to Use Language in Two Modes," begins with a fundamental distinction between two ways of using language—using language to "get things done" and using language in story-telling, play and literature, as a way of recounting and digesting experience. Britton describes the uses of language in terms of a contrast between language in the role of "participant" and language in the role of "spectator." Subsequently, he urges us to consider the additional dimension of informal-formal modes of use, and shows how this applies within "participant" language and within "spectator" language. Britton suggests that the specialized forms of "transactional" (participant) and "poetic" (spectator) language develop out of an informal "expressive language" which is relatively context-bound, personalized, and loosely structured. While this expressive language may tend toward "participant" use or "spectator" use, it is to some extent an "all purpose" instrument which is generally replaced though not eradicated by the more differentiated, formalized modes characteristic of adult language. Young children make some distinction between practical everyday uses of language and uses of language (oral and written) in the story-telling performance mode, but at younger ages there is less differentiation between these two modes than is the case later on. In concluding, Britton cautions us about prematurely introducing formalization into the child's uses of language—a tendency all too often encountered in educational settings.

Franklin opens her paper, "Metalinguistic Functioning in Development," by drawing a distinction between performances-in-context and reflective performances; she suggests that while speaking most often occurs as a performance-in-context, there are certain occasions when it becomes a reflective performance involving a shift in the speaker's orientation to his own activity. Thus "metalinguistic functioning" is conceptualized as a special type of performance, one in which the person carries out "procedures" on aspects of language/speech taken as "objects." Following the delineation of six such "procedures," Franklin discusses several questions fundamental to her conceptualization: What determines whether a given aspect of language (e.g., a word) can become an "object" for further metalinguistic operations? How should we conceptualize relations between competence and performance in relation to metalinguistic functioning? What understandings of language-in-relation-to-context are requisite for engage in metalinguistic performance? With regard to this last question, Franklin briefly describes early phases in the child's understanding of language/speech in relation to context, pointing to the progressive differentiation of speaking from other activity and from the here-and-now context of objects, persons and events. In this connection, emphasis is given to the child's first understandings of the referential nature of language. It may be noted that such understandings—varying in stability in the early years—necessarily enter into the acquistion and use of category labels as discussed by Anglin in this volume.

Part IV of this volume, *Symbolism and the Mythic World*, consists of a single paper—Kaplan's "Symbolism: From the Body to the Soul." Taking note of prevailing divergences in definitions of "symbol" and "symbolization," Kaplan makes clear his intent to focus on phenomena of "primary symbol formation." These include hypnogogic and dream imagery, as well as other phenomena displaying the realization of abstract, intangible content in concrete form. Kaplan asks us to consider the question of how ideational content can be realized in a concrete medium, how disparate domains are conjoined in the process of symbol formation. It is suggested that this is not only involves "dynamic schematizing activity" (cf. Werner and Kaplan, 1963; Smith, this volume) but adopting a particular stance, here referred to as "mythopoetic," in which certain distinctions are suspended. Such states of mind are presumed to be more typical of children than of adults, but are pervasive in adult thinking as well—although too often unrecognized by contemporary cognitive psychology. Kaplan takes issue with the classic psychoanalytic view that symbolizing moves from the corporeal (the "true" referent) to the more ephemeral and that symbol interpretation thus rests on "referring downwards." He urges us to consider the Jungian view that symbols "refer upwards," to the spiritual and ineffable, and comes to the conclusion that the symbols of "primary symbol formation" should be regarded as referring upwards and downwards simultaneously and that, in fact, it is this double reference which provides their distinctive integrative force.

This brief sketch of the contents of the volume is intended to make clear the nature of specific contributions, and to provide some sense of the whole. Clearly, some of the authors are primarily concerned with encompassing theoretical formulations; most are directed toward the investigation of symbolic functioning in particular domains. It will be seen that few of the papers are exclusively theoretical, and that those concerned with research are theoretically anchored. Research cited, whether the author's own or coming from other sources, is predominantly developmental—concerned with changes in modes of functioning as related to developmental level. Many of the authors draw freely on less formal material—observations of children at play, children's stories and comments. Taken together, the papers comprising this volume not only provide a view of work on different modes of symbolic functioning but of various approaches—theoretical and empirical, systematic research and less formal observation—to the task of understanding symbolic functioning in childhood within a developmental framework.

REFERENCES

Bruner, J., Olver, R., & Greenfield, P. M. *Studies in Cognitive Growth*. New York: Wiley, 1967.
Piaget, J. *Play, Dreams and Imitation*. London: Wm. Heinemann, 1951.
Werner, H. & Kaplan, B. *Symbol Formation*. New York: Wiley, 1963.

NATURE AND DETERMINANTS OF SYMBOLIC FUNCTIONING

1 Developmental Origins of Structural Variation in Symbol Form

Nancy R. Smith
School of Visual Arts, Boston University

INTRODUCTION

Symbols occur in dismaying profusion. We think and live in complexes of symbols. Yet the structure of symbols is little understood. A symbol is said to be distinguished from other phenomena which convey meaning in that it communicates something of the nature of the entity to which it refers. It calls to mind the qualities of being of an object or "state of affairs." It is so constructed by its maker, and such is its effect on the percipient. But how does it do so? Of what is a symbol made? What are its parts? How are the parts related to each other?

One of the factors contributing to the uncertainty about symbols is the great variation in their elements and structures. Symbolic media such as gesture, play, language, dreams, art materials, myth, and cultural ritual each offer different characteristics to be used in forming symbols. The connotations surrounding a referent can go far afield and in so doing both enrich and obscure meaning. The mode of correspondence between the material form of a symbol and its referent can be representational, conventional, or an analogy of pattern or concept. Individual symbols can be combined into larger symbol systems, and several levels of meaning can be attached to one symbolic entity. In short, symbols are made from a wide range of elements and in a variety of structures.

Interestingly, the basic elements and structures of this variability appear in early childhood when symbolization begins. While the symbols of adults are complex and far reaching, they nevertheless exhibit flexibilities similar to the simple, more "primitive" symbols of young children. Probably the very looseness of form facilitates development of the capacity, and probably it is an evolutionary advantage to be able to construct symbols with great flexibility and in many contexts.

To examine the nature of this flexibility more closely it will be helpful to identify basic elements and structures of symbols.[1]

ELEMENTS AND STRUCTURES OF SYMBOLS

A symbol is composed of a stimulus that constitutes the vehicle or signifier and the conceptual referent to which it refers.

The Vehicle

The word *vehicle,* a term preferred by Werner and Kaplan (1963), will be used to refer to the symbolizing medium whether formed or unformed, whether simple or complex. This term is helpful because it denotes the function of the medium as a carrier of meaning (a "referrer") and at the same time recognizes its separate identity.

There is a variety of basic vehicular media: body movement, language, two- and three-dimensional graphic materials, objects such as toys, play, dreams, and mental images. Each of these media has variations and elaborated forms. These forms may be stacked or embedded within one another. For example, body movement is used in motor imitation, formal and informal body gesture, reenactment of movement sequences, children's play, drama, dance, and cultural rituals. Among children there may be the direct imitation of clapping hands in "patty cake," or there may be hand clapping integral to enactment of the role of spectator embedded in the dramatic vehicle in "playing circus." Among adults there are more complex amalgams and stackings of vehicular forms. Balanchine's formalistic ballet *Agon* uses as one vehicle patterns of movement in space to suggest contemporary concepts of sophistication, playfulness, exuberance, tension, complexity, and technical precision. These patterns are built from the movements of the dancers, some of which are formalistic and some imitative enactments. Such movements are vehicular elements embedded in the larger vehicle of the spatial patterns.

Different types of vehicles may be combined in a compound symbol. The child riding a stick enacts galloping a horse, utters the word "giddiap," and selects a functionally appropriate stick to stand in for the horse (cf. Gombrich, 1951). Body movement, sound, and the stick are vehicles combined within the broader vehicle of the play scenario.

---

[1]The scheme set forth in the following section owes much to discussion over the years with my friend and very generous coeditor, Margery B. Franklin. She is not responsible, of course, for its shortcomings.

The Referent

The counterpart to *vehicle* is *referent*. This term denotes the concept of the experience being represented as it exists in the mind of the symbol maker and later in the mind of the percipient. It connotes that the concept of a state of affairs or the experience of a phenomenon is not an exterior absolute but a construct, dependent on personal response and the symbols available for its formulation. The term is applied to the concept of the referent as independent and also as dependent, interactive, the object of the vehicle in the symbol.

Dynamic Schematization-Interaction

Conventional understanding of symbol formation contrasts sharply with that of Werner and Kaplan. Symbol making is commonly thought of as a process (1) of pushing the medium into a representation of an object or event, (2) of stipulating such a relationship, or (3) of putting in conjunction two preformed but aptly suited entities. In each instance the referent is thought of as already formed; the vehicle is in one fashion or another fitted to it.

In *Symbol Formation,* Werner and Kaplan (1963) assert a more dynamic, organic interaction between vehicle and referent. They propose that, as part of the process of reality construction, there is ongoing and interdependent dynamic schematization of both vehicle and referent—that the symbol maker constructs vehicle, referent, and the relationship of "fit" between them concurrently.

> When a symbolic vehicle is taken to "represent"a referent, it is our view that the vehicular structure functions to "depict" or "reveal," through some sort of correspondence or analogy, the connotational structure of the referent. It should, however, be emphasized... that correspondence or analogy is not, in our view, "given objectively" in and by itself, but is *established through an intentional act....*
>
> Note that, in our view, symbolizing enters directly into the construction of the "cognitive objects" determining how events are organized and what they mean. Our thesis is thus opposed to the widespread view which treats symbolic vehicles and referents as two fully formed entities that are externally linked to each other through contiguous pairing (and reinforcement). (p. 15)

During the making and using of a symbol, the concept of the referent is in the process of being formed or reformed. The way the symbol is formed depends in part on the medium, and the requirements of referent modify the concept of medium. The way each (concept of vehicle, concept of referent, configuration of symbol) is formed depends on the other. The child's understanding of the enclosingness of a house is clearer having built one of blocks, and his understanding of the enclosingness of blocks is clearer having built a house with them. An idea is shaped by the words it is put into; the phrases take on new meanings in the context of the idea. Werner and Kaplan (1963) state

> ... the *establishment of semantic correspondence* between the vehicular pattern and the referential object—the formation of the symbol—comes about through the operation of schematizing, form-building activity which shapes the pattern on the one hand, and the referent on the other. Correspondence is achieved when both pattern and object are rooted in similar or identical organismic states, the formation of these states being directed and regulated by the underlying activity of schematization. (pp. 23-24)

Salient Features

In the form-building process, the shared salient features of vehicle and referent are the consequence of dynamic schematization and constitute the basis of the bonding interaction. These features are qualities perceived in each based on the purpose of the symbol maker. Sometimes adult logic and common practice enter into the purposes and schematizations of the symbol maker, and sometimes they do not. (This issue is pursued further in the section on *referential connotation*.) The child forming a bond on the salient feature "enclosingness" to build his house of blocks in a circle is using the spatial logic of the child—while producing a symbol which is anomalous to the adult.

Modes of Correspondence

This term reflects the possibility that the relationship between vehicle and referent sometimes has sensory feature part-to-part correspondence, as in representation, and sometimes does not. Among the modes of correspondence are the following: those based on sensory features (form, color, movement, duration, etc.); those based on similarity of function (as in the example of the hobby horse in Gombrich, 1951); those based on similarity of pattern or structure of elements, no matter whether they are concrete or conceptual ("analogues of states of affairs" Langer, 1942); and those based on relationships which are arbitrary or stipulated, in which the sensory forms of the vehicle bear no relationship to any qualities of the referent (language is commonly thought to be of this type, an opinion disputed by Werner and Kaplan, 1963).

Structural Extensions of Vehicle and Referent

One of the consequences of the centrality of dynamic schematization in symbol formation is flexibility in forming relationships, the variety of forms, and the extensions of vehicle and referent. One vehicle can call to mind different referents; one referent can be summoned up by different vehicles.

Multireferentiality

Multireferentiality (*plurisignificance* in Werner and Kaplan, 1963) denotes the capacity of one vehicular configuration to represent a variety of different referential entities. Often which one of these the percipient "sees" is a consequence of the context, local or cultural; the personality of the maker or percipient; and the psychic state of the maker or percipient. For example, a gesture indicating tenderness to one may be seen as aggressive by another. Or a color may symbolize a number of different phenomena depending on context, as Turner (1967) makes clear in his discussion of the ritual of the Ndembu, a people of south-central Africa.

> Certain dominant or focal symbols conspicuously possess this property of multivocality which allows for the economic representation of key aspects of culture and belief. Each dominant symbol has a "fan" or "spectrum" of referents, which are interlinked by what is usually a simple mode of association, its very simplicity enabling it to interconnect a wide variety of *significata*. For example, the associational link provided by "whiteness" enables white clay (mpemba) to stand for a multiplicity of ideas and phenomena, ranging from biological referents as "semen" to abstract ideas such as "ritual purity," "innocence" from witchcraft, and "solidarity with the ancestory spirits "(p. 50).

Often the different referents of vehicles within a symbol system refer to experience at different levels of concreteness, from the directly phenomenal to representation of concepts of social values, as in the ritual Turner describes.

A loosely structured or more abstract configuration leaves itself open to more interpretation. Thus the more neutral or transparent the vehicle, the more likely there is to be multireferentiality, and similarly, the loose structures of young children's thought make it possible for them to reinterpret the meaning of a symbol from moment to moment.

Another aspect of extension is "vehicular stacking."

Vehicular Stacking

Vehicular stacking refers to the possibility that upon one basic vehicular sensory phenomenon there may be piled or stacked a complex of elaborated and systematized vehicular forms. The hobbyhorse example of children's play stacks the dramatic narrative on top of the sensory phenomena. The foundation of every symbol is sensory; there is something to cause sensation in the maker and in the percipient of the symbol (see Fig. 1.1). Layered on top of this stimulus may be increasingly complex and sophisticated compounds

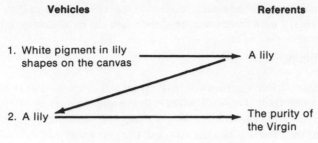

FIG. 1.1.   Referent becomes vehicle.

and systems which carry meaning by means of the patterning of vehicular elements into analogues of states of affairs, as, for instance, in the Balanchine ballet *Agon* or in the Ndembu ritual discussed by Turner (1967).

In language, words—those "little mouthy noises" (Langer, 1942)—are linked by syntax, often employ metaphor, are arranged in a particular narrative form, and are "nuanced" by style. Sounds, words, syntax, metaphor, narrative form and style are all vehicles. Each has the capability of being selected and shaped from among others by a symbol maker and of calling to mind a particular object, event, state of affairs, emotion, or concept.

The referent in any symbolic pair may become the vehicle in the next layer of the stack. Sounds are the vehicle for words. Words are the vehicle for metaphors. Metaphors are one vehicle of narrative form. Style in literature, it may be noted, can be the consequence of choices the symbol maker has made of sounds, words, syntax, metaphor, literary form, and content. Compound symbols and symbol systems may use elements from any layer in the stack.

A simple example of how a referent becomes a vehicle is provided by the iconographic convention in Renaissance painting. Ferguson (1954) describes the significance of the lily in paintings of the Annunciation as follows:

> The lily is a symbol of purity, and has become the flower of the Virgin. . . . One incident in the life of the Virgin, the Annunciation, is particularly associated with lilies. In many of the scenes of the Annunciation painted during the Renaissance, the Archangel Gabriel holds a lily, or a lily is placed in a vase between the Virgin and the Announcing Angel. (p. 33)

The shift from referent to vehicle in these paintings is diagrammed in Fig. 1.1.

In the analysis of a symbol it is important to determine if the referent in one bonded pair is the vehicle of another and if, as a consequence, there is vehicular stacking.

Referential Connotation

In addition to multireferentiality and vehicular stacking there is another aspect of structural extension in symbol formation: the connotational power of the referent. The term *referential connotation* identifies the property of the referent to call forth many associations and thus to distill out meaning from among the associations of the concept denoted. The organismic theory of symbol formation sees meaning as a complex of associations focused toward the center of a referent.

Associations are called up in accord with the purpose or goals of the symbol maker. All the known examples of a dog species help to define and flesh out the concept of the genus dog. This is one of the possible trains of connotation for the symbol *dog*. Another might have to do with common understandings of actions, functions, and molecular structure, as Langer's (1942) list of qualities of water demonstrates: falling from clouds, colorless, a substance found in ponds, chemical composition H_2O. Or the string of associations may have to do with spatial and temporal contiguities in a particular personal experience, as, for example, the sensations and recollections Proust wrote of associated with madeleines.

The principle that governs the associative string in each of these examples is different. For the word *dog* the principle is that of biological classes, for *water* the associations and attributes selected by common understanding, and for *madeleines* a very personal assembly of remembrances. The type of associated connotations surrounding a referent depends on the purpose of the symbol maker. The relevent connotations flow from the intended referent and back to it, helping to flesh out meaning.

The extension of vehicle and referent in *multireferentiality, vehicular stacking,* and *referential connotation* makes for richness in symbols and ease and economy in structuring them into symbol systems. These three forms of extension are schematized in Fig. 1.2.

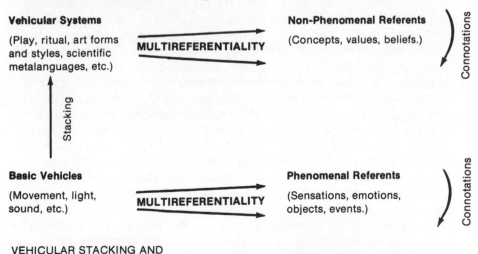

FIG. 1.2.   Extensions of vehicle and referent.

Analysis of Symbols—Summary of Terminology

In the analysis of any symbol it is helpful to establish all the *vehicle*(s) and all the *referent*(s). Since the phenomenon of vehicular stacking involves transposition of referent into vehicle from level to level, it may be necessary to determine each *vehicle* which may be *stacked* and/or combined in a system, the referent each denotes, and then the *salient features* which are shared by each vehicle-referent pair. Once this has been determined it is possible to establish the *mode of correspondence* in which each pair is bonded and thus to understand the elements of a given symbol system. The capability of symbols to be *multireferential* can produce several pairs made from the same vehicle. Also, *referential connotation* can blur the identity of the denoted referent. But establishing pairs of vehicle and referent and their type of relationship generally establishes the core identity of each vehicle and each referent and eventually the structure of the symbol system, no matter how flexibly constructed.

DEVELOPMENTAL ORIGINS OF VARIATION IN SYMBOLS

The developmental stage of the symbol maker affects his concept of vehicle, referent, and the type of correspondence possible between them. Of course, the symbol maker's prior experience influences the content and form of the symbol, too. An experienced, motivated child building the symbol of a structure he knows and likes with blocks, will make a richer symbol. His use of the vehicular material (blocks) will be informed by his greater understanding of their possibilities. He has more information about the referent to choose from. But the overall nature of his thought, his basic form of dynamic schematization, will be consistent with others of his age.

How does the flexibility of symbolization begin? The child begins life as a sensory-motor organism without the capacity to remember or organize experience. Gradual modifications in sensory-motor responses make it possible for him to attain object permanence, to differentiate experiences.[2] The search for absent objects one of the signs of object permanence, indicates that the object is symbolized in the mental imagery of the searching infant. Motor imitation, particularly "deferred imitation" (Piaget, 1951), is early symbolization. These examples of motoric symbols seem to imply generalization or conceptualization at a very early age. Piaget (1951) offers the following example:

> At 1:4 (0) [1 year, 4 months] L. tried to get a watch chain out of a matchbox when the box was not more than an eighth of an inch open. She gazed at the box

---

[2]See Chapter 2 for discussion of the very important affective component of early symbolization.

with great attention, then opened and closed her mouth several times in succession, at first slightly and then wider and wider. It was clear that the child, in her effort to picture to herself the means of enlarging the opening, was using as "signifier" [vehicle] her own mouth, with the movements of which she was familiar tactually and kinesthetically as well as by analogy with the visual image of the mouths of others. (p. 65)

It appears that Lucienne (L.) has begun to construct some concept of *open* or *opening* since the vehicle she uses, the movements of her mouth, are so remote from the referent, movements of opening the box. The salient feature shared between the two is a general idea about movements of opening—and apparently it can be perceived across very different forms.

Movement as a concept is one of the fundamental categories of thought, beginning in very primitive forms in the presymbolizing infant and coming to be one of the first salient features by which vehicle is linked with referent. Strong emphasis on the movement aspects of phenomena is one of the dominant characteristics of dynamic-physiognomic thought.

Dynamic-Physiognomic

Dynamic-physiognomic is a term used by Werner (1948) and Werner and Kaplan (1963) to characterize the kind of thought used by children between the years of 1 and 6 and by adults whose thought is taking place in that form. It is an aspect of the type of thought called "primary process" by Freud and "prelogical" by Piaget. *Dynamic-physiognomic* thought relies on motoric and sensory phenomena in forming concepts, on qualities of affectivity, expressivity, and energy. In contrast to objective or technical thought it appears loose, willful, and weak at organizing logical systems of category and causality. The mode of correspondence of many symbols is formed in dynamic-physiognomic terms.

Dynamic-physiognomic thought is structured on very fundamental sensory concepts such as movement. It allows experiences to be collected or associated in loose aggregates and to be formed into syncretic wholes. Because of their motor-sensory nature, many of these concepts are also intersensory; they are based on perceptions which occur frequently in the phenomenon of synesthesia. Among the motor-sensory qualities that young children (and adults) conceive and respond to are

1. In the area of movement, such qualities as direction, force, balance, rhythm, speed, enclosingness.
2. In the area of the tactual-kinetic, such qualities as soft, heavy, hard, angular, poking out, rigid, cold.
3. In the area of visual responses, such qualities as bright, dull, warm, dark, the "thingness" of forms, the movement of forms, the expressive

proportions of forms, the expressive contours of forms, simple size relations.

4. In the area of auditory responses, such qualities as loud, soft, sweet, hard, warm, sharp.

It is not hard to imagine corresponding qualities for the senses of taste and smell, and the degree to which these qualities are experienced across a variety of senses is obvious. Two other qualities which apply widely are simple spatial orientations such as together/apart, inside/outside, and above/below, and the simple numerical concepts, many/few.

Such sensory concepts do not lend themselves to logical objective systemization, but they do lend themselves to fluent symbol formation—the kind of rough-and-ready symbolization we so frequently observe in young children. They make for schematizations which cross sensory modalities and cross physical substances; salient features are everywhere at hand for the bonding of vehicle and referent. Dynamic-physiognomic thought makes it easy for children to form symbols. It is also a rich and potent condition for experimentation in symbolization, as analysis of the relation between creativity and primary process has shown. Finally, it contributes to the flexibility of symbol systems which helps to make them more socially effective. (This topic is carried further in the *concluding remarks*.)

The Nature of Materials

Even after object permanence (Piaget, 1954) objects are identified with the self; they are "stuff to move with." As self is further differentiated from other, materials begin to be "things to think about." There is a shift from "things-of-action" to "objects-of-contemplation" (Werner & Kaplan, 1963). The developmental shift to objects-of-contemplation makes it possible for the child to learn the nature of materials and to construct concepts of the physical and visual characteristics of each. By about 1½ years he can differentiate the substance of a material from his own actions sufficiently to produce changes of form in the material and to learn from these changes. Prior to this time he may have attempted to eat the material, to drop and retrieve it, to seek and find it, to wave and bang it, and so forth. Now as he does these things he responds more to the nature of the material; he manipulates it with more attention to its own inherent nature, though still with motor-reflexive and primitive motor coordinations.

In the beginning the movements are very similar in each material. However, because of the particular nature of each material, the same limited, motor-rhythmic movements by the child produce different results. He pats a lump of clay with his hand—it becomes flattened. He pats paper with a paint brush— dots accumulate. He pats a block of wood with his hand—nothing happens, or the block is displaced in space.

In each instance, there are pleasant kinesthetic and sound sensations. In most instances a new and interesting visual stimulus is created. These pleasurable sensations motivate the child to continue. Over time, with many such visual-motor experiences, the child builds basic physical and visual concepts of each material. Such physical qualities as soft/hard, sticky/smooth, firm/malleable, and discrete/mixable are obvious early learnings; less obvious may be various visual qualities such as particular aspects of line, shape, color, mass, and space.

The child learns these concepts from the material itself. He does what he does, it does what it does, and the child accommodates to the consequences. His experimentation is based on prior experimentation, discovery, and integration. One discovery leads to the next as he responds to the material and as the material responds to him. Concepts are differentiated in sequences of increasing complexity. Earliest experiments are motoric; in time visual concepts develop, and the child exhibits rudimentary forms of visual-motor coordination; finally he can coordinate complex combinations of concepts, as in the elaborate painted designs of 4- and 5-year-olds. For much of the time he has no intention to represent; he is simply intent on mastering the visual qualities of the material.

For example, exploring the inherent visual qualities of lines in paint, the child goes through (approximately in order) the following sequence: movement, continuity, discreteness, beginning and ending, curvedness and straightness, direction relative to itself, orientation relative to the paper space, length, width, combinability, capability of defining shape, and capability of defining and separating two contiguous shapes. This whole process of construction of concepts of graphic lines may take him from his third through his fifth year. Of course, he is constructing concepts of color, shape, and paper space concurrently with those of line.

Just as Piaget's daughter demonstrated a generalized motoric concept, openingness, so too do children demonstrate generalized visual concepts. By observing the development of their paintings, the limitation, repetition, and variation of marks, it is possible to observe the discovery, experimentation with, and mastery of visual concepts (Smith, 1972).

Materials have similar and dissimilar physical and visual qualities. In clay the child discovers and constructs concepts of density and form, of plasticity and structure, of weight and balance, and of texture. The nature of wood and the prestructured organization of a set of Carolyn Pratt blocks causes construction of concepts of rigidity and discreteness, of weight and balance, of form and structure in space, of repetition and proportion, of ordering, and of almost infinite possibilities of reordering. There are, for example, 40 distinctly different ways to arrange just 2 unit blocks in relation to each other.

The three media paint, clay, and wood are similar in that they all make shapes or forms in space. They are different in that clay is plastic and wood rigid; paint is two dimensional and wood and clay three dimensional; paint and clay are infinitely variable in form and size and blocks predetermined in modular units; and the forms made with paint and clay can be permanent (they are "stuck" together), and the forms made with blocks are impermanent (they are held together by balance and gravity). Paint has changeable color; blocks and clay do not. Thus there are some concepts which may be generalized and some which may not.

With each of the symbolizing media, the child seems to go through a period of learning prior to using the material in symbolization. He carries out a series of experiments and as he does so discovers and constructs concepts of the basic physical and visual qualities of the material.

Expressivity of Objects and Materials

Symbolization begins with simple movements in imitation of other movements which evolve into more complex patterns of movement enactions in play combined with language, according to Piaget (1951). In these forms, the medium is the child's body, the movements and sounds produced by his body. The first evidence of symbolization with tangible materials is a form of protosymbolization in which the child applies names after the fact to the consequences of motoric movements with materials. The configurations of the material are schematized by the child according to dynamic-physiognomic qualities and so identified verbally. Thus a very early motor-rhythmic, zigzag "scribble" is called "grass" by the child after he has stopped drawing. Grass here is a word referring to a string of associations of things that go up and down, have lots of parts, and perhaps are very thin. These are salient features of similarity between the lines and grass. For the child grass is a referent of the moment. The bond, probably based on the physiognomic quality of up and down movement, is very loose. Grass is one association in a possible string of "up and downnesses." In a few minutes the child might label the same drawing "rain" or "stairs."

There are two important characteristics of the earliest concepts constructed of vehicular media; they are both physical and expressive, physiognomic concepts. The more physical aspect of these concepts makes possible simple, direct control over the configurations of the medium; the more expressive aspect makes symbolization possible. The child understands a world of objects and events in which things move slowly or swiftly, are soft or hard, are large or small in mass, and so forth. These kinds of properties have both physical and expressive characteristics and may be used to define objects and events and also to bridge across them. In dynamic schematization the kinds of expressive qualities listed earlier become salient features upon which to form symbolic bonds. Werner and Kaplan (1963) state that the capacity to form such concepts is inherent and develops prior to the capacity for symbolization.

The nonrepresentational construing of objects as *expressive* is basic, and genetically prior, to the use of expressive properties in representation. Dynamic-vectorial characteristics, physiognomic qualities, rhythms, etc., inhere in the objects and events of our perceptual experience as much as do the geometrical-technical properties. Such expressiveness also inheres in the actions of organisms, for example, in their bodily movements, in their vocalizations, and so on. (p. 20)

Much of the variability in symbol formation derives from the use of expressive qualities as salient features. Their very fundamentalness predicates variability. Similar expressive qualities may be seen in a variety of very different objects and events. This phenomenon is called the "transcendence of expressive qualities" by Werner and Kaplan.

It is characteristic of organismic schematization of events in terms of expressive features that the same dynamic-physiognomic qualities may be perceived in a variety of objects and actions—phenomena which are markedly different from a pragmatic-technical standpoint. It is this *transcendence of expressive qualities,* that is, their amenability to materialization on disparate things and happenings, that makes it possible for one to feel and see equations and similarities that find no place in the physical-technical construction of the word—a construction oriented towards manipulation, control, and prediction. Such transcendence prompts the formation of similes, metaphors, analogies, etc., or at least provides the basis for such formations. It also provides the basis for the manifestation of similar expressive qualities in entities otherwise as unrelated as a sound-pattern and a perceptual or conceptual object. (p. 21)

The transcendence of expressive qualities bridges senses, objects, and events; nevertheless, because of the interaction between vehicle and referent, the physical nature of vehicular media does influence which qualities will be perceived as viable salient features. Very clear examples of the perception of expressive qualities in tangible materials occur during the period of protosymbolization in which the nature of the material directly determines the type of referent named by the child. The child has not formed the material with a referent in mind, but it takes forms to which the child responds with dynamic schematizations which he reveals verbally. Compare how the three very different media—paint, clay, and blocks—have influenced form and thus suggested different referents to children:

1. Paint: fire, rain, "a box of smoke," snow, grass, "prickers," bees, snakes, roads, and vehicles.
2. Clay: food (pizza, cake, candy, "my bowl of Wheaties with butterscotch sauce,"), snakes, worms, balls, sidewalks, roads, and vehicles.
3. Blocks: buildings, tunnels, things to carry (guns, pocketbooks, crutches, skis), roads, and vehicles.

(The examples are drawn from Biber, 1932; Bland, 1957; Guanella, 1934; Hartley, Frank, and Goldenson, 1952; Johnson, 1933; and Smith, 1972.)

The plasticity of clay as well as its bits and pieces suggest food. The smeariness of paint suggests smoke, fire, and rain. Its lines and dots suggest movement and "thingness," and sometimes "sharp-thingness" as in bees or "prickers." The discrete structural nature of the blocks prompts buildings, spaces, and portable objects. The nature of the vehicular material influences which expressive qualities will be perceived and thus influences the choice of referent in these examples.

The extremely fundamental dynamic-physiognomic quality of movement pervades these responses. It is the one quality appearing in the objects named in all the media. Roads and vehicles are symbolized in all three, often accompanied by imitative movements and sounds. Lines in paint or clay or blocks suggest roads. In the three-dimensional media the child often moves the lump of clay or block, symbolizing through the movement of an indistinct, lumpish form. Perception of the dynamic physiognomic quality in movement is early and powerful; it is the basis of many symbolic bonds, influencing the schematization of vehicle and referent. Movement as one of the expressive qualities of objects and events has a vast range of variations and extensions.

CONCLUDING REMARKS

Dynamic schematizations of vehicle and referent construct salient features in both, which features constitute the link in symbolic bonding. Developmentally the first dynamic schematizations are made in the physiognomic mode, and thus the first and fundamental form of interaction between vehicle and referent is in the physiognomic mode. Among the consequences both for children and adults are multireferentiality, vehicular stacking, referential connotation, and compound vehicles.

Dynamic schematization is one fundamental source of variation in symbol forms, as also is the physiognomic mode of thought. In physiognomic thought experience is conceptualized in cross-sensory, cross-substance categories based on physical, sensory, expressive properties. One of the most universal of expressive properties is movement, as examples of the protosymbols constructed by young children reveal. In childhood and also in adulthood all objects and events may be schematized physiognomically, but in early childhood physiognomic schematization is the natural state of affairs.

Another source of variation is in the environment, in the inherent properties of objects and events. Expressive qualities of vehicles and referents may "transcend" conventional logic, but they are constructed in relation to the nature of objects and events, and each of those objects and events offers its own idiosyncratic cluster of cues for dynamic schematization.

Thus variation is of the essence of symbol forms. Cassirer (1944) emphasized the importance of this often unrecognized fact when he wrote,

> A genuine symbol is characterized not by its uniformity but by its versatility. It is not rigid or inflexible but mobile. It is true that the full awareness of this mobility seems to be a rather late achievement in man's intellectual and cultural development. (p. 40)

Earlier it was suggested that the capacity for physiognomic perception might have an evolutionary advantage because it offers the growing child an optimal mode of thought in which to expand his symbolizing capacity. In addition, there are functional advantages accruing from symbol variation in adulthood. Discussing this issue, Victor Turner (1975) surveys contemporary anthropological thought. Symbols such as myth and ritual are seen as instrumentalities of moral , political, economic, and other social forces. As such they express conflicts between coherent systemic order and pragmatic issues which continually intrude. However, it is their susceptibility to such intrusion which keeps symbols reflective of the real world of happenings, and thus effective for societies:

> These properties of symbols—multivocality, complexity of association, ambiguity, open-endedness, primacy of feeling and willing over thinking in their semantics, their propensity to ramify into further semantic subsystems—are connected with their dynamic quality. Symbols are triggers of social action—and of personal action in the public arena. Their multivocality enables a wide range of groups and individuals to relate to the signifier-vehicle in a variety of ways. (p. 155)

In theory and in educational practice, it may be productive to keep in mind the fundamental bases for and functional efficacy of variation in the structure of symbols.

REFERENCES

Biber, B. *Children's drawings.* New York: Bank Street College of Education, 1932.

Bland, J. *Art of the young child.* New York: The Museum of Modern Art, 1957.

Cassirer, E. *An essay on man.* New Haven: Yale University Press, 1944.

Ferguson, G. *Signs and symbols in christian art.* New York: Oxford University Press, 1954.

Gombrich, E. Mediations on a hobby horse, or the roots of artistic form. In L. L. Whyte (Ed.), *Aspects of form.* London: Percy Lund Humphries & Co., Ltd., 1951 (also Bloomington: Indiana University Press, 1964).

Guanella, F. Block building activities of young children. In R.S. Woodworth (Ed.), *Archives of Psychology,* December 1934, No. 174.

Hartley, R., Frank, L., & Goldenson, R. *Understanding children's play.* New York: Columbia University Press, 1952.

Johnson, H. *The art of block building.* New York: Bank Street College of Education, 1933.

Langer, S. K. *Philosophy in a new key.* Cambridge, Mass.: Harvard University Press, 1942.

Piaget, J. *Play, dreams and imitation in childhood.* New York: Norton, 1951.

Piaget, J. *The construction of reality in the child.* New York: Basic Books, 1954.

Smith, N. R. *Developmental origins of graphic symbolization in the paintings of children three to five.* Unpublished doctoral dissertation, Harvard University, 1972.

Turner, V. *The forest of symbols.* Ithaca, N.Y.: Cornell University Press, 1967.

Turner V. Symbolic studies. *Annual Review of Anthropology,* 1975, *4,* 145–161.

Werner, H. *Comparative psychology of mental development.* New York: International Universities Press, 1948 (original English publication, 1940).

Werner, H., & Kaplan, B. *Symbol formation.* New York: Wiley, 1963.

2 The Affective Context and Psychodynamics of First Symbolization

Jan Drucker
Sarah Lawrence College

INTRODUCTION

I had an experience recently which raised a number of issues pertinent to the affective and interpersonal context in which symbolization is born and some of the psychodynamic factors which I believe influence its development. (Much of the following discussion will center on play, but I use it as paradigmatic of symbolization generally and ask that the reader keep in mind the other domains of symbolic functioning which are equally interesting and important.) The experience I refer to took place when I was visiting friends, one of whom was 4-week-old Joshua. Joshua had been nursing, and I called upstairs to his mother, "Is Josh still eating?" "No," she replied, "he's playing now." I rushed up to see—what more tempting invitation than the announcement that an infant was "playing?" I found Joshua lying partly cradled in his mother's arm, on her bed, gazing around him. "Playing?" I asked. "Well, he's not eating and he's not sleeping, and look at how he's waving his arms and poking his tongue in and out, and chirping, and looking so bright-eyed and contented."

I understood what Joshua's mother meant—there he lay, not immediately gratifying any biological need, in an ego state psychologists term "alert" to indicate how available the organism is at such moments to receiving and organizing sensory impressions, clearly experiencing pleasure and performing a variety of activities from his ever-expanding behavioral repertoire. It is significant, however, that already these activities were somewhat divorced from their origins in biologically determined patterns—the tongue motion was derived from but now relatively independent of nursing movements;

27

hand waving was no longer simply an aspect of total body discharge but a motion recreated for its own sake, for the pleasurable stimulation it afforded. Bühler's (1930) notion of "functional pleasure" as well as our everyday sense that what is playful is that which is done for the "fun of it" are invoked in this description, and we have arrived at a beginning definition of play.

Joshua's mother wisely did not say that Josh was "*just* playing," for his activity was undoubtedly serving a number of functions and exercising important evolving capacities. I have elsewhere discussed the ways in which what we generally term "play" is multiply determined and multiply functional and have explored some of the problems and possibilities inherent in the development of a theory of play which attempts to integrate a number of its cognitive and affective dimensions (Drucker, 1975). However, the scene I observed delineates the setting from which Joshua will eventually develop the capacity to symbolize and the desire to do so in a communicative fashion, and it is to these processes that I now turn.

Looking back on that scene, we can already identify many antecedents of what 18 or 20 months hence we shall feel comfortable calling Joshua's "symbolizing activities"—whether in gesture, play, or language. These precursor components can be roughly conceptualized as four major aspects of Joshua's situation after 4 weeks of life, each of which will be taken up in turn below. (1) We see, even after 4 weeks, the *ego apparatuses* embarked on their maturational course, which, through interaction with environmental stimuli, will lead to sophisticated perceptual, motoric, and cognitive processes, which will in turn make possible and directly influence the *form* of later symbolic functioning. (2) We see the close relationship of biological needs—with their psychic representations, the *drives*—to the themes, modalities, and motivations of play and other activities, which will ultimately have a major impact on the *content* of symbolization. (3) In a related consideration, we see the early intimate relationship between thought and action, the *body context* of early ego functioning generally, which will lend first symbolization its particular tie to the properties of bodily experience and therefore its distinctive *shape and texture*. (4) And, finally, we see the *interpersonal setting* within which the first symbolic acts will occur and which, I believe, influences the development of symbolization into not only one among the functions of the ego but an *ego organizer* and a central component in the growth of *object relations*.

Of the first of these factors—the role of ego development in first symbolization—I will say little here, for in most of the current literature on symbolization in children it is the various aspects of ego functioning involved which are emphasized. The importance of perceptual, motoric, and general and specific cognitive development for symbolization can never be excluded from consideration, and although in the present discussion they are left in the background, one further observation of Joshua will perhaps serve to underscore the point. Three months have passed—Josh is just 4 months old—and once again I am delighted in watching him at play.

Joshua can almost sit without support now, and he has just been given a low "walker chair." Looking a little surprised and very much pleased, he gazes around him from his new upright, yet not being held, position and fingers the edge of the plastic tray surrounding the walker. In his attempts to keep his balance he slips slightly sideways, and one foot grazes the floor. Reflexively, he kicks, and suddenly he is moving, chair and all, several inches backwards. His eyes widen, his face registers astonishment, and he vocalizes loudly. Then he tries the same foot movement again—it works! He looks over at his father sitting nearby and watches him as he continues to move himself across the room—imagine what it may be like to experience for the first time a self-initiated shifting distance from an object! Needless to say, Joshua now has a new schema, one he will repeat endlessly over the next days and weeks and one which, as it happens, dramatically expands his perceptual, motor, and cognitive world and thereby his interaction with human objects as well.

This observation illustrates briefly not only the input of ego development to play but also the importance in development of interaction with the environment—and the need for that environment to provide adequate and appropriate opportunities, in line with evolving interests and capacities. A week earlier Joshua had responded to being placed in the new chair with some mild fearfulness and had slumped forward in what seemed to be an uncomfortable way; 1 week later he was maturationally at a much better point to make use of the new play experience.

THE RELATION OF BODILY NEEDS AND EXPERIENCES TO FIRST SYMBOLIZATION

Freud postulated and more recent psychoanalytic thought affirms that the ego is first of all a body ego—that not only one's sense of oneself but also the modalities by means of which one experiences and formulates aspects of external reality are built up through experience of the own body, its parts, processes, periphery, and dynamic properties. It is interesting to consider the ways in which some fairly diverse developmental theorists address this issue and the ways of approaching the study of symbolization to which they are led by it.

Within the psychoanalytic school we find first of all Freud's discussion of dream symbolism; for example, in "Introductory Lectures on Psychoanalysis" (1961a) he says, "The range of things which are given symbolic representation in dreams is not wide: the human body as a whole, parents, children, brothers and sisters, birth, death, nakedness—... and the sexual life" (p. 153). It was entirely consonant with the rest of his work that those things most represented in dreams—and in communications from the unconscious generally—should have to do with the two most universal aspects of experience, the body and family relationships, whose centrality is the cornerstone of psychoanalytic developmental theory. Ferenczi (1950) suggested in 1913 that the beginning of symbolic development occurred when one body part was first equated with another and eventually replaced by it in psychic operations, that is, when the mechanism of displacement was first employed by the child. More recently, Greenacre (for example, 1971), Galenson (1971, 1978), Kestenberg (1956), and others have explored the role of particular patterns of stimulation and particular body areas in symbolic functioning. For example, in summarizing her own (1971) paper on play Galenson (1978) writes, "We described the way in which all young children use projection, or externalization, of bodily experiences in certain aspects of their play behavior, and we proposed a structural model for the analysis of play based upon the presence of structural and configurational similarities between body experiences and their correlated play behaviors. According to this structural model, the biting teeth, the cutting knife, and the grasping hand all share similar vectorial properties and would presumably have had similar original dynamic determinants" (p. 3).

In general, psychoanalytic approaches to play and to its usefullness in child psychotherapy have been derived from the principle that bodily needs and patterns shape not only the content but also some of the organizing modalities of play. Peller (1954), in relation to libidinal phase development; Erikson (1950), in relation to the concept of psychosexual and psychosocial zones, modes, and modalities; and Anna Freud (1946) and Klein (1932), in relation to clinical psychoanalytic practice, have been among the leaders in this work. As stated by Klein in 1932, "The child expresses its fantasies, its wishes, and its natural experiences in a symbolic way through play and games. In doing so it makes use of the same archaic and phylogenetic mode of expression, the same language, as it were, that we are familiar with in dreams; and we can only fully understand this language if we approach it in the way Freud has taught us to approach the language of dreams" (p. 29).

From quite different perspectives, the work of Piaget (e.g., 1962) and Werner and Kaplan (1963) also emphasizes aspects of the close relationship between body function and thought. Piaget's concept of the sensorimotor period in which bodily action comprises the content of mental schemata and Werner and Kaplan's formulation of the dynamic and vectorial (body) properties through which experience, and hence knowledge, are organized are most relevant here. We can assume with these writers that only very gradually does cognition come to be separated from sensory experience, and then only to a degree. I shall return to these ideas after a brief digression to note two related clinical phenomena.

In a most interesting paper, Ralph Greenson (1950) tells of a patient, raised abroad, who was able to keep out of her analysis (and her awareness) much crucial early material, connected with her feelings toward and memories of her mother from the pre-Oedipal period, until she began to use her mother tongue, German, in her analytic sessions. Comparable technical problems arise in attempting to deal with *preverbal* experience; for example, in work with emotionally disturbed young children, it has often been found that it is only through nonverbal experiences in the therapy that the important preverbal sources of the pathology can be explored. Greenson's report helps to elucidate the fact that it is not a *current* lack of ability to verbalize experience which serves as an impediment but the nature of the encoding of the experiences at the time in development when they occurred. In seeking to give symbolic expression to presymbolic experience, the child relies on the sensorimotor experience of the world which was its first organizer.

FIRST SYMBOLIZATION AND THE EVOLUTION OF OBJECT RELATIONS

We come now to a consideration of the human object relationship which provides the setting in which first symbolization takes place and to the variety of ways theorists have attempted to conceptualize its role. Some—for example, Werner and Kaplan (1963) and Gardner (1973)—build a communication paradigm into their concept of symbolization. For Werner and Kaplan, first symbolization occurs in the context of the "primordial sharing situation," characterized by the child's sharing with his mother his first experiences of the external world. Later on, progressive differentiation of the addressor from the addressee, as well as of the symbolic vehicle from its referent, is achieved, culminating in the use of shared symbols, freely and deliberately employed for communication. In most views of the symbolic functions of language, gesture, drama, and other adult artistic productions the notion of a sender, a message, and an audience is implicit, and symbolization is in large part regarded as an interpersonal phenomenon.

Returning to the psychoanalytic perspective, we can examine first symbolization in relation to the *separation-individuation process*. This apt term of Margaret Mahler's refers to the emergence of the child from the normal symbiotic fusion with the mother which characterizes the psychological situation of the second to fifth months of life. Mahler and her colleagues (see particularly Mahler, Pine, and Bergmann, 1975) have studied normal mother-child pairs over the period of more than a decade and have formulated and described the dual process by which the child comes to an awareness of his separate identity (separation) and the establishment of an array of autonomous ego functions (individuation). Four subphases are detailed: (1) *differentiation,* from about 5 to 7 months on, when the first push toward autonomy takes place; (2) *practicing*—initiated by free locomotion and characterized by the elated mood described by Greenacre as a "love affair with the world"; (3) the rapproachment crisis, at about 18 months, precipitated by the child's increasing awareness of separateness and panic about loss of the object as well as the further vulnerability of self-esteem and mood attendant on the realization of his own lack of omnipotence; and (4) the partial resolution of these anxieties as well as the child's ambivalent attachment to the mother through the consolidation of unified (i.e., not split) but separate mental representations of the self and the other which aid the child in tolerating both psychological separateness and temporary physical separations. Mahler calls this subphase "on the way to libidinal object constancy" to emphasize that the achievement is relative—continuing throughout development and remaining highly subject to regression with the vicissitudes of drive, ego, and affective states.

The significance of this model for symbolization appears to be twofold: First, it is during the height of this process that the first symbols are used and that they are first brought into relation with one another, for example, in syntactic utterances or play involving several symbolic forms or props. From a theoretical point of view, a crucial relationship suggests itself between the process of self-object differentiation and both the capacity and impetus for using symbols. Recent work elaborating and comparing definitions of mental representation and of both object permanence in the cognitive sense and object constancy in the emotional sense has raised important questions about the necessary and sufficient conditions for the maintenance of mental images of things and people in such a way as to permit their manipulation in symbolic activity (see, for example, Pine, 1974, and Fraiberg, 1969). I shall suggest below that one condition for the development of symbolization is the establishment of separate mental representations of self and object and that it may be to the period when such representations are still being established that we must look for the precursors of true symbols as well.

The second dimension of interrelation between symbolization and self-object differentiation lies in the major communicative functions of symbols and the way early symbolization can be used both to establish connections with other people and to explore the me/not-me aspects of experience. To take just one example, the child's early verbalizations, one-word utterances which sometimes stand for a whole thought, must often be misunderstood, even by the most sensitive adults, and through a myriad of such experiences the child is assisted in his awareness of his separateness from the object and the process of relinquishing his fantasies of omnipotence.

Through play the child can also make up for some of the devastations of the separation-individuation process itself. Ekstein (1972) has written, "The original pre-play is around the original object. But actual play later on will frequently constitute a fantasy about an object loss, a past object, or an object regained, by means of external objects such as toys... he will attempt through his play to create what he has fantasized: feeling of self, mastery, and the love of others" (p. 6). As a summary comment on play, he goes on to say, "Through play the child conveys to us what he means. His play also is a form of language; a form of thought; the play activity itself permits us to draw conclusions concerning the level of thought. The play then is not merely repetition of past unconscious conflict, the catharsis as reaction to trauma, the mastery of that conflict, the imitation of others, the trying out of roles, but is also an attempt to reach the love object as well as to restore self, and to master anxiety" (p. 21). And, as a final contribution to this theme, we have from Winnicott (1971), whose work has been so germane to this line of thought, the comment that "Playing implies trust, and belongs to the potential space between (what was at first) baby and mother-figure, with the baby in a state of near-absolute dependence, and the mother-figure's function taken for granted by the baby" (p. 51–52). This potential space, the first "playground," is the setting for first symbolization, and the restitution of that sense of lack of separateness may be an important motive in some of the first symbol-creating activities; I shall return to these ideas after a brief consideration of the definition of "symbolization" itself.

ON DEFINING SYMBOLIZATION

As von Bertalanffy (1965) has pointed out, "In spite of the fact that symbolic activity is one of the most fundamental manifestations of the human mind, scientific psychology has in no way given the problem the attention it deserves. Furthermore, there is no generally accepted definition of 'symbolism'" (p. 28). Although attention is increasingly being directed to the "problem" of symbolic activity, issues related to the definition of terms remain central in the field. The dictionary defines *symbolization* as the process of "representing or identifying by a symbol," a *symbol* here being "something that represents something else by association, resemblance, or convention, especially a material object used to represent something invisible" (*American Heritage Dictionary*, 1969). There are many intriguing ideas touched upon by this statement—for example, the question of the various types of relationship between the symbol and that which it represents, a question which interested Freud so much in his study of dream processes; the idea of the material symbol conveying an intangible meaning; and so on. To complete this somewhat circular dictionary definition, we need to know that in this case *represent* means "(1) To stand for or symbolize; (2) To depict or portray; (3) To present clearly to the mind."

One can also approach the problem of definition from the point of view of *function*, both what the intent of the symbolizer may be and what purposes are served by the symbolic activity—and these range widely. For Werner and Kaplan (1963), the symbol is the instrumentality through which man conquers the world's confusion and chaos and his own disorientation, through *knowing;* for Piaget (1962), the symbol is the unit of representational intelligence and basic to all further intellectual development; for psycho-analysts, the symbol conveys, in disguised form, meaningful psychic content and thereby serves a crucial function in the maintenance of psychic equilibrium. From this consideration of function it becomes clear that a cognitive psychologist and a psychoanalytic writer may have quite different referents in mind when discussing symbolization.

The main differences between the psychoanalytic and cognitive views of symbolization, however, have less to do with considerations of form or content than with the symbolizer's own awareness of his activity. In Piaget's (1962) view, as in Werner and Kaplan's (1963), the subject himself selects, or "forms," the vehicle or symbol and is aware in some sense of its distinctness from and yet relation to that which it represents. On the other hand, psychoanalytic writers speak of symbols as "the manifest expression of an idea which is more or less hidden from the subject's conscious awareness; that is, when the connection between the signifier and that which it signifies is an unconscious one" (Galenson, 1978, pp. 3–4), whether the symbol appears in a dream, an artistic production, or a symptom. Although the line of reasoning developed in the pages which follow emphasizes some ways in which these two schools of thought have similar and complementary notions about symbolization, the basic distinction between them ought to be kept in mind. (For further discussion of this point, see Sarnoff, 1970.)

A PROPOSITION REGARDING THE DEVELOPMENT OF SYMBOLIZATION AND ITS RELATION TO DIFFERENTIATION[1]

In the definitions cited above, as is often the case, the terms *symbolization* and *representation* are used somewhat interchangeably. I would propose, however, that we conceive of the process of symbolization as having two related but distinct aspects, or part processes, the developmentally later of which I would call *representation* and define as the use of an aspect of tangible experience for the transmission of meaning, of information about another aspect of experience, within a given symbolic system, making use of a particular medium, be it graphic, linguistic, gestural, etc. Further, I would specify, with Piaget, that the relationship between symbol, or vehicle, and the symbolized, or referent, not be arbitrary or by convention alone but reflect

---

[1]Many of the ideas presented here grew out of discussions with my friend and colleague Margery Bodansky Franklin, whose thinking on this and related topics has greatly influenced my own.

some conceptual link potentially identifiable through the associations of the symbolizer, whether conscious or unconscious at the moment of the formation or use of the symbol. This definition of representation emphasizes its active use of a medium, its generally communicative context, and the importance of the tangible production of a symbol as its end point and, consequently, its requirement of a relatively advanced developmental status. *Representation* seems an appropriate term for this aspect of the symbolizing process, conveying as it does the idea of "presenting again," but presumably in a new form, some prior content.

These considerations lead us now to that aspect of symbolization which I am suggesting predates representation both ontogenetically and in any given symbolic act (that is, microgenetically) and which I will call the *"endowing process."* By the term "endowing" I refer to a psychic operation in which an aspect of personal experience is embued with subjective "meaning," however organized or mentally represented. No requirement is made at this point that the symbol thus created be communicated, nor communicable, nor that it be expressed tangibly. Rather, this is a hypothesized process, taking place entirely within the mental apparatus—one, and perhaps the central, means by which human beings organize their experiential world, at least for themselves. (Within this model, one could conceive of a third stage in which, as has been explored by a number of investigators, it becomes possible to respond to instructions from someone else to represent meaning in a given medium and a fourth in which one is able to take a self-reflective stance toward the whole process—a kind of metasymbolic awareness—but this leads to a different topic, which must be put aside for the present.)

A great deal of attention has been paid to aspects of the symbolizing process I am calling representation, and it is to a preliminary consideration of the endowing process that I turn now. The work of Winnicott is especially important in this context—in particular the reader is referred to his *Playing and Reality* (1971). Winnicott has expanded Waelder's (1933) notion that playing involves the weaving of unreality around a real object; in older children and adults this can be conceived of as a "leave of absence from reality, as well as from the super-ego" (p. 222). The focus for Winnicott is a developmental one, that early stage of life when there is not yet a clear distinction between fantasy and reality or between me and not-me. The original, prototypic, creative act, then, is the endowing of a not-me, or partially not-me, aspect of experience with meaning derived from the mother-infant experience of mutuality—the constitution of what Winnicott calls a transitional object. This is the most rudimentary observable form of what I am calling the endowing process.

The *context* for this genesis of endowing is the early mother-child relationship, particularly as it enters the phase of self-object differentiation. As described above, both psychoanalytic and cognitive developmental theories posit the establishment (by 18 months to 2 years) of separate mental representations of the self and of animate and inanimate objects. It seems likely that this achievement of a dual (binary) cognitive organization of the world is a necessary condition for the child's ability to comprehend relationships between symbolic forms and referents. It is interesting that developments in the cognitive domain and those in the sphere of object relations are both organized around "twoness" at this point—fairly soon, triangularity in both object relations and relational thinking will make an appearance (for further discussion of this idea, see Abelin, 1971). Whether cognitive advances precede and make possible new levels of object relatedness or vice versa is an issue not easily resolved: What is clear, however, is that the young infant neither distinguishes self from object nor is able to manipulate symbols, and it is proposed here that the emergence of each process is importantly interrelated with that of the other.

There is interesting evidence from work with very young psychotic children supportive of this interconnection. Such children, who are characterized by their failure to achieve and maintain self-object differentiation and who either indicate little or no awareness of the maternal object or maintain a delusional fusion with their mothers, usually manifest serious defects in evolving symbolic capacities. Often language is entirely absent, and where it appears it frequently is not used in a socially communicative fashion. The level of abstraction is often inappropriate—either overly concrete or overly abstract. Symbolic play is absent or highly idiosyncratic. And as such children grow older, as well as in the schizophrenias of later childhood and adulthood, the parallel distortions of object relations and symbolic functioning continue to be dramatic and central. The underlying causal relationships here are open to debate, but the mirroring in pathology of the normal intertwining of these developmental lines lends force to the idea that endowing is at once a cognitive process and one which is attendant upon a certain level of progress in emotional and interpersonal development.

In attempting to understand and propose a model for this process of endowing we return to our comparison of the several theoretical approaches which have been taken to symbolization in general. Werner and Kaplan (1963) speak of "protosymbols," which are not yet fully representational but can be transformed into true symbols through the progressive differentiation of vehicle and referential meaning, of addressor and addressee. Piaget (1962) emphasized the distinction between symbol and symbolized and spoke of symbolization as having its roots in imitation, starting very early in the sensorimotor period (about 6 months of age). The developmental process involves for Piaget an eventual detachment of representations from the subject's activity and the immediate context and their interiorization as mental schemata, Mahler et al. (1975), Winnicott (1971), and other psychoanalytic writers speak of the differentiation of self from object and the internalization of mental representations which are both separate and (eventually) stable.

All three major theories of development, then, stress the processes of differentiation, distancing, object concept, and the need to constitute the object (and implicitly therefore the self) before one can constitute a true symbol. In considering the first 2 years of life, the theorists' notions of what the child must achieve are strikingly similar. If we are dealing, then, with a basic "truth" about development, there is much to be gained by examining these processes at an intermediate stage, when they are far enough along for there to be tangible evidence of their existence but still primitive enough to shed light on the nature of the evolving capacities. This leads us to a more detailed consideration of those first fruits of symbolization: protosymbols, semisymbolic play and gestures, consistent forms in prelinguistic language development,[2] perhaps also first words, and other expressive forms of the toddler era.

Such phenomena are just beginning to be studied in a systematic fashion, for it has taken a long time for even those interested in symbolization to turn their attention to the antecedents and early forms of the process. We can perhaps take as paradigmatic of the endowing process, as well as what may be its first visible manifestation, the behaviors Winnicott drew attention to in his discussion of transitional objects and transitional phenomena. Winnicott was describing by these terms those first appropriations by babies of objects (or routines) for their own purposes—the use of blankets or crib sheets, or special toys or songs, for self-comforting. (Linus' blanket is the most famous of these.) He supposed that these behaviors reflected a projection onto the inanimate object of feelings and meanings attached originally to the mother-me unit and experiences associated with it. The transitional object thus represents both me and mother (perhaps in different degrees at different times), and its endowment with meaning is the first truly creative act the baby performs.

A transitional object is not yet a true symbol in anyone's sense of the term—Piaget and Werner and Kaplan would point to the blurring of self and object as well as the closeness of the thing selected to the actual mother-child interaction as indicative of its not yet being a symbol, while psychoanalytic observers note the as yet undeveloped state of the psychic structures which would be necessary for repression of the connection between symbol and referent. However, it has all of the components of an endowing act and indicates the baby's readiness to select an aspect of his experiential world as the repository for a set of meanings accrued in another aspect of that world.

---

[2]See Dore, Franklin, Miller, and Ramer (1976) for a discussion of phonetically stable forms which appear to precede first words.

Although it may not be the first manifestation of the endowing process, it is often the first one visible in the child's behavior and can serve as a prototype for later, more subtle and invisible ones.

Transitional phenomena not involving objects per se are equally useful examples of the endowing process, and a description of one such behavior may help delineate the point. Becky, another young infant of my acquaintance, was breast-fed from birth to 11 months. Very early on, within the first month, she developed the habit of placing her hand on the breast as she nursed, part of her hand resting at the same time on her cheek. At about 6 months of age, Becky began to place her hand on her cheek, partly covering one eye, just as she did while nursing, but in a variety of situations in which she was tired and/or needing comfort. She maintained this means of self-soothing for many months, used it as an accompaniment to sucking on her pacifier, and continued to employ it long after she weaned herself from the breast. I would understand this pattern as Becky's use of a part of the nursing situation, one over which she had control, to in some way summon up for her the affective gestalt of the pleasureable event; that is, she endowed the touch of her hand on her cheek with the soothing quality of the whole experience of nursing and was able to make use of this to ease the separation entailed in going to sleep and to comfort herself at times of stress.

CONCLUSIONS

We have been examining the approaches of several major developmental theories to the process of symbolization in hopes of moving toward a more integrated understanding of this complex and fascinating area. We note the convergence of these theoretical emphases in notions about the importance of *differentiation* of several types during early development, despite important differences in both definition and manner of conceptualization. We have seen, further, that the second year of life may be a particularly fruitful arena for the study of symbolization in that it offers numerous examples of presymbolic activities which shed light on the process as a whole—by looking at the ontogenesis of symbolization, we may also learn something about the microgenesis of any given symbolic act. Specifically, I have proposed a division of symbolization into a first endowing stage and a second representational one and have suggested that endowing is the developmentally earlier aspect, one we can examine in status nascendi in the development of transitional objects, play, and language in the presymbolic era.

All of this points to the necessity of further investigation of first symbolization. There would appear to be a great deal to learn from such studies, with relevance to an understanding of both normal and pathological symbolic functioning. However, there are many methodological problems to be grappled with in the translation of the kinds of hypotheses presented in this discussion into operationalized studies. It would appear that the investigations of the symbolic activities of individual children both across domains and over time, beginning very early in life, may hold the key to some of the data required—some such studies are now underway (for example, Howard Gardner's work at Harvard, the work of Drucker and Franklin at Sarah Lawrence College, etc.), but our understanding and approaches to such questions are as yet tentative beginnings. Nonetheless, the potential yield of such work is great and holds promise of furthering our knowledge about the interaction among evolving ego functions, the organization of the ego, and the development of object relatedness.

Finally, an examination of the roots of the symbolic process may bring us closer to understanding its most complex form, the creative process in the artist. It is possible that in cultures like ours, where shared, somewhat routinized, symbolization is so much emphasized, we tend to lose touch with the developmental wellspring of the endowing process. Freud (1961b) wrote, "Every playing child behaves like a poet, in that he creates a world of his own, or more accurately expressed, he transposes things into his world according to a new arrangement which is to his liking. [There is a clear parallel here to Piaget's notion of assimilation, but Freud continues as follows.] It would be unfair to believe that he does not take this world seriously; on the contrary, he takes his play very seriously, he spends large amounts of affect on it. The antithesis of play is reality, not seriousness" (pp. 143–144).

Increasingly, psychologists have been taking play "seriously," and I suggest that we begin to take very early play (and symbolization generally) very seriously indeed.

REFERENCES

Abelin, E. The role of the father in the separation-individuation process. In J. McDevitt & C. Settlage (Eds.), *Separation-individuation.* New York: International Universities Press, 1971.
American Heritage dictionary of the English language. New York: American Heritage, 1969.
Bühler, K. *The mental development of the child.* New York: Harcourt, Brace, 1930.
Dore, J., Franklin, M. B., Miller, R., & Ramer, A. Transitional phenomena in early language acquisition. *Journal of Child Language,* 1976, *3,* 13–28.
Drucker, J. Toddler play: Some comments on its functions in the developmental process. *Psychoanalysis and Contemporary Science,* 1975, *IV,* 479–528.
Ekstein, R. *From the language of play to play with language.* Paper presented at the New York University Post-Doctoral Colloqium, New York, 1972.
Erikson, E. H. *Childhood and society.* New York: Norton, 1950.
Ferenczi, S. On eye symbolism. In *Sex in psychoanalysis.* New York: Basic Books, 1950.
Fraiberg, S. Libidinal object constancy and mental representation. *Psychoanalytic Study of the Child,* 1969, *XXIV,* 9–47.
Freud, A. *The psychoanalytical treatment of children.* London: Imago, 1946.

Freud, S. Introductory lectures on psychoanalysis. In J. Strachey (Ed.), *Standard edition of the complete psychological works of Sigmund Freud* (Vol. XV). London: Hogarth Press, 1961. (a)

Freud, S. Creative Writers and Day-dreaming. In J. Strachey (Ed.), *Standard edition of the complete psychological works of Sigmund Freud,* (Vol. IX). London: Hogarth Press, 1961. (b)

Galenson, E. A consideration of the nature of thought in childhood play. In J. McDevitt & C. Settlage (Eds.), *Separation-individuation.* New York: International Universities Press, 1971.

Galenson, E. *The capacity for symbolic expression: An ego function.* Paper presented at the Sarah Lawrence College Conference on Play. Manuscript submitted for publication, 1978.

Gardner, H. *The arts in human development.* New York: Wiley, 1973.

Greenacre, P. *Emotional growth* (Vol. I, II). New York: International Universities Press, 1971.

Greenson, R. The mother tongue and the mother. *International Journal of Psychoanalysis,* 1950, *XXXI,* 18–23.

Kestenberg, J. On the development of maternal feelings in early childhood. *Psychoanalytic Study of the Child,* 1956, *XI,* 257–291.

Klein, M. *The psychoanalysis of children.* London: Hogarth Press, 1932.

Mahler, M., Pine, F., & Bergmann, A. *The psychological birth of the human infant.* New York: International Universities Press, 1975.

Peller, L. Libidinal phases, ego development, and play. *Psychoanalytic Study of the Child,* 1954, *IX,* 178–198.

Piaget, J. *Play, dreams and imitation in childhood.* New York: Norton 1962.

Pine, F. Libidinal object constancy: A theoretical note. *Psychoanalysis and Contemporary Science,* 1974, *III,* 307–316.

Sarnoff, C. Symbols and symptoms. *Psychoanalytic Quarterly,* 1970, *39,* 550–562.

von Bertalanffy, L. On the definition of the symbol. In J. Royce (Ed.), *Psychology and the symbol.* New York: Random House, 1965.

Waelder, R. The psychoanalytic theory of play. *Psychoanalytic Quarterly,* 1933, *2,* 208–224.

Winnicott, D. W. *Playing and reality.* New York: Basic Books, 1971.

Werner, H. & Kaplan, B. *Symbol formation.* New York: Wiley, 1963.

3 Mundane Symbolism: The Relations Among Objects, Names, and Ideas

Mary C. Potter
Massachusetts Institute of Technology

Symbolization is the representing of an object or event by something other than itself. Three aspects of symbol comprehension will be discussed: (1) *recognition* that a given symbol refers to a particular object; (2) *discrimination* between the symbol and the object itself; and (3) *interpretation* of the similarities and differences between the symbol and the object. The first of these aspects is the most central and is the one on which we focus in this chapter. Brief consideration of the other two aspects will follow.

Two theories of symbol recognition that stem from different theories of mental representation can be contrasted. According to the *dual coding* theory, symbols such as the names of objects succeed in referring by eliciting verbal associations and by activating the appearance or image of those objects. According to the *conceptual* theory, names refer by activating amodal concepts (ideas) that are neither perceptual nor verbal. The importance of distinguishing between these two theories, for the study of symbolization, is that the theories disagree on the status of verbal symbols. The dual coding theory allots a special abstract status to words and their associations, distinct from the concrete nature of perception. Because abstract classes such as *furniture* or *democracy* have names but do not have a single perceptual equivalent, verbal thinking is given a power denied to imagery. In contrast, the conceptual theory of representation puts perception and imagery more nearly on a par with verbal comprehension, because all knowledge (apart from names and appearances) is considered part of a single system. Since each view has profound implications for intellectual functioning and development, including the development of symbolization, the two theories are reviewed in detail. To anticipate, we conclude that the conceptual theory is supported by the preponderance of evidence.

One implication of the conceptual theory is that comprehension of symbols such as words parallels perceptual comprehension, since both processes depend on the activation of the same abstract ideas. The similarity between the two processes of perception and symbol comprehension is evident not only for recognition, but also for the second and third aspects of symbolization: discrimination and interpretation. The development of perceptual competence, it is argued later in the chapter, parallels and foreshadows all three aspects of the development of symbol comprehension. The parallel suggests that percepts can be regarded as mundane symbols of object concepts, symbols whose mastery leads to comprehension of both the iconic symbols of art and the conventional symbols of language.

RECOGNITION OF A SYMBOL

How are symbols such as words and pictures understood? The first step is recognition that a particular symbol—say, the spoken word *chair* or a sketch such as

—refers to an already familiar entity, a chair. In representational art and in the use of spoken or written names, the problem of figuring out what object is being symbolized may seem trivial to an adult, but of course it is not. To discover what a word names, children have to divide the world of experience into a set of objects and events that correspond to the names in the language they are learning; how such a division is made is not always obvious (Quine, 1960). Only then can they learn name-object associations in spoken and finally in written language.

Symbol recognition is apparently less difficult for drawings or photographs than for words and least difficult for realistic sculpture and theatrical performance. The more closely the symbol resembles the referent, the easier the recognition process, at least during learning. Goodman (1968) has argued that pictures do not resemble visual appearances very precisely, but clearly there are similarities of contour and color or relative brightness between pictures and perceived objects. To recognize the referent, however, the viewer must overlook the patent differences, such as the flatness of a painting or picture. Even a young child seems to be capable of disregarding these differences and recognizing photographs and drawing of objects, as Hochberg and Brooks'(1962) dramatic experiment with a 19-month-old child who had never seen pictures demonstrates.[1]

---

[1]When pictures are deliberately made difficult to understand, for example, by blurring a photograph, there is a marked improvement with age in the ability to recognize what is pictured (Potter, 1966). In such conditions, however, problem-solving skill interacts with ordinary perceptual recognition.

In an unpublished study with eight children about 3 years of age Potter and Faulconer (1973) compared children's ability to name real objects and line drawings of the objects. The children had little difficulty recognizing simple line drawings of objects and in fact were able to name them about as rapidly as they named the real objects. The same is evidently true for brain-injured patients with some degree of aphasia—if they can name at all, they do about as well with drawings as with the objects themselves (Corlew & Nation, 1975). Although there have been some reports to the contrary, most studies show that adults and children who have not seen pictures before have surprisingly little difficulty in recognizing what is depicted in a photograph or realistic line drawing (see Hagen, 1974, for a review of this issue and a discussion of ways in which pictures may resemble what they depict).

Although a piece of representational art may correspond with what it symbolizes in contour, color, and the like, any picture still has many conventions that have to be learned. The most obvious of these stem from the two-dimensional representation of three-dimensional objects and spatial layouts. The mimicking of perspective as it would appear if viewed with one eye from a fixed point, disregarding the true distance of the picture surface, is only one way in which the idea of the third dimension might be represented. In another convention, more distant objects are placed higher in the picture without shrinking their size. What looks realistic in one era or culture, in consequence, may look mannered or artificial in another.

The one nonphotographic form with which young children may be most familiar is the cartoon and its static equivalent, the comic strip. Curiously, these forms have numerous conventions, and yet children seem to have little difficulty comprehending them. Studies of Brooks (1977) and Friedman and Stevenson (1975) suggest, however, that action lines and other cartoon conventions are not fully used by children until as late as the ninth grade. Eventually they appear to be understood as automatically and directly as the iconic aspects of the cartoon; their arbitrariness becomes invisible.

Thus, symbols may be recognized either by their resemblance to their referents or (as in the case of words and the conventions of art) by learning. Just what mental events underlie each type of recognition? Consider the simplest case, recognition of symbols for concrete objects. In the chair example already mentioned, one sees the word *chair* or a sketch of a chair and thinks of a chair. But what is "thinking of a chair" in each case? Two different accounts follow.

Two Theories of Mental Representation

Dual Coding Theory

According to dual coding theory there are two distinct systems or codes of mental representation, one verbal and the other pictorial or image-like (Paivio, 1971, 1975a). One system represents knowledge about the appearance, feel, or sound (if any) of objects such as chairs. Thinking of a chair, in this knowledge system, is activating stored images based on previous perceptions of chairs. These memory images may be somewhat schematic, but they share the spatial characteristics and other sensory qualities of perception. The other system of knowledge, according to dual coding theory, is language-based knowledge, consisting of associations among words. The word *chair* may activate associated words such as *table*, superordinate words such as *furniture*, functions such as *sitting*, and so on.

The two systems of knowledge are linked by learned associations between images and names: A chair image is associated with the word *chair* and vice versa. Understanding the symbol *chair* thus includes activation of two sorts of knowledge: verbal associations and images. Similarly, understanding a sketch of a chair consists of classifying it (by similarity) into the appropriate image category which in turn activates its name and other associations in the verbal system.

Because the word *chair* first enters the verbal system, an extra step is required to evoke the corresponding image. That step takes time and does not invariably occur when we read or hear *chair*. Conversely, when we see a chair or a picture of a chair the image representation is first activated, and an extra step is needed to evoke the chair's verbal representation, that is, its lexical entry or name.[2] Again, the step takes time. An asymmetry between verbal and image codes is hypothesized, however. When one looks at an object or a drawing of it, its name is automatically activated (given sufficient time), whereas when one reads or hears a word naming a concrete object, the corresponding image is not necessarily activated. The dual coding theory is diagrammed in Fig. 3.1.

Although concrete objects such as chairs are represented both in the verbal and in the imaginal system, the meanings of many words that refer to abstract entities (such as *liberty* or *infinity*) are represented almost entirely in the verbal system. The verbal system develops as a symbol system of words mapped onto objects—tables and cars and dogs—but through intraverbal connections it becomes autonomous, capable of representing functions, relations, and structures that are abstract rather than perceptible. Thus the verbal system is specialized for representing abstract knowledge whereas the image system represents perceptual properties of objects such as their shapes, colors, and sizes. Since speech is temporally ordered, the verbal system is specialized for the representation of serial order, whereas the image system is specialized for the representation of simultaneous spatial position.

---

[2]The lexical entry of a word includes information about its sound, spelling, and articulation; that is what is meant here by *name*. Whether the lexical entry is a necessary route to knowledge about a *pictured* object (such as its semantic category) is the theoretical point at issue.

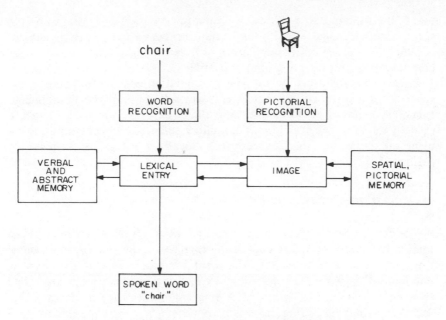

FIG. 3.1. Dual coding model of picture and word representation.

Evidence for Dual Coding Theory.   There are many experimental results that have been cited in support of the dual coding theory, of which I will mention only the major findings.

1. *Naming time.* It has been known for a century or so that people take longer to name objects (or drawings) than to name (i.e., read aloud) words. That is exactly what the theory would predict, since an extra step, between systems, is required to get from the image to the name of an object.

2. *Recall.*   Drawings are recalled more often than words in experiments in which a list of unrelated words or drawings is learned. Since a drawing rather automatically activates its name, according to the theory, drawings are dually encoded. Words are less likely to activate images spontaneously, and so they are not dually encoded during learning. On the reasonable assumption that two memory representations are better than one, the advantage of drawings in later recall is explained by the theory. In further confirmation of the theory, deliberate imaging of words greatly enhances their recall. In addition, abstract words (which are difficult or impossible to picture) are more difficult to remember than concrete words, just as expected.

3. *Rapid serial presentation.* When a sequence of unrelated words or drawings is presented for immediate recall drawings are, if anything, worse than words. Why does a dual coding theory make this prediction? A drawing

takes time to name, so a sufficiently rapid presentation will result in only a single code, the image code. For immediate recall, especially when the subject is required to recall in the same order as in presentation, the verbal system (specialized for representing temporal order) has an advantage.

4. *Hemispheric specialization.* The accumulating evidence for hemispheric specialization of function is consistent with dual coding theory. Language functions are found predominantly and almost exclusively in one hemisphere (usually the left), and certain spatial abilities such as face recognition, map-using capacities, and the like seem to be localized in the right hemisphere (Milner, 1971, has a useful review).

Conceptual Coding Theory

The conceptual theory of mental representation claims that in addition to images and words there are conceptual representations, that is, representations of the idea of an object. The mental concept *chair*, in this view, is common to the word *chair* and a picture of a chair and is directly accessible from either the word or the object. A diagram of this theory is shown in Fig. 3.2. As in the dual coding theory, there is a structural distinction between one's memory for the appearance of an object and one's memory for the word

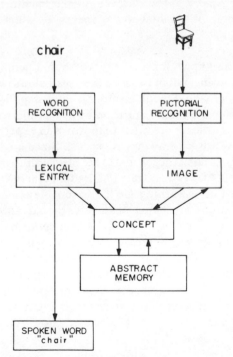

FIG. 3.2. Conceptual model of picture and word representation.

naming the object, but the conceptual theory claims that there is in addition a more abstract conceptual representation common to both.

The conceptual theory proposes that "thinking of a chair" consists of the activation of a concept or idea that is neither verbal nor perceptual. Except for stock phrases and idioms, words are not associated with each other; rather, concepts are associated. When we understand a word, we must first locate it in a lexical "dictionary," but its meaning and associations are not found there. According to this theory, the lexical entry is only a route to the conceptual system in which ideas that correspond to words are stored. When we understand a sketch of a chair, that same chair concept is activated, this time via stored information about the appearances of objects. In this case, the name of the object plays no role in understanding. Instead of two functionally distinct systems of knowledge, one concretely perceptual and the other verbal and hence inherently symbolic and abstract, the conceptual theory proposes that words and appearances are simply way stations on the route to a conceptual representation. Words, pictures, and perceived objects are all equivalent in that they converge on a single concept.[3]

Accounting for the Evidence. The conceptual theory can also account for most of the evidence just cited for the dual coding theory.

1. *Naming time.* The slower naming of a drawing than a word is predicted by this model also, as inspection of Fig. 3.2 will show.

2. *Recall.* The relative advantage of drawings over words in recall experiments may be attributed to greater depth of processing of drawings. The recognition of a written word could stop at the level of the lexical entry without evoking the concept; for example, one could read a word aloud without necessarily becoming aware of its meaning first. Rehearsal of a word might involve only the lexical representation, not the concept. A drawing or perceived object, however, seems invariably and automatically to continue past the pattern-recognition process to the level of conceptual meaning. If the viewer adopts the strategy of naming drawings and rehearsing the names, he will still be obliged to activate the drawing's concept in order to retrieve its name.

Thus, images may be automatically understood, but words—especially in a list-learning experiment—may not be. This assumption is a modification of

---

[3]A concept is regarded here as a point or node in mental and neural processing which, when active, makes information about an object or entity available to thought. Just what kinds of information are included in a concept and whether the information becomes available as a packet or piecemeal are theoretically important questions that remain to be answered. In computer models of mental representation such as that of Lindsay, Norman, and Rumelhart (Norman & Rumelhart, 1975), a concept is represented as a node in a network. The "meaning" of the concept is the position of that node in relation to other nodes and ultimately its connection with the inputs ("perceptions") and outputs ("productions") of the whole system.

the assumption of the dual coding theory that images are automatically named but words are not automatically imaged. The modified assumption explains why drawings are more readily recalled than words: They are more likely to have been processed at the conceptual level (Craik & Tulving, 1975). Further, asking a subject to image a word would ensure that it, too, was processed conceptually, since the only way to retrieve the image corresponding to a word would be to retrieve its concept. That would account for the finding that instructions to image increase the probability of recalling words. (A residual advantage of pictures over imaged words may reflect the novel detail present in a picture, detail that may not appear in a self-produced image; cf. Nelson, Reed, & Walling, 1976, and Potter, Valian, & Faulconer, 1977.)

There remains the question of why abstract words are harder to remember than concrete words. One possibility is that abstract words have a less focussed conceptual representation, a less clear-cut meaning, than concrete words. Consistent with that possibility, people produce fewer word associations to abstract than to concrete words (Paivio, 1971) and they rate sentences containing abstract nouns as more difficult and less meaningful than those with concrete, imageable nouns (Johnson, Bransford, Nyberg, & Cleary, 1972). The memory disadvantage may not be in the lack of an image corresponding to an abstract word but in the relative diffuseness of the representation in the conceptual system.

3. *Rapid serial presentation.* The third class of evidence cited above for the dual coding theory concerns the rapid presentation of a series of items. When drawings are presented rapidly there may only be time for activation of the image schema and concept, not the name. With rapid presentation of words, however, the lexical entry is quickly activated, and it includes a representation of the sound and articulation of the word. These sound (or motor) codes can be entered into an acoustic-phonemic short-term memory (e.g., Baddeley, 1976; Crowder, 1976; Penney, 1975) where they can be rehearsed in order, as the dual coding theory also claims.

No corresponding short-term memory appears to exist for *sequences* of visual images (Potter & Levy, 1969). (It is not clear whether a serial short-term memory exists for concepts apart from their names.) Thus either for immediate ordered recall or for recall after very rapid serial presentation, words may be equal to or superior to pictures. At slower rates or when recall in serial order is not required, drawings will be equal or superior. That is just what investigators have found (Nelson, Reed, & McEvoy, 1977; Paivio & Csapo, 1969, 1971; Paivio, Philipchalk, & Rowe, 1975). Moreover, a recent experiment obtained no support for the dual coding prediction that at a high rate of presentation a picture's naming latency would be negatively correlated with the likelihood that it would be retained (Intraub, 1979).

4. *Hemispheric specialization.* As for the evidence that the two hemispheres are specialized in the way that the dual coding theory predicts, the conceptual theory also claims that images and names are represented in distinct systems and might therefore be analyzed in different hemispheres. Since there are large parts of the cortex that are not known to be specialized for language, spatial functions, perception, or motor activity, it is entirely possible that amodal conceptual representation is subsumed by those areas.

Tests of the Two Theories

Both theories can account for most of the evidence so far described. Is there a critical test of the theories, or are they impossible to distinguish? The key difference between them is that the dual coding theory identifies abstract knowledge with the verbal system, whereas the conceptual theory separates abstract knowledge from both the verbal and the image systems. The dual coding theory claims that to retrieve from memory abstract information about an object—for example, its superordinate category—one has to enter the verbal system. Since it takes longer to name an object or drawing than to name aloud a written word, it should also take longer to *categorize* an object abstractly than to categorize the object's written name, according to the dual coding theory.

In contrast, the conceptual theory claims that abstract information is part of the conceptual system and can therefore be retrieved directly when an object or drawing is perceived, without first naming the object. Thus, although it takes longer to name an object than to name a word, it will not necessarily take any longer to categorize the object.

Naming Versus Categorizing Pictures and Words.   An experimental test of the two theories was carried out by Potter and Faulconer (1975), who contrasted two tasks: naming and categorizing. The method used was the following. We started with a large set of line drawings of objects and their written names. The first step was to make sure that the drawings and words to be used in the experiments were equally easy to see as visual patterns. We measured the minimum time that each item had to be in view in order to be seen correctly, using a masking procedure. For the group of 96 items that were used in the subsequent experiments, the average times were very close: 44 msec for the drawings and 46 msec for the words. Thus, the pattern-recognition stage (see Fig. 3.1 and 3.2) was roughly equal for the two types of material. The next step was to obtain naming times. A group of eight college students named each item in one or the other form, and the time to start pronouncing the name was measured using a voice key. Just as earlier

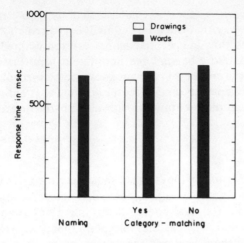

FIG. 3.3. Mean response times to name a word or drawing and to decide whether it is a member of a previously named category (from Potter & Faulconer, 1975).

investigators had found, it took almost 40% longer to name the drawings than it did to read the words aloud.[4]

Finally, in the critical experiment a new group of 16 students categorized the items. The 96 items fell into 18 superordinate categories such as food, furniture, clothing, and tools. Just before each item was shown to the subject, the experimenter named a category. The task of the subject was to say *yes* if the drawing or word matched the category that had just been named and *no* if it did not. (Half the time the category and item did not match). Again response time was measured. The results for both the naming and category-matching experiments are shown in Fig. 3.3. Even though drawings took 260 msec longer to name than words, it took subjects about 50 msec *less* time to decide on the category of a drawing than a word, contrary to the prediction of the dual coding theory.

It might be argued in support of the dual coding theory that the superordinate category of a concrete object such as a cow or shoe—that is, animal or clothing—is itself a concrete, imageable idea. If so, a drawing could

---

[4]It has been suggested that pronunciation of a word might not require prior activation of the lexical entry for that word, because orthographic-phonemic rules can be used to map the spelling onto sound. That is, a word provides a map for pronunciation, and that alone might explain the difference in naming time of words and pictures, making the latencies an invalid measure of time to activate the lexical entry (the verbal code). Indeed, adults can pronounce regularly spelled nonwords such as *tavon* almost as quickly as real words (Forster & Chambers, 1973; Frederiksen & Kroll, 1976). Chinese characters have no equivalent orthographic-phonemic rules, and so naming requires lexical retrieval. Hence the relative naming times for Chinese characters and pictures provide a test of the orthographic-phonemic explanation of the naming time difference found in English. Using native Chinese speakers, Potter, So, Ng, and Friedman (1978) found that characters are named much faster than pictures, exactly as in English. Since lexical retrieval is markedly faster for Chinese words than pictures, there is no reason to attribute the difference between English words and pictures solely to the use of spelling-sound rules.

be matched in the image system and a word in the verbal system, processes which might take similar times. A little reflection, however, will make clear that a category such as *animal* or *clothing* cannot be imaged except by thinking of a particular exemplar. Although cows look enough alike that an image of any particular cow may resemble most other cows, an image of any particular animal certainly does not resemble all other animals. To take another example, all shoes may look somewhat alike, but shoes and hats and coats do not look alike. This point has been established clearly by Rosch, Mervis, Gray, Johnson, and Boyes-Braem (1976), who use the term "basic level object" to describe the level of classification at which exemplars resemble each other.

The items used in Potter and Faulconer's experiments were basic level objects, in Rosch's sense. The superordinate categories, however, were at a level too abstract to permit category matching on the basis of perceptual features common to all members of the category. Instead, each item would have to be recognized at the basic level (e.g., as a shoe) before it could be compared with the category *clothing*. The theoretical issue, to repeat, is whether associations such as that between *shoe* and the abstract category *clothing* are part of a verbal system or are part of an amodal, conceptual system. The results we obtained support the latter hypothesis.

Other Picture-Word Tasks. In a series of subsequent experiments (Potter, 1978; Potter & Elliot, 1978; Potter, Klein, Faulconer, Feldman, So, & Garrett, 1978; Potter, So, Ng, & Friedman, 1978; Potter, Valian, & Faulconer, 1977) we verified the conclusion that both drawings and words have rather direct access to a wide range of conceptual knowledge about the object, including not only its superordinate category but also its value, associations, and even its name in another language. Only the sound characteristics (such as what a word rhymes with), the articulation, and the orthography of a word seem to be represented as part of the verbal system. Even when one is reading a sentence serially at a high rate, a picture can replace a word without disrupting comprehension (Potter, Kroll, & Harris, 1979; Potter, Kroll, Yachzel, & Cohen, 1978).

As for the image system, apart from features such as the shape of an object that are obviously more available in a drawing than in a word, there is as yet no clear evidence that knowledge about nonpictured sensory attributes (such as familiar size) are more directly available when one looks at a picture than when one looks at a word. Rather, there appears to be a small but consistent advantage of drawings over words in getting at abstract information such as an object's category as well as at quasi-perceptual information such as usual size (Banks & Flora, 1977; Paivio, 1975b; Pellegrino, Rosinski, Chiesi, & Siegel, 1977; Potter, 1978).

The findings just described support the conceptual theory's claim that in addition to a lexical system and a perceptual or imagery system adults have a third memory system in which concepts are represented amodally. We can now raise briefly a question about the development of these three systems of representation before turning again to the main issue of symbol recognition.

Development of Representational Systems

Since the apparatus of object perception is largely innate whereas a language has to be learned, it might seem reasonable to suppose that a child first represents knowledge in a form close to perception. Further, since words (other than proper names) categorize experience by referring to classes of objects whereas perceptions are necessarily of single instances, it might also seem reasonable to suppose that the growth of abstract concepts is precipitated by and closely tied to the acquisition of language. This view is more consistent with the dual coding theory just rejected than with the conceptual theory, since it gives language a special function in the organizing (and hence probably in the retrieval) of concepts.

Dual Coding in Childhood? Is it possible, then, that dual coding occurs early in development, to be replaced later by conceptual coding? That is, early in the acquisition of concepts, are they bound separately to words and to percepts? That idea was tested in a number of studies carried out by E. J. Gibson and her students. Gibson, Barron, and Garber (1972) hypothesized that if young children have two somewhat independent systems of representation for objects and for words, then they should experience greater difficulty in comparing a word and a drawing than in comparing two words or two drawings. Rader (1975) had children decide whether two objects—either two written words, two pictures, or a word and a picture—belonged to the same or different categories. Although second graders were much slower on words than drawings, the mixed pairs took no longer than the average of word pairs and drawing pairs, contrary to the dual coding prediction. Rosinski, Pellegrino, and Siegel (1977) used the same task and obtained a similar result: Children of grades 2 and 6, like adults, can deal about as well with a mixture of pictures and written words as they can with words alone or pictures alone.

The task of comparing superordinate categories, however, requires an abstraction that cannot be represented in a perceptual-imaginal system, I have argued. Therefore, the paradigm used by Rader and by Rosinski et al. may be unsuitable for testing Gibson's idea that dual coding precedes conceptual coding in development. What other evidence have we that young children do or do not have a single concept for objects and their names? In experiments with adults, Bransford and Franks (1971) presented a set of sentences about a single event or scene. The subjects spontaneously integrated the information into a single representation, making whatever inferences were necessary to do so. In consequence, they later had difficulty distinguishing between the exact sentences they had been presented and new sentences that were consistent with an integrated conceptual representation. Paris and Mahoney (1974) asked whether children (in grades 2 and 4) integrate sentence information as adults do and in addition asked whether a set of pictures containing information like that in the sentence sets would lead to the same kind of integration. They found that children did integrate both sentence sets and picture sets. Further, they found that picture-set integration transferred almost completely to test sentences. A child who saw two pictures, one showing a box to the right of a tree and the other a chair on top of the box (but no tree), was quite likely to report falsely that the sentence "The chair is to the right of the tree" corresponded with a picture.

Interference Tasks. Another sort of evidence for a single conceptual system common to words and objects has been obtained, for adults, in Stroop-type interference experiments. For example, naming a page of drawings of objects takes longer when names of other objects are printed in the center of the drawing. That is, an adult cannot help processing the written words even when he is trying to attend only to the drawings (Ehri, 1976; Rosinski, Golinkoff, & Kukish, 1975). Would children show less interference, as though they can process in each mode independently? The same experimenters tested children in grades 2 and up. At all ages, the incongruous words slowed naming; the only exception was a group of slow readers in grade 2 who were not affected by the incongruous words (Ehri, 1976). At least when the task is to produce a name, words are processed automatically even when a child is attending to a picture. The converse is also true, as Willows (1975) and Rosinski et al. (1975) found when children read words superimposed on drawings. The automatic merging of verbal and pictorial information, at all ages, is more consistent with a conceptual than a dual coding account.

Conceptual Representation in Infants? The experiments just described were carried out with children who could read. What about younger children? K. Nelson (1974) argues for a single conceptual basis of knowledge in children from the earliest age. She suggests that the core of an object concept is normally a functional, sensory-motor scheme, to which are attached other attributes such as an object's name and appearance. This view is consistent with the conceptual hypothesis, but the empirical evidence for it remains somewhat elusive. How we should characterize the system or sytems of mental representation of a child as young as 2 or 3 continues to be problematical.

Development of Memory for Pictures and Words. Another approach to the dual-systems question is to look for possible age changes in memory for pictures and words. For adults a word list is harder to remember than an equivalent list of pictures. Are words even more disadvantaged for children? The answer appears to be no: The relative advantage of pictures remains roughly constant. For example, Perlmutter and Myers (1976) gave children of 37 and 53 months lists of objects in the form of drawings or spoken names or both drawings and their names. The drawings were easier to remember than their names (in a yes-no recognition task), but the effect did not interact with age. Equally interesting is the lack of an interaction between the form of the item in learning and in the test. It was harder to learn words than pictures and harder to recognize a named item than a pictured one, but there was no *additional* disadvantage to being tested in a different format from that of learning. The implication is that names and pictures had the same core conceptual representation.

To summarize, these studies of children agree with those of adults in suggesting that words, pictures, and perceived objects all have direct access to a single underlying conceptual system. Entrance to that system does not require naming, and conversely reading a word aloud does not necessarily require prior access to that word's concept. The dual coding model is correct in claiming that word names are stored separately from the images or appearances of objects, but in addition to the imaginal and verbal systems of representation there is a third more abstract system present in children at least as young as 6. Even in children, then, much of thought may be conceptual rather than specifically linguistic or imagistic.

Percepts as Symbols

The evidence that has been presented on timed responses to pictures and words shows that when we retrieve knowledge about an object it matters little whether we are cued by a picture or by a word. What about perception of a real object? Is it a fundamentally different process from perception of arbitrary symbols such as words and iconic symbols such as pictures? Evidence already discussed suggests that pictures can be understood with little or no learning, which suggests in turn that recognition of pictures makes use of some of the same processes that lead to recognition of real objects. It seems, then, that word, picture, and object comprehension are closely related.

Images as Representations of Meaning?   Since we already rejected the notion that the relation among an object, its name, and its picture consists of convergence on the name or verbal code, could we say instead that they all converge on a perception-like representation, that is, an image? The answer is no, both on logical and on experimental grounds. On logical grounds, the image theory of mental representation is unworkable. There is no single perceptual experience that is necessary for me to know that this object is a pencil, and in fact an entirely new perceptual experience (such as feeling it under a rug with my toes) could inform me of its identity. A prototypical image cannot be the core representation of an object, since surely I do not constantly refer to such an image to understand atypical exemplars. If I encounter a mechanical pencil that looks like a pen, I know it is a pencil despite its appearance, not by imaging a typical pencil in its stead. A prototypical image may help me to identify a new instance of a pencil, but the product of identification is a pencil concept that unites information not only about typical appearance but also about function, material, cost, places in which it is likely to be found, and an indefinite amount of other information.[5]

On experimental grounds, Potter and Faulconer's evidence against a verbal basis for concepts also allows rejection of an imaginal basis. Although pictures of objects are understood somewhat faster than written words, the difference of about 50 msec is too small to permit a word to be imaged. Tasks that do require imaging (such as recalling whether given lowercase letters have risers or descenders) take 500 msec or more per image (Weber & Castleman, 1970).

Conceptual Representation of Perceived Objects

Word, picture, and object comprehension are thus fundamentally similar in that all depend on the activation of a conceptual representation of the object. One recognizes an object when the sensory array leads to the activation of a mental representation that includes knowledge retained from previous experience with that object or similar objects. The same conceptual representation is activated when the object's name or picture is understood.[6] In an important sense, then, the appearance or percept of an object can be regarded as a *symbol* for the object's concept. Unlike words, of course, the perceptual "symbol system" is for the most part innately determined, so that people who share the same five senses share much the same perceptual language.

Even though the capacity to acquire concepts on the basis of perceptual experience is innately programmed, it takes time to mature. Piaget's work is an outstanding guide to the stages of development of the capacity to represent

---

[5]A discussion of the issue of images as representations of meaning is found in Fodor, Bever, and Garrett (1974) and Fodor (1975) and a debate about the nature of imagery in Pylyshyn (1973), Kosslyn and Pomerantz (1977), and Anderson (1978).

[6]There is an important conceptual distinction between a definite object such as this pencil and an indefinite class of objects such as pencils. Introduction of the distinction complicates the theory but does not change the main conclusions reached here.

a permanent object, one that persists even when it is out of sight or has altered in appearance. Just as an arbitrary symbol such as a word is understood when the appropriate concept is activated, so a child comes to understand a particular percept when he has built up a concept that abstracts away from fluctuating sensory experience. The concept achieves stability by correlating perceptual information from several senses and joining with it conceptual information acquired through language, pictures, and other symbol systems. Concepts, not appearances or names, are the enduring mental representations of reality.

The apparently innate ability to correct for changes in illumination, distance, angle of view, and the like and to perceive the same object despite such differences in sensation, called perceptual constancy, is the forerunner of a more general ability to use a variety of symbols as direct routes to a single concept. That is, whether the association between a particular set of perceptual experiences and a mental concept was programmed during evolution or whether it is acquired through learning, the relation is that between a symbol and a concept.

Summary: Symbol Recognition

The first stage of symbol comprehension is to recognize what object or entity a symbol represents, that is, what mental concept the symbol refers to.[7] In the perception of objects the first, protracted step in development is to set up those mental concepts. Initially an infant does not have the cognitive capacity to develop an enduring concept of any object. Once object concepts have been established, then perceptual constancy, generalization to new but similar perceived objects, and activation of the concept by pictures and by spoken words or gestures all become possible. The evidence strongly suggests that words and simple drawings of objects activate the relevant concept rapidly and directly, even in young children. The ready responses of 1- and 2-year-old children to spoken language and pictures does not appear to be discontinuous with their ability to recognize and understand real objects. In this account, perception of objects itself requires a semiotic capacity; the ability to recognize symbols such as words and pictures grows directly out of that capacity.

---

[7]Note that in this case a symbol such as a word is considered to refer to or represent a mental *concept* of an object, rather than the real-world object. The processes under discussion do not have information about real-world objects except via percepts of the objects, perceived symbols, and mental concepts. Within this system, percepts and perceived symbols refer to (represent) object concepts. From the point of view of an outside observer, however, one can talk about the relation between real physical objects and their representation in a person's percepts and concepts. Which usage of "represent" is intended should be clear in context.

DISCRIMINATION BETWEEN SYMBOLS
AND PERCEIVED OBJECTS

Once a symbol such as a word or drawing becomes capable of activating the appropriate underlying concept, a second problem may arise. Since on other occasions the same concept may be activated perceptually by the real object, how does the perceiver distinguish between the presence of the object and a symbolic mention of it? How is it that symbols such as words and pictures *represent* real objects, whereas real objects don't represent anything—they simply *are* objects? The appearance or feeling or sound of a real object is not the object itself (if we speak carefully); rather, a percept is a mental event that innately and through learning is able to activate the concept of the object.[8] Since the percept coexists with the concept, however, the total mental event is different when a real object is perceived than when it is mentioned. A word does not look or sound (ordinarily) like the thing it symbolizes. Hence an adult knows that a perceived pencil can be used to write and can break, whereas the word *pencil* cannot. Conversely, the word can be loud or soft, whereas a perceived pencil cannot be. Similarly, pictures are flat and static, so they fool the eye only under special circumstances.

Since the same concept is part of the mental representation in all cases, however, one might expect occasional failures to discriminate between symbols and object perceptions. Although an infant soon learns not to eat the picture of an apple, he may remain reluctant to touch the picture of a spider or snake. In adults as well as children, the impact of a play or television drama depends in part on such failures to distinguish between symbol and reality; only by suspending disbelief can we participate in the events and feelings portrayed. As we know, children are fascinated by play acting and as-if situations as long as a proper tension between the symbolic and the real is maintained. When the balance tips too far, a child or even an adult may be terrified or shaken with sorrow.

The failure to distinguish between a symbol and the real object is ordinarily unidirectional: The symbol is treated as a real object, not vice versa. It has been suggested, however, that the opposite can happen. The reality of an event may become thin and insubstantial when it is experienced only through perceptions that are removed in time and space from their real objects (such as

---

[8]In the history of perception that goes back to the ancient Greeks, explanations of how we see objects have only slowly moved away from the misconception that percepts convey knowledge of objects because they resemble them to the realization that systematic correspondence between physical stimuli and neural patterning is the basis of veridical representation (Held, 1965). In Held's words, "the identity and continuity of objects can be regarded as the outcome of this [perceptual] processing rather than as its cause. The establishment of correspondence then becomes tantamount to discovering the laws of operation of the perceptive mechanism" (p. 54).

television news films of a war). Or a symbolized experience becomes bigger than life; one owner of a wall-sized television screen said that it had become uninteresting to meet celebrities in person.

Vygotsky (1962) points out still another kind of confusion that may arise during development. To quote,

> for a long time the word is to the child a property, rather than the symbol, of the object... the child grasps the external structure [i.e., the association] word-object earlier than the inner symbolic structure.... (p. 50)

> [Hence] preschool children "explain" the names of objects by their attributes. According to them, an animal is called "cow" because it has horns, "calf" because its horns are still small.... When asked whether one could interchange the names of objects, for instance call a cow "ink," and ink "cow," children will answer no, "because ink is used for writing, and the cow gives milk." An exchange of names would mean an exchange of characteristic features, so inseparable is the connection between them in the child's mind. (p. 129)

In the present formulation, the children studied by Vygotsky (and those described more recently by Osherson and Markman, 1974–1975) did not confuse words and real objects: They failed to distinguish words from their concepts. That is, they acted as though the question being asked was why the concept of a cow (not the name *cow*) is connected with perceived cows, and quite correctly they argued that the concept includes the information that cows have horns and give milk but cannot be used for writing. The problem was that they had difficulty considering a word as an entity in its own right.

Although the first step in symbol learning is to connect the symbol with the appropriate concept, the acquisition of this link has a cost: It becomes difficult to think of the symbol as separate from the concept. Similarly, the achievement of perceptual constancy has a cost: It becomes difficult to treat a percept as an experience separate from the concept it compellingly activates. Even adults have difficulty in treating a scene as a two-dimensional retinal array in order to paint it or in registering the perceived rather than the known color of objects or in adjusting to lenses that shift the usual correlation between visual and tactile space. And even adults may doubt that a rose by the name *pig* would smell sweet.

INTERPRETATION OF THE RELATION BETWEEN A SYMBOL AND A CONCEPT

The comprehension of a symbol might stop at the point when a person had recognized the conceptual referent and also realized that the symbol is not identical to the concept. That is, the symbol could be transparent to the level of meaning (Foss & Swinney, 1973; McNeill & Lindig, 1973) so that the concept would be activated along with a representation of the word or percept that enables the viewer to discriminate between a symbol and perception of the real object. A symbol, however, is a kind of metaphor. It is an object in its own right and yet it maps onto another object, its referent. As in the case of metaphors, interpretation may be possible on at least two levels. A painting of a person, for example, may convey by its style a comment on the person, but appreciation of this comment requires simultaneous awareness of the person depicted and the painting as an object with its own stylistic properties.

Its style or poetic aspect are what distinguish a symbol that one would call a work of art from the pedestrian symbols that tell us how to get to the subway or what happened on the stock market today. Functional symbols such as public signs, news reports, passport photographs, and the like are deliberately self-effacing; one reads the message and ignores the medium. When the purpose is to communicate a message, there is an advantage in using as symbols things uninteresting in themselves. In Langer's example, "a succulent, ripe, real peach" would be a poor symbol for plenty because "peaches are too good to act as words; we are too much interested in peaches themselves. But little noises [or little black marks] are ideal conveyors of concepts, for they give us nothing but their meaning" (1942, p. 61).

A work of art, in contrast, juxtaposes the characteristics of the symbol and those of the concept to make an indirect comment on the concept. If that were all, however, a political cartoon would be the epitome of art. A work of art as an object in its own right has properties that are amusing, pleasing, or evocative, arising from the pattern it makes on the canvas, its harmonious or discordant colors, its alliteration and rhythm (in poetry), and the other attributes that make up style.

In the greatest works of art, the style of the symbol as an object and the comment made about the conceptual topic produce a combined structure that transcends both topic and style. Consider Michelangelo's sculpture *David* as a familiar example. To understand its higher-order structure requires the simultaneous awareness of the topic (this is a representation of the biblical David), the comment (perhaps his nobility and youthful sweetness), and the sculptor's style (the marble, the slight distortions of proportion, the choice of scale, the stylization of details, and so on). What is required is a metaperception similar to the metalinguistic awareness discussed elsewhere in this volume. That awareness at several levels simultaneously is what constitutes full experience of a work of art. Taken separately, there is only a reminder of the historic David, or a nice-looking man, or an enormous hunk of sculptured stone.

Again, as in symbol recognition and discrimination, there is a parallel between the interpretation of a symbol and the interpretation of a percept. Like a symbol, a perceptual experience has particular qualities that may be appreciated apart from recognition of the identity of the objects seen or heard. And just as a symbol makes a comment on its topic, so a given perceptual encounter provides a particular subset of information about the object, showing it from a particular angle, making visible some details rather than others and the like. Since nature is not an artist, such perceptual comments on the object are haphazard; we ourselves decide which moments to frame. A landscape in the evening light is not simply identified but relished as a perceptual experience in much the way that one may enjoy a painting. The interesting sense in which nature imitates art is not in literal resemblance but in the role art may play in enabling us to look *at* our perceptions, not just through them to the concepts they symbolize.

Development of Symbol Interpretation

The ability to interpret all three facets of meaning of a symbol—its conceptual referent, its own qualities as an object, and the relation between the two—is initially absent in a child. The appreciation of the symbol as an object in its own right detaches it from its representational character. That is most obvious in production, when a young child may start a painting or sculpture or sentence with the intent of representing an idea and then get absorbed by the properties of the paint on paper or the tactile qualities of clay or the repetition of a word.

A child's limited ability to hold two or more things in mind simultaneously may prevent him from realizing the relation between the properties of the symbol and those of the referent. Either he focusses on the conceptual referent, or he looks at the symbol as an object: The sculpture is a big stone. The development of the ability to apprehend the identity of the symbolic medium at the same time as the identity of the referent has been studied by Elkind and his colleagues (e.g., Elkind, 1969) using pictures in which an object such as a man is constructed of other objects such as fruits. The development of the ability is related, in Elkind's account, to Piaget's theory of the development of logic-like perceptual regulations.

Similarly, a young child seems to be a *perceptual* literalist, not always able to recognize the conceptual equivalence among different views of a given object and not fully aware of the distinction between the conceptual object and the particularities of a momentary percept. The development of conservation of quantity, which requires a child to distinguish between the unchanging conceptual object and a misleading perceptual change, is closely allied to the ability to distinguish between symbolic play and reality, according to a study by Golumb and Cornelius (1977). They found that a measurable increase in the number of conservers occurred after three sessions of "pretend" games during which the experimenter led the child to confront the difference between pretense and reality.

A sign of development is a child's fascination with ambiguities that come almost within his grasp, such as a picture with hidden objects, Escher graphics, and verbal puns. The play acting already mentioned becomes possible as a child develops the ability to see or be two things at once. Still, a child is unlikely to appreciate the "style" of a perception (for example, the beauty of a particular landscape) until much later, just as the understanding of style in art comes late. Noticing style requires a metaconception of which a child is not initially capable.

PRODUCTION OF SYMBOLS

Although the present account has been concerned with the comprehension of symbols, not their production, there are obvious implications for an account of production. The production of an intentional symbol presumably begins with the production of a "real" object or action such as a hand wave. The infant's second step is recognizing that the chance or imitative production is a member of a certain class of actions for which he has already developed a concept. Later, as that event (produced by others) comes to be recognized as a symbol of (say) going away—that is, activates the concept of going away—the child may become able to produce that symbolic action when thinking of going away, just as he can take the "real" action of going away. At that point, he may have the same difficulty distinguishing between the real and symbolic productions that he sometimes has in symbol comprehension. A young child may be outraged that his bye-bye does not immediately result in going away.

In the production of symbols, as in their comprehension, children seem unable initially to command a symbol's potentiality for commenting on its referent and for exhibiting stylistic characteristics of its own. As already mentioned, a young child may play with clay or paint as an object itself or switch to a literal claim that he has produced the object he wants to symbolize, disregarding the communicative inadequacies of the symbol. He knows what concept his painting activates in him, and so he assumes that you see the same thing. A similar failure in young children to appreciate the communicative value of a given verbal expression has been studied by Glucksberg, Krauss, and Weisberg (1966). Gradually, a child develops a critical appreciation of the attributes of his painting or words or actions and their fit or misfit to other perceptual or symbolic representations of the concept. Thus he is increasingly able to predict what concepts his paintings and words will activate in others.

SUMMARY: THREE ASPECTS OF
SYMBOL COMPREHENSION

I have suggested that the comprehension of a symbol has three aspects: *recognition* of the symbol's conceptual referent, *discrimination* of the symbol from the concept it evokes and from perception of the real object, and *interpretation* of what the symbol says about the concept and about itself.

Symbol recognition occurs when the symbol activates the appropriate mental concept. In the case of concrete objects, the same concept may also be activated by perception of the object itself. Discrimination between the symbol and concept may not occur unless the symbol's distinctive properties are also identified. A full appreciation of the comment a symbol makes about its concept requires a simultaneous awareness of properties of the symbol and the remembered object embodied in the concept.

MUNDANE SYMBOLISM

The perceptual process leading to the recognition of real objects is not different in principle, I have argued, from symbol recognition. Each requires a process of inference, of going from sensory experience to the appropriate concept. Activation of the concept of a given object or event does not depend on any particular sense experience but abstracts away from perception just as it abstracts away from words and drawings in the experiments described earlier. We see objects rather than "mere dissolving sensa" (in Langer's phrase) because Gestalt-like principles organize our perceptions into wholes and because at a further level of abstraction percepts activate concepts.

Of course, a symbol differs from an object percept in being both a percept and a symbol—a written word is both a collection of black marks (one concept) and a symbol for something else (a second concept). We cannot stop seeing a word as black marks because the perceptual apparatus does not know how to turn off (and we would be in trouble if it did). Thus, the black-marks concept is activated along with the concept that the word symbolizes, even though we are hardly aware of the former.

Still, the basis of both perceptual and symbolic comprehension is activation of a mental concept. Mental concepts, not percepts or words or images, are the primary elements of thought. In acquiring the ability to activate an appropriate concept from a wide range of percepts, an infant is preparing the ground for activation of that concept through some other experience such as a word or picture. In learning to discriminate between the qualities of the momentary sensory experience and those of the enduring (conceptual) object, a child is readied for understanding that symbols are not the same as their referents. Finally, in becoming able to enjoy the conflict between conceptual knowledge and contradictory sensory experiences, as when seeing the room still spinning around after a twirling game, a child is learning to interpret the relation between the qualities of a symbol and its conceptual referent.

In a sense, then, a particular perception is a "mundane symbol" for an object. The abstract notion we have of the object is brought to mind by a glimpse or a touch, just as it can be brought to mind by words and other symbols. So the symbolization process is foreshadowed by the development of perception. The growth of a child's ability to understand and produce the cultural symbols of speech, written language, and the representational arts is part of his increasing understanding of the natural symbols of mundane perceptual experience.

ACKNOWLEDGMENTS

This work was supported by NIMH Grant MH-27536 to the author and by a Spencer Foundation Grant to the Psychology Department, M.I.T. I thank Virginia Valian and Barbara Klein for valuable comments on an earlier draft.

REFERENCES

Anderson, J. R. Arguments concerning representations for mental imagery. *Psychological Review*, 1978, *85*, 249–277.

Baddeley, A. D. *The psychology of memory*. New York: Basic Books, 1976.

Banks, W. P., & Flora, J. Semantic and perceptual processes in symbolic comparisons. *Journal of Experimental Psychology: Human Perception and Performance*, 1977, *3*, 278–290.

Bransford, J. D., & Franks, J. J. The abstraction of linguistic ideas. *Cognitive Psychology*, 1971, *2*, 331–350.

Brooks, P. H. The role of action lines in children's memory for pictures. *Journal of Experimental Child Psychology*, 1977, *23*, 98–107.

Corlew, M. M., & Nation, J. E. Characteristics of visual stimuli and naming performance in aphasic adults. *Cortex*, 1975, *11*, 186–191.

Craik, F. I. M., & Tulving, E. Depth of processing and the retention of words in episodic memory. *Journal of Experimental Psychology: General*, 1975, *104*, 268–294.

Crowder, R. G. *Principles of learning and memory*. Hillsdale, N.J.: Lawrence Erlbaum Associates, 1976.

Ehri, L. C. Do words really interfere in naming pictures? *Child Development*, 1976, *47*, 502–505.

Elkind, D. Developmental studies of figurative perception. In L. Lipsitt & H. W. Reese (Eds.), *Advances in child development and behavior* (Vol. 4). New York: Academic Press, 1969.

Fodor, J. A. *The language of thought*. New York: Crowell, 1975.

Fodor, J. A., Bever, T. G., & Garrett, M. F. *The psychology of language*. New York: McGraw-Hill, 1974.

Forster, K. I., & Chambers, S. M. Lexical access and naming time. *Journal of Verbal Learning and Verbal Behavior*, 1973, *12*, 627–635.

Foss, D. J., & Swinney, D. A. On the psychological reality of the phoneme. *Journal of Verbal Learning and Verbal Behavior*, 1973, *12*, 246–257.

Frederiksen, J. R., & Kroll, J. F. Spelling and sound: Approaches to the internal lexicon. *Journal of Experimental Psychology: Human Perception and Performance*, 1976, *2*, 361–379.

Friedman, S. L., & Stevenson, M. B. Developmental changes in the understanding of implied motion in two-dimensional pictures. *Child Development*, 1975, *46*, 773–778.

Gibson, E. J., Barron, R. W., & Garber, E. E. The developmental convergence of meaning for words and pictures. Appendix to final report, *The relationship between perceptual development and the acquisition of reading skill*. Project No. 90046, Grant No. OEG-2-9-420446-1071 (010) between Cornell University and the U. S. Office of Education, 1972.

Glucksberg, S., Krauss, R. M., & Weisberg, R. Referential communication in nursery school children: Method and some preliminary findings. *Journal of Experimental Child Psychology*, 1966, *3*, 333–342.

Golomb, C., & Cornelius, C. B. Symbolic play and its cognitive significance. *Developmental Psychology*, 1977, *13*, 246–252.

Goodman, N. *Languages of art*. New York: Bobbs-Merrill, 1968.

Hagen, M. A. Picture perception: Toward a theoretical model. *Psychological Bulletin*, 1974, *81*, 471–497.

Held, R. Object and effigy. In G. Kepes (Ed.), *Structure in art and science*. New York: Braziller, 1965.

Hochberg, J., & Brooks, V. Pictorial recognition as an unlearned ability: A study of one child's performance. *American Journal of Psychology*, 1962, *75*, 624–628.

Intraub, H. The role of implicit naming in pictorial encoding. *Journal of Experimental Psychology: Human Learning and Memory*, 1979, in press.

Johnson, M. K., Bransford, J. D., Nyberg, S. E., & Cleary, J. J. Comprehension factors in interpreting memory for abstract and concrete sentences. *Journal of Verbal Learning and Verbal Behavior*, 1972, *11*, 451–454.

Kosslyn, S. M., & Pomerantz, J. R. Imagery, propositions, and the form of internal representations. *Cognitive Psychology*, 1977, *9*, 52–76.

Langer, S. K. *Philosophy in a new key*. Cambridge, Mass.: Harvard University Press, 1942.

McNeill, D., & Lindig, K. The perceptual reality of phonemes, syllables, words, and sentences. *Journal of Verbal Learning and Verbal Behavior*, 1973, *12*, 419–430.

Milner, B. Interhemispheric differences in the localization of psychological processes in man. *British Medical Bulletin*, 1971, *27*, 272–277.

Nelson, D. L., Reed, V. S., & McEvoy, C. L. Learning to order pictures and words: A model of sensory and semantic encoding. *Journal of Experimental Psychology: Human Learning and Memory*, 1977, *3*, 485–497.

Nelson, D. L., Reed, V. S., & Walling, J. R. Pictorial superiority effect. *Journal of Experimental Psychology: Human Learning and Memory*, 1976, *2*, 523–528.

Nelson, K. Concept, word, and sentence: Interrelations in acquisition and development. *Psychological Review*, 1974, *81*, 267–285.

Norman, D. A., & Rumelhart, D. E. *Explorations in cognition*. San Francisco: W. H. Freeman, 1975.

Osherson, D. N., & Markman, E. Language and the ability to evaluate contradictions and tautologies. *Cognition*, 1974–75, *3*, 213–226.

Paivio, A. *Imagery and verbal processes*. New York: Holt, Rinehart & Winston, 1971.

Paivio, A. Neomentalism. *Canadian Journal of Psychology*, 1975, *29*, 263–291. (a)

Paivio, A. Perceptual comparisons through the mind's eye. *Memory and Cognition*, 1975, *3*, 635–647. (b)

Paivio, A., & Csapo, K. Concrete-image and verbal memory codes. *Journal of Experimental Psychology*, 1969, *80*, 279–285.

Paivio, A., & Csapo, K. Short-term sequential memory for pictures and words. *Psychonomic Science*, 1971, *24*, 50–51.

Paivio, A., Philipchalk, R., & Rowe, E. J. Free and serial recall of pictures, sounds, and words. *Memory and Cognition*, 1975, *3*, 586–590.

Paris, S. G., & Mahoney, G. J. Cognitive integration in children's memory for sentences and pictures. *Child Development*, 1974, *45*, 633–642.

Pellegrino, J. W., Rosinski, R. R., Chiesi, H. L., & Siegel, A. Picture-word differences in decision latency: An analysis of single and dual memory models. *Memory and Cognition*, 1977, *5*, 383–396.

Penney, C. G. Modality effects in short-term verbal memory. *Psychological Bulletin*, 1975, *82*, 68–84.

Perlmutter, M., & Myers, N. A. Recognition memory in preschool children. *Developmental Psychology*, 1976, *12*, 271–272.

Potter, M. C. On perceptual recognition. In J. S. Bruner, R. A. Olver, & P. M. Greenfield (Eds.), *Studies in cognitive growth.* New York: Wiley, 1966.

Potter, M. C. Mental comparison: Images and meanings. Article in preparation, 1978.

Potter, M. C., & Elliot, B. *Probing the meaning of scenes.* Article in preparation, 1978.

Potter, M. C., & Faulconer, B. A. *The ability of 3-year-olds to name pictures and objects.* Unpublished experiment, 1973.

Potter, M. C., & Faulconer, B. A. Time to understand pictures and words. *Nature*, 1975, *253*, 437–438.

Potter, M. C., Klein, B. V. E., Faulconer, B. A., Feldman, L., So, K.-F., & Garrett, M. G. Lexicon and concept in first and second language. Article in preparation, 1978.

Potter, M. C., Kroll, J. F., & Harris, C. Comprehension and memory in rapid sequential reading. In R. S. Nickerson (Ed.), *Attention and performance VIII.* Hillsdale, N.J.: Lawrence Erlbaum Associates, 1979, in press.

Potter, M. C., Kroll, J. F., Yachzel, B. R., & Cohen, J. S. *Pictures in sentences: Conceptual and lexical representation in language comprehension.* Article in preparation, 1978.

Potter, M. C., & Levy, E. I. Recognition memory for a rapid sequence of pictures. *Journal of Experimental Psychology*, 1969, *81*, 10–15.

Potter, M. C., So, K.-F., Ng, K.-F., & Friedman, R. Reading in Chinese and English: *Naming versus understanding.* Article in preparation, 1978.

Potter, M. C., Valian, V. V., & Faulconer, B. A. Representation of a sentence and its pragmatic implications: Verbal, imagistic, or abstract? *Journal of Verbal Learning and Verbal Behavior*, 1977, *16*, 1–12.

Pylyshyn, Z. W. What the mind's eye tells the mind's brain: A critique of mental imagery. *Psychological Bulletin*, 1973, *80*, 1–24.

Quine, W. V. *Word and object.* Cambridge, Mass.: The M.I.T. Press, 1960.

Rader, N. L. Developmental changes in getting meaning from written words. In R. W. Barron (Chair), *Getting to the meaning of written words: Implications for the development of the reading process.* Symposium presented at the meeting of the Society for Research in Child Development, Denver, 1975.

Rosch, E., Mervis, C. B., Gray, W. D., Johnson, D. M., & Boyes-Braem, P. B. Basic objects in natural categories. *Cognitive Psychology*, 1976, *8*, 382–439.

Rosinski, R. R., Golinkoff, R. M., & Kukish, K. S. Automatic semantic processing in a picture-word interference task. *Child Development*, 1975, *46*, 247–253.

Rosinski, R. R., Pellegrino, J. W., & Siegel, A. W. Developmental changes in the semantic processing of pictures and words. *Journal of Experimental Child Psychology*, 1977, *23*, 282–291.

Vygotsky, L. *Thought and language.* Cambridge, Mass.: The M.I.T. Press, 1962.

Weber, R. J., & Castleman, J. The time it takes to imagine. *Perception and Psychophysics*, 1970, *8*, 165–168.

Willows, D. M. Influences of background pictures on children's decoding of words. In R. W. Barron (Chair), *Getting to the meaning of written words: Implications for the development of the reading process.* Symposium presented at the meeting of the Society for Research in Child Development, Denver, 1975.

4 The Concept of Décalàge as It Applies to Representational Thinking

Rodney R. Cocking
Irving E. Sigel
Educational Testing Service, Princeton, New Jersey

> Building a theory is a matter of developing an appropriate concept by analogy.
> This is the essential heart of science, because it is the basis of explanation.
> —Harré (1972, p. 171)

THE DISCREPANCY MODEL FOR UNDERSTANDING DEVELOPMENT

Development is construed as a transformational process, where change occurs in the structural and functional aspects of the total organism. This involves changes in (1) the mode of constructing and organizing experience, for example, from motor action to ideation; (2) the degree of specialization, resulting in increased ability to carry out different classes of activities appropriate to their ends; and (3) the organization of the various components into hierarchically integrated wholes.

Transformations can occur as a function of discrepancies between the state of the organism and the environmental demands (or experiences). Change will occur when the state of mismatch between the organism and the environment requires rectification. A mismatch is a condition in which the organism comes into contact with particular environmental events (objects, people) and in the course of this engagement comes to perceive a discrepancy which can be resolved only by the organism's altering its approach. The child who wishes to build a tower and has only a set of nesting cubes illustrates the point: The motivation is sufficient, but the resources are insufficient unless the child reassesses the possibilities of the objects.

Development generally is propelled when discrepancies between the existing state of child and the environmental demands are resolved.[1] Discrepancies create conditions which instigate and activate mental activity. We can designate three types of discrepancies: (1) between two external events, for example, two diverse interpretations of an event; (2) between an internal and an external activator, for example, a wish on the one hand and an action on the other; and (3) between two internal states or constructions, for example, ambivalent feelings about a person or an event.

Cognitive growth, as expressed in the development of representational activity and symbol formation, occurs as a function of these discrepancies. Humans cannot tolerate such discrepancies, and the consequences of this intolerance is striving to cope with the conflict. The resolutions of contradictions occur through a dialectrical process. Dialectics, particularly when addressing the problem of resolution or contradictions, provides a model for examining development since its laws are descriptive of the transformation processes intrinsic to development (Sigel & Cocking, 1977; Wozniak, 1975).

A conflict source, while always processed internally, may have its sources in the external situation. The dialectic method of teaching illustrates an external source of conflict. The tutor's antithetical challenge to the thesis that the student must defend provokes a conflict. The resolutions must be arrived at by the student.[2] It is proposed that the student might not have been pushed to these additional considerations if the tutor had not created the conflict—thus, the conflict is externally provoked. As an example, classification schemes are both broadened and refined for preschoolers when teachers present objects which challenge class membership. The child who uses four-leggedness as the criterial attribute for classifying animals is pushed toward further considerations of his scheme when asked to include a man or a kangaroo in one of the classification categories. Internal to the person himself lies the disparity between performance on some tasks and performance on related tasks.

Conflict resolution involves at least three strategies: assessing alternatives, anticipating outcomes, or reconstructing past experiences. Each of these strategies requires the individual to create symbols—mental representations

---

[1]Discrepancies are mental constructions of the individual, and their resolution occurs only in the mind of the individual.

[2]Self-regulation is the process through which Piaget says and individual fortuitously *discovers* that his organizational schemes do not adequately handle new experiences or new facets of familiar experiences. Décalàge, that is, "gaps" internal to the individual, is one source of functional discrepancy. A teaching strategy can use this same *internal* mechanism, that is, the need to resolve with discrepancy. The teacher can *provide* (i.e., externally) the discrepant information for the individual and thereby ensure that nonfortuitous discoveries are also occurring. Recognizing that external discrepant information does not come solely from teaching situations is the heart of distancing strategies of which Sigel writes (Sigel, 1970) and around which he has developed a cognitively oriented preschool program.

of choices or decisions—since the total event is not in the immediate, observable present.[3] For example, in the solution to the conservation of substance problem, when one of two equal balls of clay is deformed, the child is asked if the same amount of substance exists. The child can solve the problem in at least two ways: (1) He can maintain the image of the initial presentation, thereby representing the original state and keeping in mind that nothing was done to alter the amount, or (2) he can work from an already-learned principle that invariance of a quality may exist even though shape is altered. The latter case entails a form of representation. And unless the individual represents, the problem cannot be solved.

We are proposing that there is a relationship between the level and use of representations and solutions of problems usually analyzed in terms of level of logical operations. Stepwise progressions are evident both within stages of development and between the various stages. That individuals do not classify pictures of objects and three-dimensional objects similarly is a case of *décalàge*, a time lag in the appearance of related cognitive processes. The fact that individuals do not function at the same structural level across all tasks gives rise to the décalàge issue, and we are proposing that it constitutes a problem in representation.

Course of Development in Discrepancy Resolution

We have indicated that at least three types of discrepancies can be identified, and three strategies can be employed to cope with them. These distinctions call forth the issue of whether development proceeds in a continuous or discontinuous way. Continuity is evident at two levels: generally, an overall steady progression toward maturity, and specifically, a progression in certain growth areas, for example, physical development. On the other hand, discontinuity is obvious in the case of qualitative changes that emerge in the process of development. The child progresses from a preconceptual level to a conceptual level.[4] For this reason, we refer to such emergent and qualitative changes as discontinuous.

It is this later consideration that leads us directly to the concept of *décalàge*. Development, whether continuous or discontinuous, is not necessarily uniform in all areas. Décalàge refers to temporal discrepancies in the appearance of mental processes. Piaget describes horizontal décalàge as follows:

> At certain ages, the child is able to solve problems in quite specific areas. But if one changes to another material or to another situation even with problems

---

[3]We are not, at this point, distinguishing, as Piaget does, between the two classes of (1) "symbols" and "signs" and (2) "indices" and "signals."

[4]The fact that sensorimotor schemata are still available to the individual does not deny that the new apparent level has no direct, observable similarity to the preceding levels of functioning.

which seem to be closely related, lags of several months are noted and in some cases even of 1 or 2 years. (Piaget & Inhelder, 1971, p. 10)

Thus, the child solves conservation of mass problems prior to solving those involving conservation of weight or volume. The processes involved are the same, but for some reason substance is conserved more readily than the weight attribute or volume. This type of décalàge is called *horizontal* because the same processes are involved; only the materials vary. The other type of décalàge, or temporal discrepancy, Piaget refers to is the vertical, where "verticality refers to an ascending age scale: What the child learns at age 7 on the plane of action, he must restructure at age 11 on the plane of verbal thought" (Ginsburg & Opper, 1969, p. 112).

We consider the horizontal décalàge construct important and propose that it be viewed as follows. One can regard horizontal décalàge as the failure to apply similar operations to a variety of questions about different physical attributes of the same materials. Thus, an example of horizontal décalàge in conservation tasks with a ball of clay would be demonstrated by the child's conserving mass at one time but succeeding only later in applying the same mental operation to problems of volume or weight with that clay. Vertical décalàge refers to the employment of increasingly higher levels of logical structures. Thus, the child might first solve the problem of conservation of mass by using an addition-subtraction scheme, which would be considered an indication of functioning at one level, while later he might apply a different schema to the solution of the same problem, which would indicate functioning at another, higher level.

It is commonly said that both at the concrete and formal levels of thought the child can represent in three modes, *motoric, iconic,* or *symbolic-linguistic* (Bruner, Olver, & Greenfield et al., 1966). The argument here is that any one of these three is available to the child in the concrete operational and formal levels and are appearing by the end of the sensorimotor levels. In fact, as soon as the child indicates some understanding of receptive language and some indication of recognitory memory, one could argue that these three modalities are available to the child but are employed in qualitatively and quantitatively different manners. The general thesis is that these three modalities provide the means through which thoughts are represented. The modalities describe the internal form of the knowledge which is expressed through such media as gestures, graphic forms, and speech. The child has these varying modalities available but different degrees of competence in their comprehension when employed by others or by himself. Décalàge describes the state of the child in terms of these varying degrees of competency.

At this juncture in our discussion it is important to reiterate a point from Piaget (1973). Representations are not operations. Operations are always mental *actions*, not symbols, although symbols are required. Representations are required for internalization of operations, and an operation itself is a transformation which can be performed symbolically. It follows, also, that operations are not representations of transformations.

Early Studies

Interest in the experiential base for representational thinking stemmed from the finding by Sigel that a lower socioeconomic group of 6-year-old black children had difficulty in sorting and classifying a group of familiar black and white photographs, for example, horse, boat, truck, fireman, policeman, baby, dog, etc. Each of these pictures was *labeled* accurately. Yet, when asked to classify or sort the pictures of these familiar items, aside from occasional chaining responses, the children had difficulty creating classes or groupings, and, further, when they did succeed in grouping they had difficulty in reflecting and communicating the basis for their strategies. These pilot data were contrary to previous findings where it was found that young children (aged 7) did not differentially classify three-dimensional objects in comparison to their pictorial representations (Sigel, 1953). The later findings led to a series of studies directed at investigating sorting behavior among preschool and kindergarten children of middle- and lower-social-class backgrounds (Sigel, Anderson, & Shapiro, 1966; Sigel & McBane, 1967; Sigel & Olmsted, 1970). The results were consistent: Lower-class children tended to have more difficulty in classifying photographs of familiar and identifiable objects in contrast to their three-dimensional counterparts. Why? In spite of the fact that the pictures were labeled correctly, the children did not relate to the objects and the pictures in an equivalent way. This problem was labeled as one in *representational competence*, in which the children did not have the translation rules by which to treat objects and pictures as equivalents. This led to a discrepancy in classification scores, with responses to three-dimensional objects being easier than responses to two-dimensional photographs of these same objects. The significance of the problem became increasingly obvious as we began to ponder the significance of picture comprehension per se and the lack of explanatory statements in the literature. We also concluded that reiterating the rules of equivalence did not seem appropriate—especially with the goal of getting children to *understand* and not just *recognize* objects or representational forms.

Differences in object and picture responding have been reported in the psychological and anthropological literature. Various theories have been offered, ranging from associationistic to cultural deprivation. None of these accounts succeed in explaining the data, however, since labeling responses suggest a recognition and knowledge of the object in three-dimensional form. Apparently the children had not acquired the rule that objects can be translated into other forms (a transformation). Where do children learn the rules of equivalence? Is it through direct teaching? This seems unlikely. Consistent sorting on tasks involving materials that vary in representational level involves an awareness that objects do not lose their identity or class membership by being translated into other media—the pictorial, for example. Understanding pictures requires competencies different from those relevant to three-dimensional objects (Sigel, 1978). As Gregory (1970) says, pictures are paradoxes: "Pictures are images among objects, for they are seen both as themselves and as some other thing, entirely different from the paper or canvas of the pictures" (p. 32).

The discrepancy in classificatory responding to pictures and objects reflects a décalàge problem. The children have difficulty applying processes of grouping to two sets of materials which, while similar in content, vary in level of representation. Whereas objects may be grouped on the basis of action, pictures can be grouped only on a symbolic level.

CURRENT RESEARCH: CHILDREN'S
HOMOLOGIC AND ANALOGIC THINKING

In the theoretical statement which we have presented, we have reiterated the point that symbol formation is in the service of representational thinking. Representational thinking, further, is comprised of several subcategories, that is, symbol manipulation, re-presenting experiences, and the *presentation* of thought (such as the mathematician's proof).

Presentation of thought is the special subcategory that we have selected to illustrate the décalàge phenomena in representational thinking. We are discussing representational thought in terms of the symbol system through which these thoughts becomes expressed. Thus, we are not only concerned with the operations which are involved in symbol manipulation but also with what we regard as the more basic issue of symbol formation. We will discuss this problem in terms of data collected from children who were administered tasks requiring operative knowledge but who may be characterized as working and problem solving on the basis of figurative knowledge. Our discussion, therefore, will be organized around the child's movement from nonlogical to infralogical and finally to logical thought processes.

We began this chapter with a quote which states that scientific explanation is essentially the discovery of concepts by analogy. If the basis of this particular scientific inquiry is analogic thinking, we should look at the issues of representational thinking, such as those we have already discussed, in terms of children's discovery and invention of analogues in problem solving. By studying analogues in preoperational children, we are attempting to specify the step-by-step procedures children use in solving a problem. That is, we are trying to isolate the algorithms for tasks which require operative thought structures. We use a straightforward definition of the term analogy in describing what we are studying. An analogy is "... a relationship between two entities, processes... which allows inferences to be made about one of the things, usually about which we know least, on the basis of what we know about the other" (Harré, 1972, p. 172). The contrast to an analogue is a homologue. In organized memory, homologues depend upon *content*, while analogues utilize the *structure*. It is not the specific content but the forms of the relationships which are critical in analogies.

It should be made clear that when we describe the child's thinking as involving homologues or analogues, we do not mean to imply that the child is engaged in the same kind of thinking that characterizes adult thought. It would be helpful to conceptualize our position here in terms of Werner's (1957) concept of "analogous processes," which he defines as mental processes occurring at different growth (genetic) levels and involving different function patterns but directed toward similar achievements. For example, infants "abstract" by selecting out specific attributes from an array. Adults also abstract by selecting out different attributes from an array, but while each is "abstracting," the level of abstraction is different for the child as contrasted to the adult. The achievements are similar, but the level and function of the abstractions are different. We employ the term "analogue" to describe an achievement similar to that of the adult where the level and function differ. In summary, our work is directed toward the study of "... those processes in information retrieval which depend upon the *structure*, as opposed to the *content* of organized memory" (Rumelhart & Abrahamson, 1973, p. 1).

These thinking strategies, then, may be characterized as homologic or analogic. Homologic thinking involves superimposing relatively fixed structures onto new situations in template fashion. A conflict occurs if two situations are different; there is a resolution if they are interpreted as being sufficiently alike to evoke structurally similar operations. In other words, the same schemata that have been used in familiar or "known" situations are evoked for dealing with the new situations. We suggest that so-called rote learning is an example of homologic thinking. For example, in early language learning, productions of irregular past tenses are often produced correctly but applied incorrectly. "Went" in one situation is produced as "went" in another situation, but while "went" is correct for the *simple past tense* (I went home), it is not correct for an expression calling for an *auxiliary + past-tense* construction (I have went home).

El'konin (1969) states that preschool age is the period during which intellectual activity becomes differentiated, so that mental actions (symbol manipulation) and verbal thinking (symbol manipulation, re-presentational thinking, and presentation of thought) are separated from practical actions. One transition of which El'konin speaks is the shift to visual-graphic thinking, which he says is related to types of activities which require the reliance upon representations of the object. If the grouping of mental structures necessary for thinking about objects is the same as for grouping the objects themselves, then only the symbols (e.g., mental images) need be established as equivalent by the child in order to engage in homologic thinking. The only transformation necessary, therefore, is what we have stated previously as the shift from three-dimensional space to the two-dimensional mental image— surely a minimal transform, albeit a significant step in symbol formation. The shift of which El'konin speaks, however, involves extensive use of transformations (that is, changes in composition or structure) and these begin to appear during the second half of the preschool years. During this period we see numerous examples of the issue we have presented as the décalàge problem in symbol formation and representational thinking. This is the time during which we see the emergence of analogic thinking.

Let us provide some data on analogic thinking which were obtained from children in their later preschool period, when they were approximately 4.5 years old. These examples are from children's performances on imagery tasks (kinetic and static), a conservation task, and a language production task.

Kinetic Anticipatory Imagery

In developing procedures to assess kinetic imagery, we wished to distinguish between image content which is observed frequently and image content which is observed infrequently, if ever. We were also interested in the problem of how children anticipate events. We therefore chose a task which Piaget terms "Kinetic Anticipatory Imagery (KAI)." Thus, we focused upon both position and movement in our test of mental imagery. The task is designed to answer the question, "... given very elementary and well-known movements, [will] the image of the result of displacement be... [formed]... if the result [is] not shown in advance?" (Piaget & Inhelder, 1971, pp. 50–51).

The materials in our task consist of a piece of clear Plexiglas on which a blue square and a red square (each 2 in.) are mounted. The blue square is rigidly affixed to the Plexiglas, while the red square pivots on a visible screw from the lower, right-hand corner of the blue square (see Fig. 4.1). The red, mobile square has a "handle" extending from the corner diagonally opposite the pivot with which the examiner can rotate it in full circle. After being shown how the red square moves when the handle is pushed upward or downward, the child is asked to imagine how the configuration will look if the red square is rotated through four consecutive 90° rotations. After giving the child time to imagine what each rotation would look like, the examiner shows the child a form board with five arrays of possible positions mounted on it. In addition to the four positions of rotation which were to be imagined on the four separate trials (90°, 180°, 270°, and 360°), an "impossible" choice is also

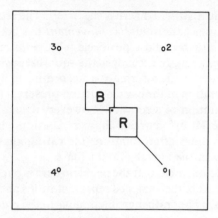

FIG. 4.1. Kinetic anticipatory imagery.

represented. The impossible choice corresponds to the initial position, with stationary and movable squares in reversed positions. The choices are pictured in Fig. 4.2.

We have already stated that we employed operational tasks with preoperational children in order to study the movement from figurative knowledge to operative knowledge. Thus we were not surprised to find this task too difficult for the children to perform correctly. Correct choices for a particular rotation, say a 90° rotation, were never beyond chance levels of responding, and therefore we shall confine our discussion to an examination of the error patterns. As we shall argue, the error patterns do, however, illustrate analogic thinking.

The children in the research sample were divided into two groups on the basis of their preschool experiences. One group had a longer-term, cognitively oriented program, while the other had a traditional preschool program (see Footnote 2). In our first assessment (T_1) of Group I, the impossible configuration was chosen predominantly, with other choices

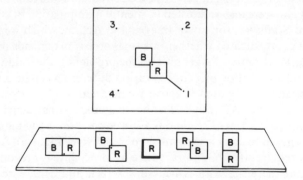

FIG. 4.2. Kinetic anticipatory imagery: choices.

randomly distributed across the array. The choice represents an analogue to the stimulus pattern in that *movement* has been represented as a rotation of the two squares whose positions relative to one another have not changed. The choice simply exchanges the squares' positions by *overturning*. This is a circumduction transformation according to Piaget, in which the imaginal representation of the circumduction preserves (conserves) the relations. It is a representation of a rotation, however, through overturning.

Group II, by contrast, chose a rotation which would leave only the red square visible after rotation, indicating that they were representing the visibility of the movable, red square.

It appears, then, that the problem here is one of spatial coordination within the context of the imagined representations and that the children's choices are not random but rather are analogous to the required rotation. It is important, in this instance, to point out that the choice is not analogous to the stimulus, as we would expect in a task of reproductive imagery. The choice suggests an analogue of the imaginal representation of the *movement*—the kinetic representation. Piaget states that it is clear that "... the difficulties associated with the representation of the image... are not connected with the representation of movement as a whole. They are connected... with the representation of its adjustment in the form of particular *relative positions* [italics added]" (Piaget & Inhelder, 1971, p. 66). While this example is the easiest of the rotations (90°), the choices illustrate the organized form of children's memory. The choices are neither randomly distributed nor a homologue of the stimulus form, which would have been evident by the identity choice on the form board. Thus, we are dealing with imaginal representations which are analogues of the task demand—anticipated movement.

Static Reproductive Imagery

In addition to the mental imagery task which required imaginal movement by the subject, we were also interested in mental manipulation of static images. The task of Static Reproductive Images and Action, which we modeled on Piaget's task, investigated whether imaginal precision depends on the modes of the subjects' activities. Piaget phrases the problem in the following way: "Is the child's internalization of a configuration different when he only perceives the configuration as opposed to actively constructing it?" (Piaget & Inhelder, 1971, p. 230). In the task, the child is shown a model constructed of different, colored geometric forms. The child is allowed to observe the model for 30 sec before he is asked to copy it with his set of blocks (see Fig. 4.3). A second trial on the task requires the child to verbalize his procedure for reconstructing an array so that the tester who is behind a screen and cannot see the child's movements is able to build the same model that the child is constructing. A

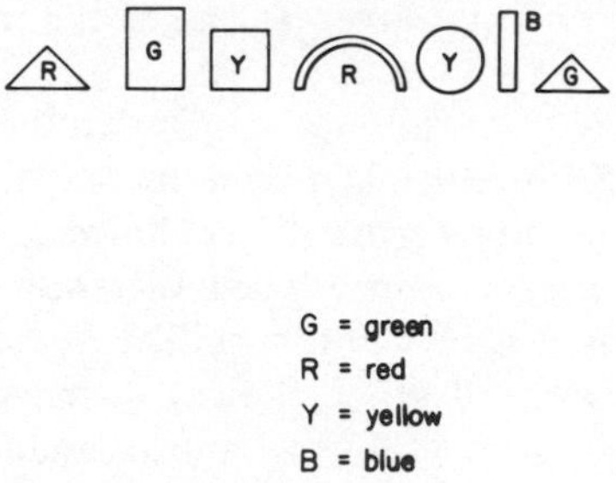

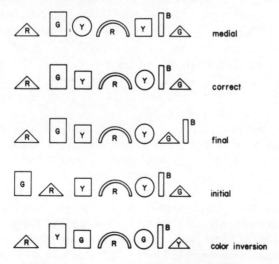

FIG. 4.3. Static reproductive imagery.

G = green
R = red
Y = yellow
B = blue

final, third procedure is for the child to choose the initial array of blocks from several choices mounted on a form board (see Fig. 4.4). The tasks, then, assess static imagery through (1) copy; (2) reproductive imagery, as the child builds the model from memory and communicates the actions to the tester; and (3) the recognitory skill, which requires a match between a static mental image and a physical representation of the original stimulus. Our purpose here is to discuss analogic thinking in static imagery; therefore, copy and reconstruction aspects of the task which relate more directly to homologies will not be considered. We will discuss only the recognitory aspect of the task demands.

Each of the five choices was labeled according to the position of the error in each choice array. Thus, we would label an error as an "initial," a "medial," or a "final" cluster error depending on whether the anomaly lay in the beginning, middle, or end of each choice cluster. In addition to these three error choices and the correct choice, there was a fifth alternative which we called an "impossible" choice. This fifth option contained a color inversion so that

medial

correct

final

initial

color inversion

FIG. 4.4. Static reproductive imagery: choices.

yellow forms replaced green forms of the same geometric shapes and vice versa.

We chose to look at our subjects' responding at two periods of time separated by 3.5 months. While our less experienced group showed randomly dispersed responding across all five choice options on the two time samplings, the more experienced nursery school group exhibited analogic thinking on both occasions. The recognitory skill at the first testing revealed two principal error forms, with all other choices distributed randomly. The two forms constituted 67% of the subjects' choices and were either a medial error (44%) or the color inversion (23%).

The question is, how do we know that the error was not made because the child engaged in homologic thinking and simply applied his template to the choice board. As noted before, the characteristic which distinguishes homologues from analogues is that the homologues are structures which have an organic unity, while analogues are structural groupings which transcend class membership boundaries. Our clue to analogic thinking is generally the child's employment of commutative principles: "If A is like A' and B is like B', then the entire structure is applicable to the new situation." In these recognitory choices, the initial and final clusters of the medial error correspond to the model which the tester built and of which the subjects formed static images. The discrepancy is embedded in the center of the array, and it appears that the match is made because initial and final clusters are alike, and therefore it is concluded that the two forms match in all aspects. The medial cluster error may be termed a color analogue, since commutative thinking might be based on color correspondences. Such a choice fails to coordinate the color similarities with the form discrepancy. The situations is a little different for the "impossible" or color inversion choices. While the color representations made the choice "impossible," the cluster array did not differ from the correct array in terms of *form*. That is, a color-blind person who viewed both arrays achromatically would not be able to distinguish between the two. For this reason, we suggest that the second dominant error form resulted from applying the form homologue (i.e., the "impossible" or color inversion choice) to the choice array.

Let us now turn to a brief discussion of the utility of the internal source of discrepancy in promoting the development of logical thought. When we tested these same children 3.5 months later, the 44% who had employed analogic thinking now demonstrated a correct recognitory imagery-object match, while the 23% who had utilized the homologic *form* match were still doing so. All other subjects were continuing to give responses which were randomly distributed among the alternatives. That is, those who employed analogic thinking at Time 1 were more likely to solve the problem correctly at Time 2 than those who employed any of the other strategies, including those who had given homologues of the correct choice.

Conservation of Continuous Quantity

Continuing with our plan to assess mental images and operations in preoperational children, we adopted the Conversation of Liquids task of Piaget. While we were interested in the conservation responses and justifications, our principle concern was for the anticipatory or prediction skills children use as they try to image physical transformations. Like the kinetic and static imagery tasks, the task assesses the interaction between figurative and operational processes. In the task, the child is presented with the standard conservation of liquids problem and asked to (1) anticipate the image of the liquid to be poured from one vessel into another and (2) observe the demonstration of pouring and then explain it. We employed two 250-ml beakers and a 50-ml cyclinder as our vessels and a glass carafe of the juice-of-the-day from the child's nursery school. Fifty milliliters of juice were poured into the standard, and the child himself established when the experimenter had put an equivalent amount into the second beaker as determined by a standard mark on the vessel.

If a homologue were employed in predicting the level of the liquid in a new vessel which is both taller and narrower than the standard, the prediction would be a projection of the mental image of the standard onto the new vessel. This type of error is generally discussed as "a perceptually based error," which is equivalent to sayaing that the mental image is superimposed in template fashion onto the new task. We would consider as analogic that thinking expressed in a predicion which projected an image of higher liquid level but which failed to employ a principle of compensation, accounting for both height and diameter differences between the two vessels. Craig, Love, and Olim (1973) discuss this response as a "proportionality response," whereby a 20%-full level in one vessel is predicted as a 20% level in any test vessel. A correct prediction, of course, would be a 50-ml response. For the discussion of our data we shall again separate our two groups because of their varying nursery school experiences.

Group I at Time 1 used the perceptual homologue at chance level, while 53% made errors interpretable as the analogic error form. Thirty-five percent made a correct prediction. While 43% of Group II made a correct prediction at Time 1, the remaining children distributed their responses between analogic (21%) and homologic (36%) predictions.

At a later assessment date (Time 2), 80% of Group I were making correct predictions, while only one additional subject from Group II moved in the direction of imaging the correct liquid level. Thus, while groups did not differ significantly from one another at Time 1, Group I changed significantly in the direction of correct anticipations over the two time periods and differed significantly from Group II at the second testing. Group II showed no significant changes over the two testings. Thus, it appears as if analogic thinking does move in the direction of logical thought and that homologic thinking does not proceed directly toward images of transformations.

Language Productions

To study "... the assembly of verbal structures ... [which] represent objects and relationships... " (Luria, 1973, p. 141), we constructed two tasks. One task assessed language comprehension by asking children to manipulate objects and toys. The task was patterned after Bellugi-Klima's (1969) comprehension scheme, where experimenter requests are made in different syntactic forms. Our parallel task for language production derives its format from the test of syntactic structures by Potts (1973). In the latter procedure, children complete story stems which are accompanied by pictures, the story tag varying in syntactic structure. We may briefly consider homologic and analogic thinking as represented in the *production* of the linguistic symbol system. The relationship between comprehension and production performances will be discussed in our summary of the décalàge issue.

We have already pointed to the example of *irregular past-tense* productions, where rote learning was evident in homologic productions used to represent two different forms for expressing past action (I went—*I have went). Anologic thinking was seen in the newly acquired rule-governed behavior as occurring somewhat later in development. *Regular past-tense* forms which add the /-ed/ morpheme illustrate the correct analogue usage (talk + /-ed/, walk + /-ed/). Inappropriate analogic forms which preserve the meaning (e.g., past time orientation) come somewhat later and clearly illustrate children's *constructions*, for they frequently result in forms which the child has never heard (Cocking & Potts, 1976; McNeill, 1970; Menyuk, 1970). In this case, the rule of the regular form is applied to the irregular verbs which were formerly produced correctly. Roger Brown (1973) has pointed out that mothers give feedback on the syntactic form, correcting the "ran'ed's" and "went'ed's," where the truth-value of the statement needs no correction. That is, the child has an adequate *representation* of the event, while at the same time he has a deficient *symbol system*.

DÉCALÀGE IN REPRESENTATIONAL THINKING

It has been argued in the course of this chapter that there is a difference between what children express as knowledge based on form or *structure* of concepts and knowledge based on *content* of concepts. Awareness and self-reflectivity are part and parcel of reflective abstraction, which, we stated, leads to analogic thinking. Homologic thinking, on the other hand, is a derivative of sensory- or perceptually based information which is relevant to *specific* bits of knowledge (Inhelder, Sinclair, & Bovet, 1974). Of particular significance is the fact that "...consciousness generates the awareness of choice.... In fact [the person]...is forced to make choices because he is aware of alternatives even when they are physically not present"(Luria, 1973, p. 146). The ability to make such choices about the nonpresent is possible because the human can re-present and anticipate his world; these are competencies which are generic to the species. Thinking in representational terms has been accomplished because of the development of symbol systems for dealing with the nonpresent.

Various contents may be represented in symbols, and the symbols may vary in medium. The medium may be mental images, oral or written language, graphics, gestures. Symbols can be said to serve the function of representation. At the same time, the term "representation" refers to the process or activity of re-presenting.

To summarize, we have stated that representational thinking can mean several things. The term may apply to the development and manipulation of the symbol system, as witnessed in the development of object constancy in very young children. We also use the term to discuss the use of symbols in the *presentation* of thoughts by the individual. Finally, representation can mean the re-presenting of previous experiences.

Our discussion of homologic and analogic thinking serves to demonstrate décalàge in representational thinking. We have pointed to an example in language development where "gaps" exist in the system for representing events. We also raised the medium/mode issue as a source for the lag in representation across related tasks: Classification skill performances varied when objects or graphic representations of those objects were used. The décalàge resides in the development of symbols for representing across various media. Finally, the discrepancy model was used to describe children's cognitive growth. Three conflict sources with which children have to deal and which promote growth through their resolution were identified in the model.

A genetic basis for representational thinking has been advanced by S. E. Luria. He has argued eloquently that there exists in the brain's neural substrate a basis for logical structures, comparable to the model by which language structures have been conceptualized. Luria (1973) states the issues in the following way:

> Language is an assembly of verbal structures representing objects and relationships. From thinking of language as a dual entity consisting of a genetically determined component inscribed in the structure of the brain and a learned component derived from experience it is an easy step to a more general conception of the human mind. As men conceptualize in thought or speech, the world around and within them, the mind analyzes these perceptions in terms of certain properties. From Aristotle to Descartes to Immanuel Kant, philosophers have long perceived these analytical categories, the elementary structures of

mental analysis, as something given rather than learned. To the biologist, it makes eminent sense to think that, as for language structures, so also for logical structures there exist in the brain network some patterns of connections that are genetically determined and have been selected by evolution as effective instruments for dealing with the events of life. Insofar as logical structures are dealt with in terms of language, this cerebral substrate of logic would be an integral component of the language structure. Perfecting of these cerebral structures must have depended on their becoming progressively more useful in terms of reproductive success. For language this must have meant becoming a better instrument in formulation and communication of meaning through a usable grammar and syntax. For logical structures in general, a selection must have been for more effective "thinking" (pp. 140–141).

We would add human consciousness as another relevant aspect to be taken into account when considering one's ability to represent his or her world. It is through reflective abstraction that people move on to the higher levels of analogic thinking involved in scientific thought. The data reported here demonstrated that even "error' analogues are an important step as children discover the analogues which explain their world.

REFERENCES

Bellugi-Klima, U. *Grammatical comprehension test.* Unpublished manuscript, rev. version, 1969. (Available from U. Bellugi-Klima, Salk Institute, La Jolla, CA.)

Brown, R. *A first language.* Cambridge, Mass.: Harvard University Press, 1973.

Bruner, J., Olver, R. R., Greenfield, P. M., et al. *Studies in cognitive growth.* New York: Wiley, 1966.

Cocking, R., & Potts, M. Social facilitation of language acquisition. *Journal of Genetic Psychology Monographs,* 1976, *94,* 249–340.

Craig, G. J., Love, J. A., & Olim, E. G. Perceptual judgments in Piaget's conservation of liquid problem. *Child Development,* 1973, *44,* 372–375.

El'konin, D. B. Some results of the study of the psychological development of preschool-age children. In M. Cole & I. Maltzman (Eds.), *A handbook of contemporary Soviet psychology.* New York: Basic Books, 1969.

Ginsburg, H., & Opper, I. *Piaget's theory of intellectual development.* Englewood Cliffs, N.J.: Prentice-Hall, 1969.

Gregory, R. L. *The intelligent eye.* New York: McGraw-Hill, 1970.

Harré, R. *The philosophies of science: An introductory survey.* New York: Oxford University Press, 1972.

Inhelder, B., Sinclair, H., & Bovet, M. *Learning and the development of cognition.* Cambridge, Mass.: Harvard University Press, 1974.

Luria, S. E. *Life—The unfinished experiment.* New York: Scribner's, 1973.

McNeil, D. *The acquisition of language: The study of developmental psycholinguistics.* New York: Harper & Row, 1970.

Menyuk, P. *The acquisition and development of language.* Englewood Cliffs, N.J.: Prentice-Hall, 1970.

Piaget, J. *The child and reality: Problems of genetic psychology.* New York: Grossman, 1973.

Piaget, J., & Inhelder, B. *Mental imagery in the child.* New York: Basic Books, 1971.

Potts, M. *A technique for measuring language production in 3, 4, and 5 year-olds.* Unpublished manuscript, Cornell University, 1973.

Rumelhart, D. E., & Abrahamson, A. A. A model for analogical reasoning. *Cognitive Psychology*, 1973, *5*, 1–28.

Sigel, I. E. Developmental trends in the abstraction ability of children. *Child Development*, 1953, *24*, 131–144.

Sigel, I. E. The distancing hypothesis: A causal hypothesis for the acquistion of representational thought. In M. R. Jones (Ed.), *The effects of early experience.* Miami: University of Miami Press, 1970.

Sigel, I. E. The development of pictorial comprehension. In B. S. Randhawa & W. E. Coffman (Eds.), *Visual learning, thinking, and communication.* New York: Academic Press, 1978.

Sigel, I. E., Anderson, L. M., & Shapiro, H. Categorization behavior of lower- and middle-class Negro preschool children: Differences in dealing with representation of familiar objects. *Journal of Negro Education*, 1966, *35*, 218–229.

Sigel, I. E., & Cocking, R. R. Cognition and communication: A dialectic paradigm for development. In M. Lewis & L. Rosenblum (Eds.), *Interaction, conversation and the development of language.* New York: Wiley, 1977.

Sigel, I. E., & McBane, B. Cognitive competence and level of symbolization among five-year-old children. In J. Helmuth (Ed.), *The disadvantaged child* (Vol. 1). New York: Brunner/Mazel, 1967.

Sigel, I. E., & Olmsted, P. Modification of cognitive skills among lower-class Black children. In J. Helmuth (Ed.), *The disadvantaged child* (Vol. 3). New York: Brunner/Mazel, 1970.

Werner, H. *Comparative psychology of mental development.* New York: International Universities Press, 1957 (original English publication, 1940).

Wozniak, R. H. Dialecticism and structuralism: The philosophical foundation of Soviet Psychology and Piagetian cognitive developmental theory. In K. Riegel & G. C. Rosenwald (Eds.), *Structure and transformation: Developmental and historical aspects* (Vol. 3). New York: Wiley, 1975.

II | PLAY, GESTURE, AND GRAPHIC REPRESENTATION

5 Some Preliminary Observations on Knowing and Pretending

Greta G. Fein
The Merrill-Palmer Institute, Detroit, Michigan

Nancy Apfel
Yale University

Much has been written about the pretend play of young children. Sustained serious research, however, has begun to appear only recently, and as yet relatively few theoretical problems have been addressed. One can step into the study of pretend play in several ways. In this chapter we shall consider theoretical and empirical issues which arise when pretense is treated as a behavioral index of the child's status, that is, his emotional condition or his cognitive competence.

Early empirical investigations in this vein drew heavily from techniques developed in play therapy and relied implicitly (if not always explicitly) upon theoretical interpretations derived from psychoanalytical theory. In the diagnostic perspective, pretend play was viewed as an access route to information about the child's "inner person" (Sears, 1947), his underlying conflicts and anxieties, and from there to information about the life experiences which produced them (Levin & Wardell, 1962; Sears, 1947). As such, it made sense to suggest that aggression in fantasy would be associated with frustration and punishment in the home (Chasdi & Lawrence, 1951). It turned out, however, that the diagnosis was complicated empirically by situational effects (Phillips, 1945; Pintler, Phillips, & Sears, 1946; Sears, 1947). It was also complicated theoretically by psychoanalytic formulations which argued that while pretend play reflects a child's "real" social and emotional experiences, reality becomes distorted in such a way that the literal *content* of pretense, whether in the expressions of anger, affection, or joy or in the details of a story and its characters, is not isomorphic with reality. Nor, taken in isolation from other sources of information, is the literal content sufficient to determine the nature of the child's latent anxiety (Gould, 1972;

Peller, 1954; Wälder, 1933). Given such a perspective, short-term laboratory studies seem precluded as a suitable research procedure. Indeed, if the linkage between affect in pretend play and children's experiences is of interest, in-depth, intensive diary records might be the best way of obtaining a glimpse of the connection between real events as viewed by adults and the pretend episode created by the child. As Piaget (1962) so vividly demonstrated, a pretend episode can change how the real event happened, its consequences, and even its affective content. In the absence of a converging operation, it is a moot question whether the child distorts *his* reality in the pretend episode or whether his initial perception of reality differed from the perception of the adult.

More recently, pretend play has been used as a basis for assessing the symbolic maturity of children during the second and third years of life (Fein, 1975; Inhelder, Lezine, Sinclair, & Stambak, 1972; Lowe, 1975; Nicolich, 1977; Sinclair, 1970). Such studies raise a host of different though comparably difficult issues regarding how pretend play functions as a symbolic vehicle, although the basis of cognitive inferences is not the same as that for affective ones. Within a Piagetian framework, the investigator takes as "given" adult categories regarding the organization and function of objects. If the child gesturally "eats" from a proper, ordinary, but empty spoon, it is assumed that at some level the child "understands" the conventional use of the object as an eating utensil. The gesture becomes significant as an index of symbolic maturity because the child seems to have decontextualized the meaning of the object by using it appropriately outside the practical context. In addition, it is tempting to argue that when children choose to eat from an empty spoon or drink from an empty cup even though real food and drink are nearby, the behavior has been decontextualized at a motivational level as well. It should be evident, however, that we have been discussing objects which have been constructed by adult designers to function as particular kinds of eating utensils. In the course of this construction, features such as shape, size, and texture have been adapted to serve functional requirements. In a sense, then, knowing how a thing is to be used probably involves considerable knowledge of what a thing looks like. What, exactly, is the state of the child's knowledge of objects used in pretending? Before describing a study which attempts to illuminate a small part of that most complex question, let us briefly describe some of the changes which appear in pretend play during the second and third years of life.

The earliest pretend behavior appears quite abruptly at about 12 months of age. The child displays it in a fleeting gesture—closed eyes, bowed head as if sleeping; empty spoon to lips, a tilt of the head, perhaps a smack of the lips as if eating. Then, over the next year and a half, these initially ephemeral gestures become elaborated and enriched. The child begins to use a doll as the recipient of food, and as he does so, the doll gradually becomes the recipient of a complex array of other care-giving activities—the doll is put to bed, dressed, patted, and spanked.

At first, the objects used in pretending tend to be similar to the things used in the real-life situations which the pretend activities seem to mimic. Gradually, the need for verisimilitude weakens, and assorted objects can be used as substitutes in pretend enactments (Fein, 1975; Piaget, 1962; Sinclair, 1970).

By 3 years of age, we see the beginnings of sociodramatic play, and by the age of 5, what began as a few simple gestures now encompasses intricate systems of reciprocal roles, ingenious improvisations of needed materials, increasingly coherent themes, and weaving plots. Then, surprisingly, as precipitously as it began, pretend play begins to decline. Although there may be disagreement regarding the actual age at which overt pretend play declines (Eifermann, 1971), there is little disagreement that it does so. A paradox badly in need of explanation is that as spontaneous overt pretending declines the child's capacity to represent actions and objects increases (Overton & Jackson, 1973).

Piaget has cast these empirical observations into a sequence of developmental levels which reflect changes in the child's cognitive competence. The levels proposed by Piaget (1962) represent a progressive decontextualization and elaboration which come from the phasing in of several discrete strands of symbolic mastery. One strand is the increasing independence of pretense from the immediate and tangible substance or thing. Initially, the child uses a spoon during mealtimes when it contains food. The first step in pretending is taken when object is separated from substance; however, the object itself in a familiar form must be present. As development progresses, the dependency of pretending on a perceivable object is reduced, and eventually the child is able to produce a purely imaginative object with no apparent reliance upon the immediate stimulus field (Overton & Jackson, 1973).

A second strand involves the substitutability of one object for another. Initially, the spoon must be "spoon-like," but eventually an object which does not appear to have any apparent spoon-like features (a leaf) can be used as if it were a spoon, provided it can be held, lifted, and fitted in some fashion to the mouth. The third strand adds a special social quality to pretend play and a social-personality dimension to its analysis. It has to do with how the child as "self" participates in a pretend sequence. Initially, the child's pretend activities are self-related in that the child functions as both agent and recipient (e.g., the child feeds himself). In time, other actors and agents are added to the pretend game, and persons as well as things become substitutable (e.g., the child can pretend to feed mother or a doll and eventually become a detached "other" who makes the doll feed itself). The final strand eventually makes the difference between a pretend scheme and a sociodramatic scenario. Once the child can combine pretend actions, agents, and recipients, it becomes possible to produce the intricate scenes and sequences which characterize full-blown dramatic play.

As indicated earlier, one emphasis in research has been to document the fine details of the development of individual strands (e.g., Fein, 1975; Lowe, 1975; Overton and Jackson, 1973), while another has been to document the interweaving of strands in the overall pattern of development (Inhelder et al., 1972; Nicolich, 1977; Sinclair, 1970). What seems to be emerging are seemingly contradictory answers to the question of what the child knows about the real world when he pretends. These contradictions appear vividly in earlier theoretical controversies regarding the psychological interpretation of pretend play.

Needless to say, the question is not a new one (cf. Bühler, 1930; Klinger, 1971; Stern, 1924). William Stern and Karl Bühler argued about it, and Stern proposed the "ignorance" hypothesis. According to Stern, the 12-month-old knows something about the world but not very much. The child has only "hazy memories and echoes." When the child treats a wooden stick as if it were a doll, the child believes, at that moment, that the stick *is* a doll. By 6 years of age, when pretend play begins to decline, the child knows a great deal about the fixedness of role relations, objects, and boundaries in the real world. Stern implied that the child knows enough by then so that his behavior can be governed by a healthy respect for reality. Bühler's succinct response to Stern's argument was in the form of a penetrating question: If the stick cried, would the child be surprised?

Piaget (1962) offers a cognitive position which is similar to Stern's in its reference to the child's ignorance but different in that it stresses the intentionality behind pretend enactments. Before the age of 12 months the child has not acquired an adequate system for representing objects and object relations. As long as the meaning of objects is governed by sensorimotor knowledge, the child cannot go beyond behaving in accord with the immediate, concrete situation. As the child acquires a mental system which can represent objects and object relations, he can ignore things as they are by assimilating the here and now to well-formed mental categories. But this phase is transitory, and as a balance (or equilibrium) between assimilation and accomodation is achieved, logical structures begin to dominate earlier prelogical forms. Make-believe play is supplanted by constructive activities and games with rules. However, the child's prelogical status does not preclude the acquisition of a system of symbolic codes (images, language) which represent the object and action knowledge he has acquired (cf. discussions of the figural aspects of thinking in Furth, 1969; Piaget, 1966; Piaget and Inhelder, 1971). In Piaget's view, the child's memories are clear enough, but he is simply not bound by a system of logical operations. As far as the child is concerned, eating from an empty spoon could produce food, and drinking from an empty cup could produce milk.

The problem of conceptualizing the pretending child's cognitive status bears indirectly upon the problem of conceptualizing the function of pretend activity. If the young child's pretense is concerned with familiar activities and objects, i.e., those which are presumably well understood and easily identified, pretend is not likely to have an important role in helping a child acquire such knowledge. If, on the other hand, pretend play is biased toward the moderately hazy or the partially mastered, the possibility that play functions to deepen and stabilize new and fragile cognitive acquisitions would be worth exploring in further depth (Sutton-Smith, 1972). But in much research, notions of familiarity tend to be fairly crude and often linked simply to the passage of time rather than to how children fill that time (Scholtz & Ellis, 1975).

Moreover, we really do not know the extent to which the earliest pretend enactments reflect deliberate and differentiated object combinations. For example, if a tool (such as a spoon or a cup) is used for pretend feeding, will it be used to feed all recipients (the child, a doll, another person) indiscriminately, or will recipients be selectively matched to tool? It seems necessary to document the haziness or, perhaps, clarity of the schemes children use when they are pretending. An additional and related question concerns the observation by Lowe (1975), Moore (1964), Pintler et al. (1946), and others that as pretend activities become elaborated and expanded they also, paradoxically, become highly conventionalized. If the sociodramatic play of older children involves a collective representation (Piaget, 1962; Smilansky, 1968), participation in such play must imply that a child has acquired communicable group symbols, i.e., that actions and core role representations have become formalized and ritualized enough so as to be understood and shared by the play group. On the other hand, there are reasons to believe that the child becomes increasingly able to introduce into his play innovations which violate social norms and conventionalized object functions (cf. Fein, 1975; Smilansky, 1968; Sutton-Smith, 1972). How can the apparent contradiction between order and disorder, convention and innovation be resolved?

A fine-grained analysis of how children use objects in pretend games should contribute to a diagnosis of the child's cognitive status. Since pretend feeding activities are among the earliest to appear (Inhelder et al., 1972; Lowe, 1975) and since they have a central role in the house play of preschool children, we decided to look at how children's choices of objects and tools related to such activities change between 12 and 30 months. Of special interest is whether children arrive at some consensus regarding object use and object relations.

METHOD

Data for the present analyses were taken from a larger study of children's development between 12 and 30 months. Thirty-eight children (19 boys and 19 girls) were observed longitudinally at 12, 18, 24, and 30 months. The same set of realistic toys and objects were presented at each age level. The set included materials likely to evoke pretend feeding activities: a doll, a pint-sized saucepan, a large wooden spoon, a metal teaspoon, a 6-in. plastic baby bottle, a 2-in, plastic doll bottle, a 6-in. plastic coffee mug, and a 2-in. plastic teacup. Although the spoons, bottles, and cups were of two sizes, only the doll bottle could be considered miniaturized. Since preliminary analyses failed to reveal stable differences as a function of size, subsequent analyses were performed on tool categories collapsed over size. To encourage elaborations of the pretend feeding theme, the toy set also included a doll crib, a blanket, a toy phone, and a large dump truck.

The child was observed in a playroom with a one-way observation window along one side. The child's mother remained in the room during the 10-min observation period. A young female adult presented the toys by setting them out on the floor in a prescribed order. She invited the child to play and then seated herself at the periphery of the toys. Pilot observations had indicated that the absence of encouragement or the presence of intrusive encouragement reduces the occurrence of pretend activity at the younger age levels. In an attempt to optimize the frequency of pretending, the experimenter casually chatted with the mother, interrupting her conversation at approximately 1½-min intervals to make the following five pretend suggestions: (1) The phone is ringing. It's daddy. He wants to talk to the baby. Let daddy talk to the baby. (2) The baby is hungry. Feed the baby. (3) The baby wants to go for a ride. Take the baby for a ride. (4) The baby is tired. Put the baby to sleep. (5) The baby is dirty. Wash the baby. Before introducing the suggestions, the mother was asked what words she would use in these sentences. With the exception of the first suggestion, the activity was not modeled. The objects which could be used to enact the pretend suggestion were placed in front of the child. The child's activities were observed from behind the one-way window by a trained observer who orally recorded the child's activities using a precoded system of verb actions.

Interobserver agreement for the six observers who participated in data collection ranged from 71% to 95% for feeding activities and 90% to 95% for tool and/or recipient. Proportions are based on the number of agreements divided by the total number of coded events. Due to the ambiguity and fleetingness of early pretend behaviors, coding categories were carefully defined. Agreement among observers was established initially in a series of training sessions which involved filmed and live episodes of play. Observer agreement was assessed during training, immediately after training, and again when the children were 24 and 30 months old. The observers were experienced assistants who participated in several studies of play over a 3-year period.

RESULTS

The data displayed in Table 5.1 are based on the number of children at each age level who engaged in at least one pretend eating or feeding activity. Note, first, changes in the number of children who pretend. The most dramatic change occurs between 12 and 18 months when the number of children who pretend to feed doubles from 16 to 32. By 30 months, 36 children (95%) pretended to eat or feed at least once during the 10-min period.

Of greater interest, however, are changes in the children's choice of recipient and tool. Whom does the child choose to feed? The bottom half of Table 5.1 portrays the percentage of children who chose a given recipient. The percentages reveal a considerable degree of selectivity at each age level as well as a changing pattern of consensus between 12 and 30 months. At 12 months the self is the most frequent recipient of food, other humans (mother or experimenter) come next, while relatively few children (19%) pretend to feed the doll. It is as if at 12 months the absence of substance can be mastered, but the absence of animation cannot. By 18 months, however, the ordering of recipients has changed considerably. Preference for the doll has undergone a fourfold increase, whereas feeding the self or an "other" slightly declines. Although the increase in doll feeding is precipitous, the decline in self and other feeding is gradual; 81% of the children feed themselves at 12 months, but only 39% do so at 30 months.

TABLE 5.1
Percentage of Children at Each Age Who Pretended To Feed by Their
Choice of Tools and Recipient

	Percentage of Pretend Feeders			
	12 Mos	18 Mos	24 Mos	30 Mos
Tool				
Cup	44	28	50	50
Spoon	69	75	71	69
Pot	25	3	3	0
Bottle	13	91	91	86
Recipient				
Doll	19	88	91	100
Self	81	69	59	39
Others	31	19	24	17
n (pretend feeders)	16	32	34	36

Unfortunately, the argument that there might be a major developmental shift between 12 and 18 months is weakened by the fact that only 16 children pretended at 12 months. It could be that if we separated "early" and "late" pretenders we would find that what appears to be a develomental shift is simply an artifact of individual differences. A comparison of early and late pretenders failed to reveal significant differences between the groups. The two groups showed similar patterns of preference at 18, 24, and 30 months. Within the "early" group, a pattern of preference is present at 12 months, changes by 18 months, and holds relatively stable thereafter. At 12 months, pretending is a barely present, fleeting activity; its occurrence during a brief 10-min period is vulnerable to short-term situational or motivational factors, but a striking consensus emerges among those children who do pretend.

Consider now the top half of Table 5.1, which shows the percentage of pretend factors who used each of the four tools. Here too, we find a major reorganization of pretending between 12 and 18 months. Again, "early" and "late" feeders do not differ significantly. Although all of the children were bottle fed, note that relatively few used the bottle at 12 months. Indeed, they were more likely to use the pot, a utensil which as far as we know, none of the children had ever been fed from. Of course, one might call upon Stern's argument that the children were simply confused. But, then, why shouldn't they be equally confused about the bottle? Clearly the spoon is the most preferred feeding utensil at 12 months, attracting 69% of the pretending group, with the cup coming in as second choice. By 18 months, the bottle comes into its own, followed by an increase in the use of the spoon. The important point is that the distribution of choices is clearly not random. The tools used at 12 months seem to be chosen selectively, and the basis of choice seems to change between 12 and 18 months.

Consider now the data in Table 5.2, which show the percentage of pretending children who use each tool/recipient combination at each age level. The table reveals considerable selectivity, even at 12 months. Note that at 12 months the bottle is used for self-feeding by only one child (6%). By 18 months, when most of the children in the study were being weaned to a cup, almost all of those who pretended used the bottle to feed the doll; indeed, 8 of the 11 who used the bottle to feed themselves also used it to feed the doll. In contrast, the cup and the spoon are the most frequently used tools for self-feeding at 12 months (44% and 56%, respectively), even though in real life children in the study rarely used a spoon to feed themselves and were just beginning to use a cup. Surprisingly, at 12 months they never used the cup to feed an adult; four children used the spoon (25%) and one used the bottle (6%) in this fashion. Use of the cup for self-feeding declines somewhat by 18 months, while use of the spoon for self-feeding holds its own. The pot was apparently a 12-month aberration. It is on its way out by 18 months, never to be used as an eating utensil at 24 and 30 months.

TABLE 5.2

Percentage of Children at Four Age Levels Who Pretended To Feed by Their Tool and Recipient Choice

	Recipient											
	12 Months			18 Months			24 Months			30 Months		
	Self	Doll	Others	Self	Doll	Others	Self	Doll	Others	Self	Doll	Others
Tool												
Cup	44	0	0	22	6	0	26	38	9	25	33	14
Spoon	56	13	25	50	50	16	35	56	12	19	61	8
Pot	25	0	0	3	3	0	3	0	0	0	0	0
Bottle	6	13	6	34	81	3	18	85	6	6	86	0
n	16			32			34			36		
Percentage of pretend feeders in total group	42			84			89			95		

It is evident from Table 5.2 that a major reorganization of tool/recipient combinations occurs between 12 and 18 months and becomes increasingly stable thereafter. The rank order correlations for the 12 cells are not significant between 12 and 18 months, marginally significant between 18 and 24 months, and significant at the .01 level between 24 and 30 months.

It is clear from Fig. 5.1, which presents the frequency of tool choices for doll and self, that the pattern of tool use for different recipients changes dramatically with age. To examine changes in children's preference for each tool/recipient combination as a function of age, separate multivariate analyses of variance were run on frequencies converted to linear, quadratic, and cubic trend scores for the four ages. Some combinations which did not occur frequently enough (e.g., bottle/other, pot/doll) were omitted from the analyses. Analyses of the use of the bottle, spoon, and cup to feed the doll yielded significant multivariate F ratios ($p = .003$, $p = .002$, and $p = .002$, respectively) and significant linear trends ($p = .003$, $p = .002$, and $p = .002$). The linear trends reflect the increasing use of the doll with all tools over the 1½-year period. The significant quadratic trend which appeared for the bottle/doll combination reflects the abrupt increase between 12 and 18 months and the slight decline between 24 and 30 months which appears as the children increase their use of the spoon to feed the doll. The use of the spoon and bottle for self-feeding also yielded significant F ratios for the quadratic trend ($p = .024$ and $p = .004$) which reflect the 18-month peak for self-feeding activities. The only other significant trend appeared for the cup/adult

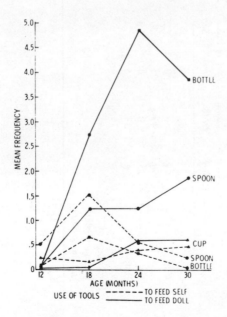

FIG. 5.1.   Frequency of pretense by choice of tool and agent at 12, 18, 24, and 30 months.

combination (linear, p = .04). This combination occurs infrequently at 12 and 18 months but with increasing frequency at 24 and 30 months.

CONCLUSIONS

The data leave us with some puzzles which warrant comment.

First, at 12 months, the pot was used more often as a feeding utensil than the bottle. The pot might be an example of Stern's ignorance hypothesis. Its appeal as a vessel to drink from might have come from its classification by the children as a "container," a global category within which distinctions are fuzzy. If so, why were the bottles not "confused" with the real thing? It seems strange that the children should pointedly ignore a familiar eating tool, while going for one which they have probably never seen used in such a way. Do they use the pot because they have not yet developed a clear distinction between eating and cooking utensils? And do they ignore the bottle because it is too well understood?

Clearly, at 12 months children are selective in their choices. It is the principle behind their selection which eludes us. At 12 months, the children sought out cups and spoons. If they are imitating, who are their models? If early pretending is governed by self-imitation, why do the children ignore the bottle? If they are imitating others, are they imitating adults who feed themselves with cups and spoons, or are they imitating adults who feed children with cups and spoons? Although imitation is a popular explanation of pretending, it is not so easy to specify who or what is being imitated.

Let's suppose that children represent in pretend play life's challenges, not life's commonplaces. At 12 months, bottles are old hat; they are things to be used when you are hungry. They are well-mastered utensils which hold litttle interest beyond their practical purpose. Cups and spoons, however, have been used but not mastered. They are, rather, intriguing, challenging objects in the process of being mastered. Whereas the child may have noted the pot being used in connection with food, the doll is an object which as yet cannot be linked to the eating activities of living things. Then, between 12 and 18 months, children seem to make a connection. The doll is discovered as a representation of a baby, and babies drink out of bottles. Surprisingly, self-feeding with a bottle increases also at the time, as if at least some children create a three-way linkage between "me," "doll," and "baby." But by 24 months, most children rule themselves out as babies who are fed from the bottles. Indeed, they relegate that status to the doll, which becomes the major recipient of nourishment. Concurrently, the doll is increasingly fed with cup and spoon. In a sense, the doll "grows up." It is tempting to suggest that the activities with the doll are a reflective commentary on the child's own developmental history.

The data suggest that the basis of selection changes over the 1½-year period. At first, selections seem to be based on the nature of interesting problems such as the use of tools not quite mastered. Then, by 18 months, selections change, reflecting the child's ability to construct a representational analogue—the relation between "doll" and "baby." Later their selections seem to reflect a social definition of "self" and "others" in terms of "who does what to whom."

It should be noted that the data index changes in the extent to which children agree on tool/recipient relations. Indeed, by 30 months, the consensus appears to be that the bottle goes with the doll. In a sense, the children seemed to have acquired a collective symbol for infant nurturance. Perhaps we see here the beginnings of a shared social symbol. If so, the socialization of symbols appears during the very age period in which the child is increasingly able to invent novel combinations.

In additional analyses we looked at non-food-related pretending with eating utensils, assuming that these would reflect novel, unconventional uses of these materials. At 12 months we find one unconventional use. A child placed a cup to his ear in a listening pose just after he had been doing the same with a toy telephone. At 18 months two children used the bottle in an unconventional way. One held the bottle to his ear in a listening pose and remarked "busy." The other child made a pouring gesture with the bottle onto the doll as if pretending to pour lotion or powder. It is at 24 months that unconventional uses mushroom. We find 12 novel pretend themes not related to the conventional functions of the tools. The spoon was used as a bat, a comb, and a tool to repair the truck and to spank the doll. One child used the bottle to put medicine on the doll's ear, and another pretended to clean the doll by pouring pretend water from the bottle on the doll, saying "dirty." The same child poured from the bottle onto the phone but made no verbalization to explain his action. One girl pretended to apply powder or lotion to the doll and then rubbed in the imaginary contents. The cup and the pot were both used as pretend hats (one child tried the pot on his mother and then on himself, and another put the cup on the doll's head). One 24-month-old girl said "baby take bath" while putting the doll in the cup. The pot seemed to be used by one boy as a vehicle when he pushed the doll around in it. This pretend was preceded by the same pretend act with the doll and a realistic-looking replica of a truck. In this instance, the child created a novel use for the cup even when the tool being represented was actually available. In sum, by 24 months, children begin to move away from pretend behaviors which mimic conventional uses. They begin to use familiar objects to represent objects not present in the immediate array.

At 30 months a countertrend appears. Although more children produce novel pretends, the number of novel themes generated drops from 12 to 6. At this age five of the six children who used the spoon in an unconventional way used it to spank the doll. But note that the use of a spoon this way may not be a symbolic transformation. Spoons were frequently used by some mothers to spank their children. A spoon and a cup were used as a drum, the cup and pot were used as bathtubs, the cup was used as a hat, and the bottle was used to lubricate the truck. We seem to be seeing here two different, even oppositional tendencies. On the one hand, there is a tendency toward expansion and elaboration which makes anything possible, and, on the other, there is the beginning of a consensus which narrows and reduces the possibilities which are realized.

These findings set out some empirical foundations for responding to important theoretical problems. Contrary to Stern's argument, early pretend play is not characterized by diffuse confusion. Children seem to avoid objects they do not understand as well as those they understand too well. The child's pretending hones in midway between the well-formed category and ignorance. In addition, two seemingly contradictory processes seem to occur as children get older. On the one hand, pretend play begins to exhibit the steroty ped forms investigators have noted in 3- and 4-year-olds (Moore, 1964; Pintler et al., 1946). On the other, it exhibits the production of transformations and novelties which have attracted the attention of so many (Sutton-Smith, 1972). If pretend play is to be used as an access route to the diagnosis of children's symbolic development, and if the function of pretend play with respect to that development is to be evaluated, it will be necessary to take into account relationships between the socialization of symbols and their invention (Fein, 1976).

ACKNOWLEDGMENTS

The research was supported by the Office of Child Development under Research Grant OCD-CB-98.

REFERENCES

Bühler, K. *The mental development of the child.* New York: Harcourt, 1930.

Chasdi, E. H., & Lawrence, M. S. Some antecedents of aggression and effect of frustration in doll play. *Personality*, 1951, *1*, 32–43.

Eifermann, R. R. Social play in childhood. In R. Herron & B. Sutton-Smith (Eds.), *Child's play.* New York: Wiley, 1971.

Fein, G. A transformational analysis of pretending. *Developmental Psychology*, 1975, *11*, 291–296.

Fein, G. *The social competence of play.* Paper presented at the annual meetings of the American Education Research Association, San Francisco, April 1976.

Furth, H. G. *Piaget and knowledge.* Englewood Cliffs, N.J.: Prentice-Hall, 1969.

Gould, R. *Child studies through fantasy.* New York: Quadrangle Books, 1972.

Inhelder, B., Lezine, I., Sinclair, H., & Stambak, M. Les Debut de la function symbolique. *Archives de Psychologie*, 1972, *41*, 187–243.

Klinger, E. *Structure and functions of fantasy*. New York: Wiley, 1971.

Levin, H., & Wardell, E. The research uses of doll play. *Psychological Bulletin*, 1962, *59*(1), 27–56.

Lowe, M. Trends in the developmental of representational play in infants from one to three years: An observational study. *Journal of Child Psychology and Psychiatry*, 1975, *16*, 33–47.

Moore, T. Realism and fantasy in children's play. *Journal of Child Psychology and Psychiatry*, 1964, *5*, 15–36.

Nicolich, L. Beyond sensorimotor intelligence: Assessment of symbolic maturity through analysis of pretend play. *Merrill-Palmer Quarterly*, 1977, *23*(2), 89–99.

Overton, W. F., & Jackson, J. P. The representation of imagined objects in action sequences: A developmental study. *Child Development*, 1973, *44*, 309–314.

Peller, L. Libidinal phases, ego development, and play. *Psychoanalytic Study of the Child*, 1954, *9*, 178–198.

Phillips, R. Doll play as a function of the realism of the materials and the length of the experimental session. *Child Development*, 1945, *16*, 145–166.

Piaget, J. *Play, dreams and imitation in childhood*. New York: Norton, 1962.

Piaget, J. Response to Brian Sutton-Smith. *Psychological Review*, 1966, *73*, 111–112.

Piaget, J., & Inhelder, B. *Mental imagery in the child*. New York: Basic Books, 1971.

Pintler, M. H., Phillips, R., & Sears, R. Sex differences in the projective doll play of preschool children. *Journal of Psychology*, 1946, *21*, 73–80.

Scholtz, G. J., & Ellis, M. J. Repeated exposure to objects and peers in a play setting. *Journal of Experimental Child Psychology*, 1975, *19*, 448–455.

Sears, R. R. Influence of methodological factors on doll play performance. *Child Development*, 1947, *18*, 190–197.

Sinclair, H. The transition from sensory motor behavior to symbolic activity. *Interchange*, 1970, *1*, 119–129.

Smilansky, S. *The effects of sociodramatic play on disadvantaged preschool children*. New York: Wiley, 1968.

Stern, W. *Psychology of early childhood*. New York: Henry Holt and Co., 1924.

Sutton-Smith, B. Play as a transformational set. *Journal of Health, Physical Education and Recreation*, 1972, *43*(6), 32–33.

Wälder, R. The psychoanalytic theory of play. *Psychoanalytic Quaterly*, 1933, *2*, 208–224.

6 Pretense Play: A Cognitive Perspective

Claire Golomb
University of Massachusetts

Play, in particular child's play, has intrigued psychologists, educators, philosophers, anthropologists, and historians for many decades; a serious interest in the subject can be traced to the latter part of the nineteenth century. Interpretations of the nature and significance of play have varied considerably and include such diverse viewpoints of play as an essentially goalless though pleasurable activity (Schiller, 1875; Spencer, 1873), the attributions of an evolutionary significance (Hall, 1906, 1916), the exercise of waning instincts in the service of species survival (Groos, 1901), and the identification of play as an important cultural factor essential for the health and preservation of a civilization (Huizinga, 1949). Recent years have seen a renewed interest in the subject of child play as evidenced by several major publications and reviews (Herron & Sutton-Smith, 1971; Klinger, 1969; Millar, 1968; Miller, 1973; Singer, 1973; Slobin, 1964). I shall refrain from a detailed review of theories of play and address myself to only one aspect of play, namely pretense play, which has also been termed symbolic play or sociodramatic play. Within this more restricted context, let me briefly review two major theoretical accounts of pretense play.

The most widely known and influential theories of child play are the psychoanalytic and the Piagetian interpretations of pretense or symbolic play. The psychoanalytic conception emphasizes the symbolic satisfaction which the child derives from play. Play is perceived as a major avenue for the expression of desires and needs, often the only means for attaining momentary wishfulfillment. In the realm of play the child operates almost without constraints, transforms reality, and recreates it according to his fancy. Play as wishfulfillment is a manifestation of the pleasure principle which serves important psychological functions. Thus, play affords the child a temporary escape from reality, fulfills desires, releases tension, compensates for weakness, and permits the expression of otherwise unacceptable impulses, for example, regressive and conflicting ones. Play also enables the child to gain mastery over anxiety arousing situations, and may provide the youngster with an opportunity to deal with reality by rehearsing his or her role in a quasi-realistic situation. The two recurrent themes of the psychoanalytic writers revolve on the expression of fantasized wishfulfillment and mastery over anxiety evoking situations. Thus play serves a dual function: It answers the child's emotional needs and helps obtain mastery over complex problems. This approach to child play has had important practical implications for clinical child psychology which frequently employs the play situation for diagnostic and therapeutic purposes.

Summarizing the psychoanalytic position we can state that it emphasizes the emotional significance of play. The adaptive function of play is only indirectly perceived in terms of maintaining or reestablishing ego balance (Erikson, 1963; Freud, 1922; Freud, 1936; Klein, 1931; Peller, 1952; Waelder, 1933).

The second most important formulation of child play can be found in Piaget's (1962) account published in 1946 entitled *Play, Dreams, and Imitation*. This book is the third work in a series dealing with the growth of intelligence and the child's construction of reality. It represents Piaget's attempt to integrate pretense or symbolic play within his cognitive framework of intellectual development. From a cognitive perspective Piaget considers symbolic play as a manifestation of the child's conceptual immaturity, an expression of a cognitive imbalance typical of an early stage of human development. Despite the cognitive limitations, however, symbolic play serves an important function: it enables the child to escape, momentarily, from the all too pressing demands of the adult social world. The child accomplishes this via the distortion of reality in symbolic play, distortions which take the forms of wishfulfillment, reconstruction of past events, compensation for undesirable outcomes, and liquidation of conflicts. Symbolic play represents a transformation of reality in the direction of wishfulfillment, and in this sense resembles the psychoanalytic version of "play in the service of the pleasure principle," and "play as a source of mastery" or being the "cause of an action." Piaget perceives symbolic play as subordinating reality to the whims of the ego; instead of accommodating the ego to reality the child assimilates reality to his needs and desires. It is this assimilation of reality which, according to Piaget, enables the child to maintain a sense of continuity and to establish a measure of ego balance. This balance, which rests on affective factors, is of considerable importance since the cognitive operations for the establishment of a genuine equilibrium have not yet been constructed.

It can be seen readily that both positions, the psychoanalytic and the Piagetian, share a common ground. Both theories emphasize the child's emotional needs during a period of cognitive imbalance and instability. Both perceive play as a somewhat regressive tendency, a retreat from reality which demands accommodation to its complex standards and customs. For Piaget symbolic play directly reveals the child's cognitive egocentricity which is characterized by undisciplined thinking and the lack of genuine class concepts. The nature of egocentric thought is clearly reflected in the child's arbitrary substitutions of one object for another, substitutions which presumably lack rhyme or reason. According to Piaget, pretense play is characterized by the child's tendency to substitute, quite arbitrarily, one object for another. It is unlike conceptual thought which is orderly, and permits only systematic substitutions based on perceptual similarity or established conventions. Thus, for example, in conceptual thought a drawing of a triangle can stand for all triangles, it is a mere representative of the class of objects called triangles. These orderly substitutions are totally unlike the substitutions which the child makes in symbolic play. The latter are idiosyncratic and willful, made at the whims of the ego. In symbolic play, according to Piaget, anything can stand for the missing object. There are no guiding rules and the child's momentary needs and fancy determine the nature of the substitution. In psychoanalytic thinking the symbol, though private, is not conceived as arbitrary. While the meaning of the substitute object may escape ordinary consciousness, and the link between the symbol and its referent is often repressed, the symbol is selected because it is in some way a fitting vehicle for wishes and needs, and frequently carries a sexual meaning. Thus, unlike Piaget's notion of the undisciplined character of the substitutions, the symbol in psychoanalytic theory obeys certain psycho-dynamic rules, the rules of the primary thought process.

The foregoing analysis illustrates that both positions emphasize the *emotional* significance of play and assign only incidental significance to the role of play in cognitive development. Both Freud and Piaget perceive symbolic play as a near-universal phenomenon due to the affective and cognitive constellation of the child. In the affective realm several conditions conspire to elicit conflicting emotions which cry out for expression and tend to find an outlet in symbolic play activity. Foremost among these is the widespread human condition of growing up in a family, the prolonged childhood dependency on the family and its attendant attachment ties which, inevitably, are associated with feelings of helplessness, jealousy, rivalry, anger, and fear of desertion. Furthermore, the preschooler's intense concern with his bodily functions leads to conflicting impulses and feelings and fosters related fantasies. In the cognitive realm the child's conceptual immaturity places severe restrictions on his ability to reason and to comprehend and leads to a distorted worldview, a prelogical view of himself and the events he observes. The differences between reality and fantasy, between physical causality and magic are not clearly perceived. In Piaget's system the fate of symbolic play is to vanish from the scene. Like egocentric language and thought, play becomes socialized and takes the form of cooperative, rule-governed games. The imaginative aspect of play is not lost for ever but is ultimately integrated into conceptual intelligence. In Freud's system symbolic play goes underground and continues to flourish in dreams, daydreams, art and fantasy.

Some minor though important voices of dissent ought to be mentioned. Lewin (1935), one of the major proponents of Gestalt psychology, emphasized the child's ability to move between the world of fantasy and reality; he attributed to the child the capacity to discriminate between them and to act accordingly. He perceived child behavior as a function of the total psychological environment, and if the situation was understood from the child's perspective, his behavior appeared to be quite reasonable, sensitive to the demand characteristics of a task and altogether less distorted than Piaget suggests. In line with this conception, one of his students, Sliosberg (1934), studied preschool children's willingness to substitute objects during pretense play and during arts and crafts activities and block building. Under these two contrasting conditions she discovered important differences in the child's selections, differences which she attributed to the effects of the task and the materials. These findings seemed to suggest that the child's play behavior in the constructive activities (block building and arts and crafts) was subject to certain implicit rules of the reality-oriented game.

Vygotsky (1966), another great psychologist, saw in play a manifestation of abstract reasoning. He considered imaginative play as the highest cognitive achievement a preschool child was capable of. Other dissenting voices should be mentioned, for example, those of Elkonin (1966) and Smilansky (1968), who perceive in the child's symbolic or pretense play the guiding influence of the adult. These authors consider play important for intellectual development and assign significance to play as an essential ingredient for later scholastic success. If adult modeling and teaching of pretense play are important, one might expect significant differences due to social-class and cultural variables, and indeed Smilansky (1968) and Whiting (1963) stress the lack of universality of symbolic play, its near absence in certain cultures (for example, the Nyansongo, a Gusii community in Kenya, and the Mixtecan community in Mexico), and Smilansky suggests additional social-class variables.

While the issue of a "cognitive significance" of symbolic play has been raised by several students of play behavior, clear-cut empirical evidence for such a function has not been provided. A series of diverse studies show that symbolic play can be trained (Feitelson & Ross, 1973; Singer, 1973; Smilansky, 1968), that it may bear some relation to creativity measures

(Feitelson & Ross, 1973; Lieberman, 1965), that play training may affect certain creativity measures (Feitelson & Ross, 1973; Rosen, 1974), that the children of the poor sometimes fail to engage in pretense or sociodramatic play (Rosen, 1974; Smilansky, 1968) and fall behind the middle-class child in terms of school achievement. However, a connection between play and cognition has not been demonstrated. Thus, the issue of a cognitive significance of symbolic play remains highly controversial. Not a single study shows a direct training effect of symbolic play on cognitive achievement. Studies that were designed to elucidate the relationship between creativity and play often failed to control for examiner expectations and also reported somewhat inconsistent findings which affected their reliability. And finally, the separation of social class and cultural variables has proven to be a difficult task, and both variables have been confounded (Rosen, 1974; Smilansky, 1968). For most investigators it is a matter of belief that symbolic play has beneficial effects, a belief which is maintained even in the absence of a firm empirical basis. The exception to this statement is perhaps the literature on role play, which has stressed that training in role taking improves a child's capacity for adopting another's point of view, which is a social and cognitive skill. Efforts to go beyond this statement to specific effects on cognitive tasks are tentative, since the studies on role play are correlational and do not tell us much about cause and effect, and some of the data are inconsistent (Feffer, 1970; Feffer & Gourevitch, 1960; Swinson, 1965; Turnure, 1975).

In view of the conflicting conceptions concerning the nature and function of pretense play and the incomplete state of the empirical evidence, I addressed myself to the following questions: (1) What is the extent of an object's substitutability, and what type of substitutions are acceptable to children? (2) What is the incidence, type, and relative complexity of symbolic play when compared with other kinds of play activities children engage in? (3) What is the role of social-class effects? (4) What is the effect of symbolic play training on a strictly cognitive task such as the conservation of quantity?

The first problem concerns the issue of object substitution and raises the question of the type of transformations children make, that is, whether all substitutions or object transformations are equally permissable or acceptable to the child. It leads to an investigation of the child's spontaneous responses when substitute objects are made available and what happens upon suggestions by the adult experimenter. This issue is of particular interest since Piaget perceives the early substitutions which characterize pretense play as an inferior form of cognition and as evidence of an unstable cognitive structure. However, from a different perspective pretense substitutions might also be viewed as evidence of a symbolizing capacity which enables the child to treat one object as representing another absent one and thus as a mark of abstract reasoning. And, indeed, the ability to pretend has been defined by some investigators as a cognitive achievement characteristic of the adult's normal intellectual operations (Goldstein, 1963). The neurologist Goldstein interprets the absence of the pretense ability as a symptom of cognitive impairment, signaling the loss of the capacity for abstract reasoning which defines the normal adult's intellectual operations.

To obtain a better insight into this issue of object substitution the following experiment was designed (Golomb, 1977).

STUDY 1

Sixty preschool children of middle-class background, ages 2.8 to 5.9, were presented with three pretense play situations: going to the beach, going to the pet shop, and feeding a hungry baby. In all three situations the child faced a revolving stage, partitioned into three sections. In "going to the beach" the stage background displayed a picture of children playing at the beach. In front of the beach was an array of objects varying in degree of similarity to what might be construed to be a child's "friend." The following objects were displayed: doll, picture of a child, tadpole photo, smile button, giraffe, stuffed form, carrot, cardboard roll, pencil, plasticene stick, string, key purse, boot, cookie. The examiner informed the child that they were going to play a game of "going to the beach" and that the child could invite a "friend" and make his selection from the objects on display. After the selection was made and the friend was brought to the beach, the examiner declared that the friend had to go home and promptly removed the selected object from the stage and out of sight. The child was encouraged to make a second selection and to take another friend along to the beach. This procedure was continued until the child selected every item or refused to do so on the ground that he could no longer find a suitable friend among the available objects. A similar game was played with the "pet shop." The child was asked to *pretend* that it was his birthday and that he wanted a kitten for a pet. In front of the pet shop was an array of objects varying in degree of similarity to the desired pet: stuffed animal kitten, porcelain kitten, picture of a kitten, stuffed animal—dog, porcupine, stuffed nondescript form, furry slipper, doll, blob of plasticene, carrot, cube, cradle. After the child made his selection the examiner declared that this pet was, unfortunately, ill and had to go to the doctor. The object was removed from the stage, and the subject was encouraged to search for another pet. This procedure was continued until all objects had been selected or rejected by the child. The third pretense play situation concerned a "hungry baby." The stage displayed a doll which, according to the experimenter, was a very hungry baby. The stage background, defined as a kitchen, was equipped with a number of different objects, some seemingly sensible ones such as bottles, a can of food, a picture of food and others tending to be incongruous or absurd such as a cardboard roll, pencil, cube, candle, rabbit, brush, toy car.

The child was encouraged to feed the hungry baby. After each selection and pretend feeding the examiner declared that the baby was still hungry and thus encouraged further selections. This procedure was continued until the subject either exhausted all available substitute objects or rejected the substitutes, maintaining that he could not find any more food. In each one of the three situations (which were presented in a counterbalanced order) the emphasis was from the very *beginning* on playing a pretense game. The examiner opened with the sentence, "Let's pretend this is. ..." The pretense nature of the situation and of the objects was made quite explicit. Since the subject was actively encouraged to search for a substitute object, the whole procedure was highly suggestive and in this sense constituted a test of the upper limits of substitutability.

The results of this study are quite clear-cut. The child's selection was neither random nor arbitrary but followed a rule: from the most suitable objects—for example, in the case of the hungry baby, food; in the case of the beach, the doll; in the case of the pet shop, the kitten—to neutral objects nondistinct in form and function; selection sharply diminished when only incongruous objects were left. This trend could be clearly observed for all age groups and held true for the three pretense situations. Some minor variations were observed: Incongruous selections in the pet shop and the beach game were higher for the youngest subjects, who also showed a higher degree of role enactment on the hungry baby game.

In the second part of this study the same subjects were presented with three different puzzle tasks: a manekin, an elephant, and a car. In this experimental situation the child was informed that puzzle parts have to be put together so that the pieces fit. After this introduction, the puzzle was presented in its near-completed form, with a *single* part missing: In the case of the manekin, the head; in the case of the elephant, the back; and in the case of the car, the rear wheel. In each presentation the missing part, that is, the standard part, was displayed among an array of pieces which varied in terms of degree of fit to the standard, that is, in terms of their power to substitute for the standard piece. In the case of the manekin puzzle the display consisted of the following 13 pieces: standard face, standard minus features, large face, small face, square face, cat's face, large oval, medium oval, small oval, disk, hand, telephone, fruit. In the case of the elephant, the following 12 pieces were displayed: standard back, standard plus incongruous drawing, large back, small back, large rectangle, small rectangle, triangle, disk, cut-out of milk bottles, driver, cat's face, tree. In the case of the car puzzle the array consisted of the following 13 pieces: standard wheel, standard plus drawing, large wheel, medium-sized wheel, small wheel, square wheel, face, cup, clock, steering wheel, flower, boot, handlebars. The child was encouraged to look over the collection of pieces and asked to find the one that would best complete the puzzle. Following the child's selection of a part, this part was removed, and the child was asked whether he could find another piece to complete the puzzle. This procedure was continued until the child's firm refusal, a statement to the effect that no such piece was available. As in the first part of our experiment, this procedure was highly suggestive and encouraged the search for substitute objects, which may well constitute a test of the upper limits of substitutability.

The results of this study are also unambiguous: The first choice was always the most appropriate one, that is, the standard part. The order of the selections followed a definite rule: from standard to neutral forms, to discrepant ones (if at all), with the latter trailing far behind the former choices. This finding held for all ages, and for the three puzzles, with only minor age and task effects. The age effect was noticeable in the youngest subjects' slightly higher acceptance rate of irrelevant or incongruous substitutes, and the task effect could be seen in the manekin puzzle, which elicited more humorous substitutions and was also easier in terms of fit. All subjects indicated a clear awareness of the absurdity of the later selections ("a telephone-man," a "cat-man"), and even for the most compliant ones (the youngest age group) there were limits to the acceptability of substitutes, with the most incongruous ones eliciting rejection.

If we compare the effects of the "realistic" situation, which the puzzle task represents, with the effects of the "pretense" play situation, we observe that both obey a common rule. Although the substitutions on all tasks were actively encouraged by the examiner, the choices, both in terms of sequence and percentage of selections, followed the same "rule" from optimal selections, fitting in terms of size, form, and meaning, to neutral ones, trailing off with the incongruous substitutes. It is true that our subjects could be induced to accept less than optimal substitutes, beginning with the "neutral" ones and ending in most cases with some effort to accept incongruous substitutes; however, eventually, some or all incongruous substitutes were rejected despite the highly suggestive encouragement provided by the adult experimenter.

If now we compare the incidence of acceptable substitutions for the puzzle and pretense tasks, we find a significant difference in the selections of "suitable" and "unsuitable" substitutes, depending on the task. If we place the objects on a continuum extending from most acceptable to least acceptable substitutes, we find that the five most acceptable substitutes on each one of the three puzzle tasks were selected 55% of the time and the five least acceptable substitutes only 21% of the time. On the pretense tasks, children made more selections, though the ratio of acceptable to unacceptable substitutes is not too different: 86% for the acceptable substitute objects and 44% for the unacceptable substitutes. This illustrates a task effect. Thus, the extent to which children transform the object to *fit the needs of the task* (as defined by the experimenter and the child's comprehension) is a function of the *nature of the task* (puzzle or pretense play) and the *characteristics of the object*. However, even in the case where the task encourages transformations, there are apparently limits to the extent of incongruous object substitution. The protocols show clearly that the children responded to the "rules" of the game,[1] that they detected fairly soon what the experimenter was after. In both situations they showed a willingness to play the game, to go beyond their "natural" choices as indicated by laughter and hesitation, making selections of a neutral kind before passing on to the incongruous selections, but for most subjects there were limits to the incongruity they were willing to tolerate.[2] Age effects were minimal (which might be due to the absence of young 2-year-olds); all subjects quickly perceived what was needed and attempted to make an optimal choice, one which was sensible and not idiosyncratic.

These results appear to challenge Piaget's account of the almost "lawless" substitutions of pretense play.[3] Piaget, as will be recalled, contrasts the undisciplined substitutions of the young child, who presumably operates on the assumption that "anything can stand for anything," with the orderly substitutions of reasoning where the image or symbol resembles the object and thus serves a communicative, that is, a social, function. This communicative function is even more apparent in the use of conventional signs typical of language and mathematics. But the symbolic activity of the young child, according to Piaget, undergoes socialization only gradually, and his pretense games in particular remain of a private and arbitrary nature. When play eventually becomes rule governed, it leads to social games, and symbolic games vanish. The spontaneous transformational activity seen in symbolic play, the "as-if" character of the child's substitute objects and actions and his extensive role taking, is seen predominantly as an expression of undisciplined thought and as a manifestation of an immature cognitive structure, a position which, in the light of our findings, needs to be revised.

---

[1]Following the first two or three selections, children quickly discovered the "rule" of the game and frequently anticipated the examiner's response, declaring that this pet was sick and had to go to the doctor.

[2]Sliosberg (1934), working within Lewin's framework, conducted an interesting study on substitutions in children's play. She differentiated between reality (constructive activities consisting of arts and crafts and block building) and irreality (pretense) play. Her data, however, are not altogether clear, and the lack of statistical analyses prevents us from determining whether an obtained difference was meaningful. She found a tendency to substitute objects more readily in pretense situations than in the realistic ones, but this was not a consistent trend. She failed to fully analyze the nature of the real and of the pretense situation and ignored the transformation of the real situation into one of pretense as a function of examiner expectations. Although she mentioned the existence of "rules" and of "limits" in the realistic situation, she dealt with neither of these in the case of pretense.

[3]It should be remembered, however, that Piaget's account is based on play in the home setting, which is frequently the stage for solitary play of a private, secretive nature and shows evidence of intense emotional involvement. While his observations do not invalidate ours, they may present a special case rather than the major form of preschool pretense play.

Now that we have established a degree of "lawfulness" in the kinds of substitutions children make under our experimental conditions, let us consider the spontaneous pretense behavior of the child in a *naturalistic* setting. The observational study reported here was conducted with children from two very different social classes, children from a middle- to upper-middle-class background and children from a working-class background.

STUDY 2

Sixty subjects, 30 of which came from a middle-class background and 30 from a working-class background, ages 3.4 to 6.1, were observed during the free play period in a nursery school, a day-care center, and kindergarten classes. The child's behavior during the free play period was recorded and classified into different play episodes, for example, motor play, exploratory play, arts and crafts, pretense play, constructive activities, conversation, sandbox or water play activities, learning activities, and games with rules. Next, the play episodes were analyzed in terms of level of complexity, social cooperation, socialized or egocentric language, and type of symbolic play.

One of the most striking findings of this study is the high (approximately 30%) incidence of pretense play for all ages, regardless of social class. Pretense games appeared to be a highly favored activity of our preschool children, even of the kindergarteners, and playing house represented the most preferred theme. In its earliest form pretense play was most frequently characterized by imitative actions and short-lived role enactment. Examples are moving a toy truck back and forth, imitating the movements and sounds of the object in reality, or wearing a fireman's hat as a mark of identity without, however, truly enacting the role of a fireman, for example, climbing ladders and extinguishing fires. These relatively short-lived episodes were often played in a solitary setting or alongside others, without genuine interaction. The latter has been characterized by Parten (1932) as "parallel" play where children engage in similar activities without coordinating their efforts. Gradually, with increasing age, the play episodes became more involved and complex, with appropriate role division among players. This involved a genuine kind of role enactment which transformed the actor and the objects of his game. The child truly identified with his role and acted accordingly, attempting to imitate as faithfully as possible the behavior of the teacher, the mother, the doctor, the cowboy, etc. In the case of the older children role play developed along more imaginative lines with greater theme variation and elaboration. Characters were derived from fairy tales, storybooks, television, and picture books, presenting a mixture of fantasy and conventional imagery. In the case of the somewhat older children an increase in the length of the episode was also noticed. These age trends were apparent for both socioeconomic (SES) groups; they were general trends and seemed predominantly a function of age. It is interesting that while the older children's role play led to more intense involvement in pretense play, more than one role transformation or character change during an extended episode was rare for both SES groups, and object substitutions were on the whole modest and fairly conventional. Pretense play, even for the youngest subjects, was frequently cooperative, involving a number of players and their adaptation to the common theme, integrating the individual player into an overall scheme. This cooperative trend became the dominant one for the 4- and 5-year-olds. Altogether, the highest level of social interaction which required give and take, perspective taking, and comprehension of multiple roles was found during the pretense episodes and was unmatched in frequency of occurrence by other play episodes. No other play activity matched pretense play in the level of the attained play complexity and the use of communicative language.

Summarizing our findings, we can state that symbolic play or pretense play shows a definite developmental progression from simple acts of imitation, short-lived identifications, and object substitutions to extensive role play and theme elaboration which is quite comparable for our two different socioeconomic groups of subjects. This genre is unique in its social and cognitive achievements. It spontaneously brings together several children in the pursuit of a common goal. The players subordinate their roles and perhaps desires to a common theme, momentarily relinquishing self-determination to the organizer of the game; they communicate successfully and adopt perspectives depending on their own role and that of the other player. It appears that pretense play, more than perhaps any other play activity, fosters cooperative behavior, successful communication among peers, multiple perspective taking, and the ability to maintain a fictional role and to assume a momentary identity for oneself and for the other players. Play illustrates the child's capacity to represent absent realities and reflects perhaps the child's highest social and cognitive achievement in the settings we have studied. It appears as a spontaneous activity, generated and organized by the children themselves, an activity which seems highly satisfying to the child and one of which he rarely tires.

Let us now turn to the last study, which examines the relationship between pretense play and cognition and uncovers a functional relation between training in pretense play and conservation attainment. The rationale underlying this study is based on the following analysis of the cognitive operations typical of play.

The most striking cognitive aspect of pretense or symbolic play is the child's capacity to maintain, simultaneously, an imaginary duality of object and role. While adopting a role and enacting it, the child does not forget his "real" identity; if need be, he can step momentarily out of his role, go to the bathroom, or answer his mother's call. The same is true of the identity he ascribes to the substitute objects. He may treat a blob of play dough as if it were a delicious cake but carefully refrain from biting into it. Moreover, the player not only maintains the duality of his own identity but that of the other actors as well. Apparently, we are witnessing in the pretense play situation of early childhood a form of reversible thought operation. In symbolic play the child is employing a kind of intuitive form of reversibility; he is performing reversible transformations which are not perceptually apparent. Every time the child adopts a role and pretends to be someone other than himself he engages in a mental transformation which is not matched by physical reality. When he discards his temporary role and readopts his usual identity the imaginary transformation is reversed and his former self is reinstated. If this kind of analysis has any validity, then the pseudoreversibility of thought, which one is tempted to attribute to symbolic play, may well be related to the reversible thought operations which characterize the attainment of conservation. In that case one might consider the reversibility seen in play as a spontaneous antecedent, a precursor of the genuine reversibility of operational thought, in which case training in symbolic play might affect conservation.

With this hypothesis in mind Cheryl Cornelius and I set out to explore the relationship between pretense play and its intuitive reversibility and conservation with its operational reversibility (Golomb & Cornelius, 1977). Children were exposed to symbolic play situations and questioned about their pretense behavior, thus *inducing* an awareness of their mental operations, and the effects of this training procedure on the child's attainment of conservation were studied.

STUDY 3

Our subjects were 30 nonconserving 4-year-olds attending a middle-class nursery school. All subjects were between the ages of 4.0 and 4.6 years. Fifteen comprised the test group and 15 the control group, with near equal numbers of boys and girls in each group. The two groups were thus matched for age, sex, socioeconomic status, and type of schooling. To ensure the nonconserving status of our subjects, all subjects were first tested on four conservation tasks using liquid and substance conservation (conservation of quantity). They witnessed the transformation of the water level as the liquid was being poured into different-sized containers and as the play dough balls were being shaped into sausages, and finally they observed the transformation back to the standard. Each trial also involved extensive and systematic questioning of the child to determine the rationale underlying his response to the task.

Following the conservation pretests and the assessment of the subjects' nonconserving status, 15 subjects constituting the experimental group were assigned to the pretense play condition, and 15 subjects constituting the control group were assigned to the constructive play condition. The experimental group was given a series of six pretense play periods extending over 3 days, followed on the fifth day by conservation posttests. The control group was given a series of six constructive play tasks (two puzzles, two mosaic games, two drawings) over 3 days, followed on the fifth day by conservation posttests. Thus, Day 1 was reserved for conservation pretests and Days 2, 3, and 4 for playing games (pretense or constructive games), while Day 5 was used for conservation posttests.

The six pretense play situations were instituted in daily sessions lasting approximately 15 min. Each game engaged the child in a pretense situation, for example, puppets riding on horseback (block) or picking strawberries (pebbles) and selecting a kitten (sponge) in a pet shop. Once the game was in full swing the examiner "stepped out of the pretense situation" and systematically questioned the child about the nature of the object and how the plaything could be two things, itself and a make-believe identity. Thus, for example, when food was prepared for the picnic the examiner professed sudden hunger and, biting into the play dough, suggested to the incredulous child that he and she do likewise. This prompted the child to explain his actions and to offer an account of the symbolic and reversible nature of his pretense play.

Analysis of the performance of the two groups on the conservation posttests revealed dramatic differences in performance. In the experimental group only 2 out of 15 subjects remained firm nonconservers, while in the control group 14 out of 15 subjects remained firm nonconservers. The 13 subjects of the experimental group who displayed a change on the conservation posttest distributed themselves as follows: Three subjects became *doubters;* they felt uneasy about their judgment, hesitated, and indicated puzzlement; there were long silences with "mmms" (tape-recorded conversations), interspersed with comments of "I don't know" and "I am not sure," but they finally trusted the perceptual cues and responded in a nonconserving fashion. Six subjects could be defined as *transitional conservers,* conserving on one to three of the total of four conservation trials. Four subjects became *genuine conservers,* demonstrating neither doubt nor confusion and offering typical conserving responses: "Well, you see, we can always make it back the way it was at first," "We didn't add any clay to it, so it can't have more," "It's just the shape that is different," and "It just looks like more water because the glass is taller and skinnier than that one, so the water goes up higher." Of the 15 control subjects, 14 remained nonconservers, and only a single subject became a conserver.

The results show an unquestionable improvement in conservation performance of the experimental subjects who underwent symbolic play training, an achievement unmatched by the control subjects. The data suggest that a similar process underlies both symbolic play and conservation attainment since training on one affects the other. The similarity lies in the ability to maintain the identity of an object in spite of its transformation. In the case of symbolic or pretense play the transformation is purely imaginary; on the conservation task the transformation is of a perceptual nature. The dramatic effect of symbolic play training and its technique of intensive questioning suggests the existence of a functional relation between symbolic play and the acquisition of conservation. These findings are provocative since the present study employed a generally accepted and stringent cognitive task. Unlike other play studies which failed to deal directly with specific cognitive skills or produced only correlational evidence, the results of this investigation demonstrate a functional relationship between symbolic play and cognition. Our data suggest that symbolic play is an important antecedent of operational reversibility, spontaneously generated and freely exercised during a period which Piaget defines as characterized by cognitive egocentrism and cognitive imbalance. These data challenge the notion that the child during the preoperational period is predominantly a victim of egocentric reasoning, a view which has forced Piaget to overlook the constructive, truly cognitive aspects of symbolic play. If symbolic play indeed fulfills a developmental function and fosters the emergence of reversible thought operations, we ought to reconsider the notion that play only represents a transitional phase characterized by cognitive imbalance. Perhaps symbolic play need not merely be outgrown but ought to be exercised.

This brings us directly to the educational implications of this work. The series of studies which we have considered have highlighted the disciplined character of pretense play. Although pretense play is characterized by an imaginative orientation which encourages object substitution and role adoption, it is rule governed almost from its inception. This highly favored play of childhood exercises important cognitive and social functions while simultaneously offering great emotional satisfaction, thus ensuring its continued fascination for youngsters. The naturalistic observations once more confirm Parten's (1932) original finding that pretense play elicits the most advanced forms of social cooperation in children and fosters, perhaps more than any other play activity, socialized language in Piaget's (1926) sense. It is an activity where children share their most private and intimate feelings and thoughts with others of similar status, their peers. The amazing result of the effects of our play training tehcnique on conservation achievement points toward the effectiveness of making discerning use of processes already available to the child and recognizable to him. In our training situation the child is encouraged to discover the solutions within himself, drawing upon his own repertoire of available responses and experiences rather than being pushed to accept outside input or reasoning beyond his developmental level. Active participation in pretense play among preschoolers as well as guided dramatic play may well represent one of the major avenues for developmental progress and achievement during the preoperational period, and its educational functions for the elementary school child ought to be fully explored.

REFERENCES

Elkonin, D. Symbolics and its function in the play of children. *Soviet Education,* 1966, *8,* 35–41.

Erikson, E. H. *Childhood and society.* New York: Norton, 1963.

Feffer, M. H. Developmental analysis of interpersonal behavior. *Psychological Review,* 1970, *77*(3), 197–214.

Feffer, M. H., & Gourevitch, V. Cognitive aspects of role-taking in children. *Journal of Personality,* 1960, *28,* 383–396.

Feitelson, D., & Ross, G. S. The neglected factor—Play. *Human Development,* 1973, *16,* 202–223.

Freud, A. *The ego and the mechanisms of defense.* London: Hogarth, 1936.

Freud, S. *Beyond the pleasure principle.* London: International Universities Press, 1922.

Goldstein, K. *Human nature in the light of psychopathology.* New York: Schocken, 1963.

Golomb, C., Symbolic Play: The role of substitutions in pretence and puzzle games. *British Journal of Educational Psychology,* 1977, *47,* 175–186.

Golomb, C., & Cornelius, C. B. Symbolic play and its cognitive significance. *Developmental Psychology,* 1977, *13,* 246–252.

Groos, K. *The play of man.* New York: Appleton, 1901.

Hall, G. S. *Youth.* New York: Appleton, 1906.

Hall, G. S. *Adolescence: Its psychology and its relation to physiology, anthropology, sex, crime, religion and education.* New York: Appleton, 1916.

Herron, R.E., & Sutton-Smith, B. *Child's play.* New York: Wiley, 1971.

Huizinga, J. *Homo ludens: A study of the play element in culture.* London: Routledge & Kegan Paul, 1949.

Klein, M. *The psychoanalysis of children.* London: Hogarth Press, 1931.

Klinger, E. Development of imaginative behavior: Implications of play for a theory of fantasy. *Psychological Bulletin,* 1969, *72*(4), 227–298.

Lewin, K. *A dynamic theory of personality. Selected papers.* New York: McGraw-Hill, 1935.

Lieberman, N. J. Playfulness and divergent thinking : An investigation of their relationship at the kindergarten level. *Journal of Genetic Psychology,* 1965, *107,* 219–224.

Millar, S. *The psychology of play.* London: Penguin Books, 1968.

Miller, S. Ends, means, and galumphing: Some leitmotifs of play. *American Anthropologists,* 1973, *75*(1), 87–98.

Parten, M. B. Social participation among preschool children. *Journal of Abnormal and Social Psychology,* 1932, *27,* 243–269.

Peller, L. E. Models of children's play. *Mental Hygiene,* 1952, *36,* 66–83.

Piaget, J. *The language and thought of the child.* New York: Harcourt & Brace, 1926.

Piaget, J. *Play, dreams, and imitation.* New York: Norton, 1962.

Rosen, C. E. The effects of sociodramatic play on problem solving behavior among culturally disadvantaged preschool children. *Child Development,* 1974, *45,* 920–927.

Schiller, F. *Essays, aesthetical and philosophical.* London: G. Bell, 1875.

Singer, J. L. *The child's world of make-believe.* New York: Academic Press, 1973.

Sliosberg, S. Zur Dynamiek des Ersatzes. *Psychologische Forschung,* 1934, *19,* 122–181.

Slobin, D. The fruits of the first season: A discussion of the role of play in childhood. *Journal of Humanistic Psychology,* 1964, *4*(1), 59–79.

Smilansky, S. *The effects of sociodramatic play on disadvantaged preschool children.* New York: Wiley, 1968.

Spencer, H. *Principles of psychology.* New York: Appleton, 1873.

Swinson, M. The development of cognitive skills and role-taking. *Dissertation Abstracts,* 1965, *26*(7), 40–82.

Turnure, C. Cognitive development and role-taking ability in boys and girls from 7 to 12. *Developmental Psychology,* 1975, *11*(2), 202–209.

Vygotsky, L. S. Play and its role in the mental development of the child. *Voprosy Psikhologii,* 1966 (1933), *12*(6), 62–76.

Waelder, R. The psychoanalytic theory of play. *Psychoanalytic Quarterly,* 1933, *2,* 208–224.

Whiting, B. B. (Ed.). *Six cultures: Studies of child rearing.* New York: Wiley, 1963.

7

Style and Sequence in Early Symbolic Play

Dennie Wolf
Harvard Graduate School of Education

Howard Gardner
Harvard Graduate School of Education
Boston Veterans Administration Hospital

Observation 1: J. (1:4:7) is offered a collection of small toy replicas—utensils, plates, teapot, among them. She picks out the teacup and goes over to her own toy box where she picks out a baby doll. She holds the cup to the doll's mouth, makes smacking noises with her lips. Then she lays the baby down on the floor, searches in her toy box for the towel that she uses as a blanket, and carefully spreads the towel over the doll, saying "night, night." She repeats the sequence of bedding down the doll twice over with some show of tenderness, even patting the doll once the towel is spread over it. She takes the toy spoon and dips it into the teapot, then lifts it several times to her own mouth. She selects a small cup and pretends to tip the pot out over it as if pouring into it. She pretends to drink from the cup. Setting it down she says, "baby" and walks across the room, returns for the cup, and, having carried it over to the doll, gives the doll a drink as it lies on the floor.

Observation 2: Presented with a collection of small toy replicas, A. (1:6:15) at first selects the teapot. She plays with the small lid, fitting it on and taking it off repeatedly. She pours it out over a cup and takes a sip. Then she sets the cup down next to the pot. This seems to suggest to her the idea of making a line of items. She adds on all the plates and other cups. She puts a spoon in each cup until she runs out of spoons. Taking the teapot out of the line she pushes it along the floor, tapping each of the items in the line with it in turn.

INTRODUCTION

From several perspectives the two children described in Observations 1 and 2 are "identical": They share age, sex, cultural background, and a certain level of cognitive sophistication. Moreover, they have been presented with the same set of materials and offered the same simple introduction to these materials: "Here are some things for you to play with." But the manner in which each child organizes these small objects and exploits her immediate surroundings of people, space, and objects is distinctive. Where the first child creates a string of situations, the second devises a series of careful spatial configurations. Where the first treats the materials as scaffolding for rich social interchange, the second discovers in them the equivalent of building blocks. The salient attributes of the materials for one child are their roles in specific human events; the qualities which appear to strike the second child are size, arrangement, number, and shape.

Individual differences like these, often striking in everyday encounters with young children, are elusive to the experimenter: They are difficult to articulate, even harder to measure reliably, and often prove unstable over time. A peculiar paradox hangs over them. On the one hand, dimensions of individuality are customarily viewed as innate or arising early, and yet they are simultaneously thought of as features which *modulate*—rather than as factors which themselves *regulate*—the course of growth (Escalona, 1968; Kagan & Kogan, 1970; Thomas, Chess, & Birch, 1970). While individual differences have traditionally been considered the "poor relations" of developmental change, it is conceivable that there are behavioral differences which arise early, exhibit stability, and affect critical aspects of growth and the course of development.

In what follows two such patterns of differing behavior, introduced briefly in the observations above, will be described; their role in the organization of early symbolic play will be outlined; and their consequences for later symbolic development will be discussed. Two themes will be highlighted throughout the discussion. First, symbolic play will be portrayed as a rich arena for the initial identification and subsequent monitoring of differences in "styles" of symbol use. Second, such early acquired styles will be portrayed as key factors in organizing symbolic activity.

Before embarking on this investigation of stylistic differences in symbolic play, two definitions and a context are required. First, *symbolic play* is considered here as the ability to represent actual or imagined experience through the combined use of small objects, motions, and language. For example, a child engages in symbolic play when she feeds a doll with a toy spoon from a block that serves as a plate, acts the part of a doctor, pretends to fall asleep, or builds a toy city in which imaginary cars, trains, and figures move about.

From one point of view, symbolic play is akin to other symbol systems— drawing, writing, clay modeling. The central achievement is twofold, requiring both the construction of an adequate "vocabulary" of signifiers for a wide range of contents and the invention of a "grammar" which permits the individual signifiers to be combined into more complex statements. However, symbolic play is quite unlike other symbolic media in a number of equally important ways. In symbolic play the fundamental process of signification is up to the symbolizer (that is, she decides which aspects of experience or imagination will be rendered and how this is to be accomplished). The act of cooking can be rendered linguistically (the child chants a series of ingredients), kinesthetically (the child pretends to stir, pour, and taste), through small objects (the child arranges a line of pots with spoons in them), or via a combination of techniques. Given this diversity of means, a child is free to capture in symbolic play precisely those aspects of experience most prominent to her.[1] Further, the grammar governing the larger structure of play activity is similarly flexible. The child can determine whether the structure of her symbolic play will derive from the logic of storytelling, the rules regulating the rendition of meaning in three-dimensional displays, or the techniques which govern pantomime. Here lies the potential of symbolic play for illuminating early styles of symbol use: While playing in this way, the child selects not only what is to be signified but also the means whereby the signification is to be effected.

In designating a *style* of symbolic play, we describe a mode of behavior which remains consistent across a range of materials and situations. Such a style has many components, including the means whereby children select information, capture it in symbolic forms, organize it into coherent messages, and transmit it deliberately to others. In the above examples, the two children exhibit complementary styles: The first attends to the social aspects of the situation and assimilates objects to schemes which bind people together; the second, in contrast, focuses largely on the attractive physical attributes of her materials, using them effectively in the course of her play.

Finally, a context for the following discussion is required. Our observations, discussions, and tentative conclusions have emerged from an intensive longitudinal study of early symbolic development in nine children—three males and six females: These youngsters are being followed from their first birthdays into their elementary school years.[2] Through observational as well as experimental techniques, a team of researchers has been monitoring developments in several major areas of symbolic growth: language, symbolic play, music, movement, two- and three-dimensional materials, and number

---

[1]It is true that the other symbolic systems, like language, can be used to capture the various aspects of experience. For instance, in language, words can describe the spatial arrangements, the rhythms, and the odors, colors, and sizes of a cooking experience, but this verbal facility is a much later and sophisticated achievement. At first, words are used only to account for moment-to-moment events. In contrast, symbolic play, even at a time when the child is a very primitive symbol user, opens vistas in each of these symbolic domains.

[2]Most of this chapter presents findings about the subset of two children who were first enrolled in the study. A tenth youngster's symbolic play has also been intensively studied for 2 years.

(cf. Shotwell, Wolf, and Gardner, 1977). The children's initial contacts with important media—such as books and television—have also been examined.

Data collection and analysis have taken a variety of forms. In the course of weekly visits, observers watch as children engage in free play and structured tasks. Parents have kept diaries and have been interviewed weekly concerning recent events and developments. Long-term findings from the structured tasks are being analyzed to yield ordinal scales for development in each of the media followed (cf. Uzgiris and Hunt, 1975). In addition, children's performances have been rated weekly according to a "working style scale": an index of personality and performance variables (e.g., tempo, pleasure in situation, degree of attentiveness, etc.). Reliability on these scales has been maintained through regular videotaping of play sessions, followed by independent ratings of those sessions by at least three trained observers. In addition to being measured by the above indices, children are tested quarterly in basic areas of cognitive development (e.g., object permanence, sorting skills, number and language skills).

FROM SKILLS TO STYLES

At the heart of this longitudinal study has been the question, "Is the course of symbolization similar across children, or are there instructive differences characterizing the manner in which individual children achieve symbolic competence?" From the start, previous developmental testing (Bayley, 1969; McCarthy, 1972) assured that, no matter how small the subject population, we would encounter differences in the rate at which children's various representational skills matured. Similarly, a long tradition of intelligence testing (Wechsler, 1949) promised that, even with a small sample, it was likely that we would observe children who exhibited differing patterns of basic abilities (e.g., verbal vs. spatial skills). But in a fundamental sense the question we had posed aimed at moving beyond profiles of specific skills—which are unlikely to suggest how an individual will negotiate novel types of problems, unfamiliar media, or further developmental milestones in the same media. In asking about individual differences in the development of symbolic competence, we have wanted to go beyond specific skills to underlying processes; we have tried to relinquish a catalog of existing abilities in favor of a description of how different basic processes were likely to affect later growth and, specifically, the development of symbolic competence.

Pilot investigation of symbolic development of preschool children left an indelible impression: Vast individual variation in specific areas of competence could be found even in a small group of children. At the outset the variations were rather narrowly captured via the two traditional characterizations already mentioned. We noted the speed of development—how quickly individual children moved forward in individual media—and we distinguished broadly only between verbalizers and visualizers (Gardner, Wolf, & Smith, 1975). *Visualizers* were children who appeared to flourish in the creation of two- and three-dimensional displays, children whose stories were often marked by the deliberate construction of a spatial milieu within which the narrative unfolded. *Verbalizers* were children who enjoyed storytelling and who, even in their use of clay and drawing materials, favored voices and descriptions above visual means of articulation.

While this characterization was consistent with the usual conception of individual differences, it also entailed two less familiar aspects. First, the distinction between visualizers and verbalizers proved to be as pronounced at age 3 as at age 5. Second, children did not simply excel in a single medium, such as drawing, clay, symbolic play, or storytelling. Instead, they tended to be expert in drawing *and* clay or in symbolic play *and* storytelling. Put differently, they excelled in either the "narrational" or the "configurational" domain. Furthermore, children gave evidence of importing their narrational or configurational skills across the boundary into the territory of their less favored domain. A verbalizer might treat a drawing like a mask, speaking through it as a means of articulating an otherwise-unsophisticated graphic rendition. Analogously, asked to tell a story using small blocks, a visualizer might build a complex construction, contributing by way of narration only the fact that "In Disneyland we saw towers like that." However, the full significance of these importations across skill domains, and of media pairings, was to become apparent only after the intensive longitudinal study both validated and enriched these early impressions.

In fact, work with our infant subjects over the past 2 years has underscored the initial distinction made between visualizers and verbalizers. By age 2, the children exhibited consistent patterns of media preference. The toys played with in the most extended and articulated manner in weekly free play sessions, as well as activities favored in between the experimenter's visits, were consistently drawn from the same domain. For example, a child favoring language activity would spontaneously and consistently select those items associated with linguistic exchange: books, puppets, toy telephones. In addition, the parents of such a child would report that spontaneous play activity included conversational exchanges over books, dolls, pictures, etc. Children's progress toward symbolic competence also mirrored their patterns of media preference. Based on performances on *Bayley Scales for Infant Development,* the children showed characteristic profiles of abilities, the areas of advancement coinciding with areas of preference. Finally, these profiles supported the notion that several of the children displayed mutually exclusive patterns of skills, their developmental profiles peaking within the visual-spatial realm *or* the verbal realm.

Other findings have refined and deepened our understanding of the original skill-based characterization of individual differences in symbolization. The first such finding concerned children's media preferences. Parental diaries and observer transcripts often reported children converting an instance of a less favored medium into a prop for activity in a preferred medium. For instance, a child favoring three-dimensional activity would override the obvious uses of a tea set, preferring instead to build complex towers out of alternating cups and saucers. In an effort to confirm these "media conversions," experimenters offered children ambiguous materials (e.g., pieces of oddly shaped wood, pipe cleaners, assorted pieces of foam rubber). In encounters with such materials, children consistently demonstrated a tendency to absorb such novel materials into their preferred realms of activity.

A final line of evidence on this issue came from the use of standardized tests. In the course of administering these instruments, the examiner is often required to test a child for several items beyond an initial failure. In observing youngsters working on problems beyond their customary reach, experimenters were once more struck by the fundamentally different styles used by children when they were required to exert a maximum effort. Indeed, it was particularly in these instances of "cognitive stretch" that underlying differences between children's styles of organization and problem solving first became clear.

TWO CONTRASTING STYLES: PATTERNERS AND DRAMATISTS

Sketched in the accompanying figures are two responses to the completion of a pear puzzle drawn from the *McCarthy Scales of Children's Abilities*. The first solution (Fig. 7.1) requires some explanation. J. (2:4:7) had previously

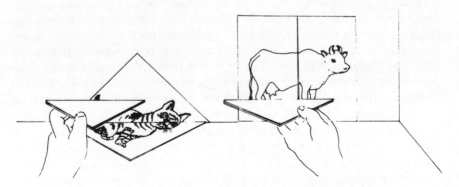

FIG. 7.1.   Dramatist's solution to the pear puzzle. Reproduced from the McCarthy Scales of Children's Abilities by permission. Copyright © 1970, 1972 by The Psychological Corporation. All rights reserved.

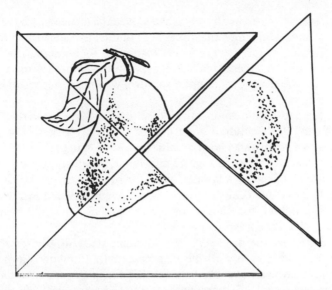

FIG. 7.2. Patterner's solution to the pear puzzle. Reproduced from the
McCarthy Scales of Children's Abilities by permission. Copyright © 1970, 1972
by The Psychological Corporation. All rights reserved.

solved puzzles of a cat and a cow. Instead of permitting the experimenter to
return them to their box, she had leaned each up against the wall, making its
appropriate animal noise and called out the experimenter's name in a high
"pretending" voice. When J. was presented with the pear puzzle (which has
more pieces and requires more sophisticated strategies for alignment), she
experienced marked difficulty. The experimenter cued her by saying, "The
pieces make a yellow pear like you eat." At this point, J. "solved" the problem
of the puzzle by making two pairs of triangular pieces, pressing them together
into sandwich shapes which she held up in turn to the cat and the cow puzzles,
saying "Eat it, eat it."

By contrast, A. (2:6:10) had solved the cat and cow puzzles quickly, even
taking the initiative to put each puzzle back in the box as the experimenter set
down a new one. When A. was presented with the pear puzzle she immediately
matched the two upper pieces, carefully aligning the portion of the leaf (Fig.
7.2). She placed a third piece, again using the strategy of matching contours,
not realizing that sheer matching is insufficient. Having incorrectly placed the
third piece, she had difficulty with the fourth, uncertain because she could not
make the contours meet. The experimenter cued her, "It makes a yellow pear
like you eat," but this information failed to help her out. She tried several
more arrangements—each one dictated by matching contours and colors,
many of them indifferent to the picture "meaning" of the pear. At last she
turned to the experimenter, asking "How this goes?"

As we came to conceptualize it, J. had solved the difficult puzzle by making an *event structure* in which the pieces are handled like something to eat even as their graphic properties are largely ignored. By contrast, even with the information that the pieces make a pear, A. pursued her solution on purely visual grounds, refusing to accept a solution which did not result in a viable visual pattern.

A parallel pattern of responses could be observed in some early attempts at classification. Both children were offered a set of 16 items—4 people, 4 animals, and 4 small and 4 large blocks— asked to "put the ones that are alike together." As can be seen in Fig. 7.3 and 7.4, J. grouped together a disparate set of objects by devising a familiar situation of a person in a house, while A. fashioned an extended construction, one apparently guided by the principles of matching colors and shapes and, more generally, by the creation of a balanced and symmetrical form.

Encouraged by the discovery of consistent patterns of preferences and characteristic ways of organizing responses with ambiguous materials and difficult tasks, which were observable both in free play and in standard testing situations, we sought to characterize the processes underlying two distinct styles of playing and problem solving. A variety of converging indices (summarized in Table 7.1) supported the basic patterns of organizing information which we had observed. In brief, one group of children, whom we came to call "patterners," displayed strong interest (and skill) in configurational uses of materials—the making of patterns, structures, and orders. These children exhibited a persistent curiosity about the object world around them; they wanted to know how something worked, how it might be named,

FIG. 7.3.   Dramatist's solution to the classification task described in the text.

FIG. 7.4.   Patterner's solution to the classification task described in the text.

how to explore and vary it. Given materials, such children were more often interested in mechanical and design possibilities than in communication or re-creation of personal experience. Patterners' complements, whom we labeled "dramatists," manifested an abiding interest in the human surrounding: what others did, how they thought and felt, how others could be contacted and affected, what links could be forged between persons. A considerable portion of these children's energies was devoted toward effective communication with others and toward dramatic sharing of their experiences.

This formulation can be most fully appreciated in the light of other findings from the longitudinal study. The first is that symbolic skills undergo not just one but two revolutions in the first 3 years. At roughly 18 to 20 months all the observed children discovered the possibility of segmenting the stream of pragmatic experience into sequential symbolic forms, for example, sentences, serial gestures, or the combinations of words, gestures, and object use typical of symbolic play. In this initial translation of action into symbols, children first captured the actor and action structures of daily events. Consequently we have seen this first phase of representational development as providing the means to represent simple "event structures."

Later, between 30 and 36 months, the same subjects' symbolic growth underwent another major development as all the children became effective producers of meaningful configurations—in the media of drawing, block building, and modeling clay. Courtesy of these later discoveries, children obtained the means to "map" the physical attributes of the object world—size, shape, color, number, contour—into symbolic forms. While it was true that both groups of children conformed to this developmental timetable, they did

TABLE 7.1
Principal Differences Between Patterners and Dramatists

Domain	Patterner	Dramatist
Language		
1. Contents of early vocabulary	High proportion of early words are names of objects, animals, locations.	High proportion of early words are proper names, greetings, expressions of feeling ("wow").
2. Contents of later vocabulary	Strong emphasis is placed on terms to encode color, size, number, physical relationships (e.g., "bigger").	Strong emphasis is placed on terms to encode emotions, moods, qualities in people.
3. Language usage typical of free play	Language used primarily to label and report actual objects and events. C. often recounts actions to self. Where nonliteral language use occurs, it takes the form of comparisons or metaphors.	Language used primarily to maintain social contact with others, drawing them into the activity. Where nonliteral language use occurs, it takes the form of storytelling or "embroidering" (e.g., coming up with elaborate designations for drawings, buildings, etc.)
Symbolic play		
1. Bases for transforming or renaming objects in the course of play	Renamings are often based on visual similarities (e.g., using a soup spoon as an ice cream cone).	Renamings occur with relative independence from visual similarities (e.g., anything that can be held and licked can be used for an ice cream cone).
2. Ability to replay familiar routines or significant experiences	Rehearsal usually occurs at a primitive level and rarely takes place spontaneously.	Rehearsal is frequent, detailed, and often sophisticated.
3. Ability to deal with entirely imaginary items	Children are uncomfortable with imaginary objects, often demanding that a real item be brought into play.	Children from an early date spontaneously introduce entirely imaginary content (make-believe companions, use of gestures to imply the presence of a needed prop).
Two- and three-dimensional media		
1. Characteristic approach to materials	Interest persistently focuses on the physical aspects of materials (e.g., how paints mix, elaborate forms balance, and building occurs with blocks).	There is a tendency to bypass physical aspects of materials in favor of using them right away to effect contact and communication with others. Later this becomes an interest in bypassing design possibilities in favor of representational uses.

(continued)

TABLE 7.1 *(continued)*

Domain	Patterner	Dramatist
	Representational operations in these media tend to exploit the "object properties" of materials (shape, color, size, etc.), coordinating them in patterns—a red round shape is likely to be called "ball" or "apple."	Representational operations in these media utilize materials rather directly for meaning—ignoring or even overriding their object properties (e.g., a red round shape may be called a "person," a "fish," a "house," depending on what a child wishes it to be).
Problem solving	Spontaneous classification tends to groupings based on object properties (color, size, etc.) or on the effort to create pleasing configurations of objects.	Spontaneous grouping tends to thematic organization (i.e., child puts items that imply an event or story together).
	Physical cues are used to guide solutions (e.g., exact fit between pieces); where a puzzle is too difficult, children match pieces of similar shapes or create symmetrical designs.	*Meaning* cues are used to guide solutions (e.g., deciding what the puzzle is a picture of, then looking for the appropriate parts of the picture).

so only broadly. A closer look at our data suggested that children might acquire the basics of symbolic competence using quite distinct vehicles. More specifically, our findings held out the possibility that children termed dramatists might exploit their sensitivity to narrational forms not only as a route to acquiring event-structure skills but also as a means for acquiring mapping skills. Conversely, it suggested that while patterners developed the simplest event structures in synchrony with dramatists, they employed their configurational abilities to construct full-blown event structures.

To the extent that these contrasting routes have been accurately described, we may have captured an underlying variability in the symbolization process itself. In their description of symbolic activity, Werner and Kaplan (1963) suggest that any symbolic act must incorporate two agents (the self and the other) and two aspects of meaning (the signifier and the signified). The act of symbolization, in their view, is profitably considered a dynamic interaction among these several components: Symbolic development involves the increasing differentiation and articulation of each element in the quartet.

It is possible to accept, and yet amplify, this analysis by considering that each component in the symbolic equation may be highlighted or neglected; the challenge of symbolization may be apprehended in diverse ways by different individuals. In the case of the contrasting styles sketched above, patterners seem to concentrate efforts on the process of rendering the signified. That is, they are particularly interested in exploring the world of objects, in mastering and organizing their various attributes and dimensions, and then in capturing these features in appropriate signifiers. In contrast, dramatists appear to emphasize the link between the self and the other— effecting the communication between the human participants in the exchange. To be sure, mature symbolization requires considerable attention to each of the components in the symbolic relation. Yet, to the degree that individuals are (for whatever reason) intent on attending to one or two aspects of the symbolic relation, the ways in which they acquire symbolic capacities are likely to vary to a significant extent. And, indeed, the strongest evidence that symbolization constitutes a different kind of problem for patterners than for dramatists comes from an examination of the developmental paths followed by our two sample subjects.

THE DEVELOPMENTAL COURSE
OF EARLY STYLES

12 Months: Emerging Differences

Observation 3: The observer presents J. (1:0:3) with a small toy tea set and several small dolls. J.'s attention is attracted right away to a small plastic spoon. She places the spoon in her mouth and wanders about the room with the spoon protruding, mugging for her mother and the observer. J. stoops over to pick up a cup, she places the spoon in the cup, stirs it hard, and makes a "mmmm" sound as if tasting something delicious. J. walks over to her mother, takes the spoon from her own mouth, and uses it to feed her mother repeatedly. Her mother enters the game, smacking her lips, saying "mmmm," and asking for more. J. moves away and comes back with a small cup that she holds out to her mother, who obligingly drinks. J. then feeds her again. Upon walking away toward the window, J. encounters the dolls. She stoops and picks one up, drops it into a nearby chair where she feeds it from both the spoon and the cup. J. then takes the cup and, balancing it on her nose, turns to show her mother, who claps.

Observation 4: Presented with a small toy tea set and several small dolls, A. (1:2:11) collects one doll, one cup, and one spoon. She sits with them on her lap a moment but then lifts them into the observer's lap. She is much more interested in the plates of various sizes that are spread out on the floor. She collects the four small ones first, making a neat stack of them. She then collects the four larger ones, also stacking them. A. then nests the stack of smaller plates inside the set of larger ones. A. places three remaining spoons on top of her stack; as she does so she makes smacking noises with her lips. She starts to offer the spoon to the observer and to her mother, simply holding it out toward each of them, but instead her attention returns to her previous interests, and the process of unstacking and then rearranging the plates resumes as before.

Even though the two children are just a year old, the general outlines of the symbolic situation are already clear. For J. objects are a way to contact others: to make them laugh, to draw them into playful exchanges. The "point" of her activity appears to be the replaying of familiar feeding situations in which she, her mother, and the observer can become mutually involved. The striking achievement, symbolically speaking, is her realization of how she, the adults, and the dolls can all take on the role of the "person fed"—the realization that many persons can fill the same role in an event. It is this sensitivity to event and role structures which characterizes the dramatist's play. Interestingly, A., too, at one point starts to feed the doll, her mother, and the observer, yet even as she grasps the possibility of reconstructing familiar events and roles, A. bypasses these options in favor of exploring the manner in which the various objects can be arranged and combined.

From a distance these children are at the same stage of symbolic development. All of our accumulated evidence indicates that both children (like others a year in age) are beginning to move from direct contact and object manipulation toward symbolic communication and the construction of signifier-signified relations.

But our findings also suggest that this passage from sensory-motor to symbolic intelligence may be achieved along at least two discrete paths. A dramatist appears to take most seriously the task of recapturing the personal world, only occasionally constructing signifiers for objects, attributes, and the causes and consequences of physical actions. By contrast, a patterner focuses on the task of reencoding her knowledge of objects and actions, down-playing the possibility of representing knowledge of others, alternative roles, and the sequence of interactions.

Profoundly concerned with establishing structures suited to the mutual sharing of experience, dramatists' earliest communications center on imitations, simple role-exchange games like peek-a-boo and teasing; their earliest signifier-signified relations concern the reformulation of significant interactions and roles. And so, early "object" substitutions arise largely in the context of replaying familiar experience; they center on gestural abbreviations for significant actions or on discovering a wide range of persons and objects which can fulfill the same role in an event. In the example above, J. experiments with *who* can take on the role of the person fed. In this situation the precise form of props or scenery is relatively unimportant; once launched into the replay of a feeding situation the child will "feed" herself, others, and even toy cars, using as a "cup" virtually any item which can be handled like one.

By comparison, a patterner might be thought of as an individual seeking effective means to capture and explore salient aspects of the object world. Interested in the possible uses and transformations of objects, a patterner's earliest communications are often "sharing" and "showing" games which center on exchange or manipulation of small objects. At the stage where manipulation gives way to simple symbols, these children begin work on the construction of the signifier-signified relation; they explore how the simplest visual-spatial characteristics of one object can be "rediscovered" or mapped onto another. Between 12 and 18 months they employ the simplest forms of correspondence—location and gesture—to suggest likenesses (e.g., a small object placed on the head can be called "hat"). In subsequent months, patterners' ability to draw likenesses between objects extends to the visual-spatial realm. Increasingly, for patterners, the precise form of props is a critical issue—while they resist treating a block as a cup, they may accept items as disparate as spools and hats, due to their physical similarities to cups.

At this age both patterners' and dramatists' symbolic play is limited for developmental reasons to simple "moves," but even within this narrow range, significant differences can be observed. In terms of simple substitutions a patterner's attention fixes on the possibilities of physically available objects. Consequently there is less imaginary replay of experience and instead a constant search for similar forms—a process which might be termed "visual metaphor." Moreover, while entirely capable of replaying simple event structures, a patterner only occasionally explores the problems of rendering actions and agents. In the example above, A. bypasses role substitutions in favor of rich exploration centered on the number and fit of the toy plates.

Even at the outset, it is important to stress that styles are a matter of emphasis. At a year, J. can also stack the plates, make lines of them, and discover which cup fits inside which other cup. At 12 months, A. is not insensitive to the possibility of feeding her mother, the observer, or a doll. The point is rather that each child's spontaneous activity over time has a characteristic profile of the possibilities which are tried first and explored most widely.

24 Months: The Consolidation of Approaches

In a sense these emphases make a patterner appear less symbolically sophisticated or possibly more imaginatively conservative than a dramatist. J. seems to be moving toward the capacity to replay experience and is already exhibiting a certain flexibility about role and object substitutions. By contrast, A. appears "more conservative"; her actions do not refer to previous events but serve to explore the possibilities of objects that are immediately present.

As the examples (Observations 1 and 2) at the outset of the chapter indicate, this impression is heightened at 18 months when dramatists have articulated a clear notion of event structure, their play thereby acquiring the connectedness of simple narrative. By contrast, the play of a patterner like A. is briefer and more segmented. In fact, its symbolic elements appear no more connected than they did months before. The major change seems to be the advent of more deliberate patterns—arrangements of objects in pairs or lines and the creation of additional and more sophisticated forms of correspondences.

Indeed, to the extent that symbolic play is viewed as the redramatization of emotionally significant routines or events (Freud, 1955), A.'s behavior still seems remote from *symbolic* play. However, where play is construed more generously to include the reformulation of experience, patterners like A. can be seen to be mastering an important facet of representational process. Here, rather than restaging the routines of mealtime, A. may be recreating the spatial structures—the orders and pairings that are, for her, the salient aspects of dinner. While patterners like A. do not replay, they do reconstruct, based on the appearance of what we have called similarities or "mapping relations." The raw materials for these mapping relations have been developed by early manipulative exploratory play in which objects have been grouped by size, arranged in rows of the same number, and matched by color. What changes toward the end of the second year, yielding patterners their own characteristic form of symbolic play, is the transition from simply noticing attributes to operating on them for representational purposes.

The differences in symbolic play resulting from children's operating on an event structure or an attribute-mapping structure can be seen in the two observations that follow. Each child, now 24 months, is presented with a set of wooden blocks painted to look like people, buildings, etc.

> *Observation 5:* J. (2:0:7) takes the set of blocks from their container and sorts through them, commenting, "Take them out... her cookies (as she touches some small flat round blocks)... this person" (naming a block with a face on it). She walks this little block across the floor toward the observer, accentuating the stepping gesture pattern she makes with a high-pitched voice which she often uses to animate small figures. Selecting still more of the blocks painted to look like people, she says, "little people... more people here." She selects a long flat brick-painted block, lays it flat on the floor, and sets up a figure at each end, facing one another. She removes the figures and makes a stair pattern by laying smaller and smaller blocks on top of one another. The last block that she places has a door painted on top of it. As she lays it in place she remarks, "Make door... Go to sleep." With this she attempts to balance one of the small figures in a lying down position on top of the door block, saying "night, night." But it continuously rolls off. On the third time, she picks up the figure and offers it to the observer: "Going go boom fall down." She places it on the block again, and then when it rolls off, she picks it up and pats it, then offers it to the observers to kiss and comfort.

> *Observation 6:* A. (2:2:15) is given the set of blocks and invited to tell a story with them. A. comments, "Make house." A. (with some help from observer) builds an arch and then places a small conical block on top of it. She changes her

mind and places the conical block in the center space under the arch. She again changes her mind and builds a tower of blocks, using the cone, beside the arch. She knocks it over all at once with a laugh but then quickly rebuilds the arch. When she again places the conical block atop it she comments, "hat."

What is striking in these instances is that both children are clearly engaged in symbolic play, and yet the forms remain clearly distinct from one another. While J. is capable of grouping together the people, or of placing blocks on top of one another, her play is clearly dominated by the structure of events. And while A. is clearly capable of labeling objects (and of substituting one object for another), her attention falls on the arrangement of a pleasing visual-spatial structure and, more generally, on the exploring of physical attributes and properties. Each child can operate briefly within the opposing style but seems wedded to her own preferred pattern of symbol use.

24 Through 36 Months: Complementarity

During the first year of symbolic growth, each child has concentrated on a particular aspect of the symbolic relation, while her attention to the alternative portions of the symbolic relation has been occasional. At the age of 24 through 36 months, however, this pattern of emphasis begins to shift. The narratives related by dramatists have now evolved to a point where they often require the skills of attribute mapping. In a parallel fashion, the constructions of patterners have become sufficiently articulate to imply specific sequences of events. This point is clearly seen from two observations of our children at 30 months.

> *Observation 7:* Offered a set of materials which includes both blocks for building as well as some human figures and animals, J. (2:4:22) is asked to take the people to the zoo. J. picks up a green snake-shaped block and waves it at the observer. "He is going to bite you. . . he's biting me. He's hurting me." She waves her hand exaggeratedly as if bitten. "We better build him a cage so he can't get out." She quickly selects four yellow rectangular blocks and builds a four-sided cage into which she drops the snake. "Another snake," she calls as she picks up a block in the shape of a tree but also painted green. She adds, "Better put him away," and she drops the tree into the cage with the snake. "Another big snake," she remarks of another still-larger tree block. "Is he going to get me?" she recoils, pretending to be afraid. The observer says, "Pick him up quickly and drop him in; then he won't get you." J. does this and then proceeds to repeat the gesture with all the other green blocks in sight, first the remaining trees and then even some of the rectangular building blocks. "There. We got 'em all. Better put them to sleep," and she constructs a roof over the "snake pit" with several additional blocks.

Observation 8: Offered the same array of blocks, A. (2:7:0) is attracted to the building blocks first. Talking quietly to herself, she builds a very orderly structure with them, saying things like "This goes here. I do this." The last part of the structure to be added is a long road-like piece out to the left. At this juncture she comments, "I made a road." Then she takes the animals from the box, walking them up the inside, then down the outside, over to the road then down the road until they make a long procession. Then she takes the people figures and, as she walks each one, she comments, "I am coming to the zoo. Here I come." As she makes them pass the animals she says, in a high voice meant to be coming from each figure, "Hi there elephant... hi there reindeer," etc. She continues their walk to the end of the animals, then reverses directions. As the people are walked past the animals she makes them say "Bye elephant... bye reindeer...." She continues walking the people right back into the box, drops them in, then picks up the animals, walks them back to the box, finally storing all the building blocks back into the box.

These observations document that each of the children has arrived at a point where she is capable of attribute-mapping skills (as with J.'s using all the green items to represent snakes) as well as simple narrative skills (as with A.'s animation of the animals and the figures). But, as our earlier descriptions indicate, they have arrived at this shared "endpoint" by different routes. The patterner has progressed from orderly object handling to very spare event structures and then through attribute-mapping skills to visual-spatial representations of objects so articulate that they can imply and support fuller event structures. The dramatist has moved from the simple repetition of ritual acts through simple imaginary events to scenes requiring props so abundant that the previously neglected attribute-mapping skills come into play.

It is critical to emphasize again that the patterning and dramatizing styles are a matter of accent and not exclusive development. No normal child, no matter how enchanted with the interpersonal world, grows up insensitive to the attributes and possibilities of objects. Conversely, no normal child, regardless of her fascination with objects, completely disregards the world of persons. What we are speaking of here is the *order* and manner in which individual children come to deal with the task of recapturing at a symbolic level the earlier, pragmatic knowledge of infancy. Even the most convinced mapper of attributes continues to relate to, be affected by, and learn from her interactions with people. And the child wrapped up in working out representations for events, characters, and feelings is not unaware of quantity, color, or likenesses.

Our overview is that, following a period of intense symbolic activity in the preferred realm, children move through a phase of complementarity, turning their attention to the still-neglected aspect of their symbolic understandings. From 2 to 3 years there appears to be a "balancing-out phase" in which children put to good use the rudiments of the complementary mode. The probable course in which these skills have evolved in patterners and dramatists can be seen in Table 7.2. Should this pattern of observations be verified, the third year of life would emerge as a period of significant developmental consolidation in symbolization, children having realized on the symbolic plane their interactions with both persons and objects.

CONCLUSION

Our findings are consistent with several earlier descriptions of mental development. Indeed, the patterner-dramatist dichotomy recalls well-established differences between a focus on language and a focus on the visual-spatial realm: In addition, it is congruent with observations of children who are either person centered or object centered (Jennings, 1975). Moreover, the findings enrich recent reports about differences in the uses of early language (Nelson, 1973) as well as different strategies in the acquisition of linguistic competence (Bloom, Lightbown, & Hood, 1975).

Our descriptions may prove to be well founded, but it must be stressed that our account is not explanatory in the usual sense. At present we can neither identify the sources of these differences nor indicate the extent to which they could be altered. Still in front of us is the task of investigating the strength and consistency of the stylistic preferences we have described. For instance, it is possible that the young patterner is capable of significant dramatizing behavior but simply elects not to demonstrate it, because this style of organizing and using information is neither undestood, appreciated, nor taught in her home, school, or culture. It is also possible that, under the right circumstances, a dramatist might produce lengthy instances of patterning behavior if she were not brought up to suspect "such things are for boys." Our observations suggest that these contingencies are unlikely, but such possibilities deserve—in fact, demand—exploration.

Given the small size of our sample and the preliminary stage of our data analysis, it is premature to draw strong conclusions from our study. Even as the results reported here are offered as suggestions from work in progress, we would also like to share some possible implications of this work. Our observations of older children, and our reflections on the intellectual processes of adults, suggest that these differences in styles are more than "matters of interest." While most individuals acquire skill in both symbolic approaches—indeed, everyday interchange requires both patterning and dramatizing skills—traces of these contrasting modes can still be observed at much later stages of development. In our studies of elementary school children, for instance, we find a significant minority who can still be characterized reliably as strong patterners or strong dramatists. Moreover,

TABLE 7.2

Hypothesized Time Line for the Emergence of Patterner-Dramatist Differences

	12 Months *Emerging Differences*	24 Months *Consolidation of Approaches*	36 Months *Complementarity*
Dramatist	The emergence of the child and other (person) as the primary dyad of interaction in the symbolizing situation: The emphasis of earliest symbolic activity appears to be effective communication.	Symbolic play is strongly narrational—a way of telling stories or recounting experience. Emphasis falls on replaying roles and events to the exclusion of interest in props or scenery.	Previously dominant event structures are complemented by attribute-mapping skills; e.g., the child in dramatic play about a zoo selects ambiguous blocks to serve as animals (on the basis of shape, size, color).
Patterner	The emergence of the child and the object with its possibilities as the primary dyad of interaction in the symbolizing situation: The emphasis of earliest symbolic activity appears to be discovering, naming, and calling attention to what objects can be made to do.	Symbolic play persists as atemporal configurations. While such arrays are "indifferent" to role and event structures, they capture, with increasing detail, the visual-spatial relationships characterizing situations being referred to (e.g., in playing house the child may build an elaborate structure with many openings, each opening containing a small figure or group of figures).	Previously dominant attribute-mapping skills are complemented by the appearance of late-emerging event-structure skills. A child's displays and arrangements become so articulate as to imply events and suggest characters; e.g., the child builds an elaborate "zoo"—adds blocks for visitors and animals and tries them out in different positions, eventually treating this spatial play as representing trips and chases.

even if most of us can adopt either cognitive style, it may well be that each individual retains a characteristic "strength" or "leading position." These strengths may be particularly manifest when we engage in playful activity in which only our impulses are at stake or when we confront a new and unfamiliar material.

To illustrate the persistence of such styles we offer one more set of observations which portray the two children as they work toward the acquisiton of a new symbolic form—number. In this situation both children were presented with an array of objects: specifically, two lines of objects, the longer one containing a smaller number of large objects and the shorter one containing a larger number of small objects. The experimenter used a puppet to ask the child "Where are there more things?" and then to say "Show me." Finally, the puppet asked the children to "Make it so there are the same number in each line."

Observation 9: J. (3:0:15) is shown an array of two lines of objects; the upper one contains three circular counters and the lower one four small blocks. When asked to show where there are more, J. points to the line of counters, without bothering to count. When the experimenter tells her "Show me," J. points to each of the counters in turn at the same time counting quickly to 5. She makes no move to count the contents of the other row. When the experimenter asks her to make the same number in each line, J. turns to the puppet and explains to it. "No, you can't have any more donuts." Through the puppet, the experimenter then asks, "Why not?" to which J. replies, "No, you see you have to leave some for other people.... No, the other people ate them all up."

Observation 10: A. (3:2:23) is shown an array of two lines of objects: The upper one contains eight large buttons and the bottom one six smaller blocks. When asked to show where there are more, A. points to the line of buttons. When asked to support that, A. carefully counts the items in each row, tapping each with an index finger as she counts it. But she draws no conclusion from having counted eight buttons and six blocks. Through the puppet, the experimenter then asks her to make the same number in each line. Working with precision, A. carefully tries to place a button atop each block. But the buttons are so much larger that her strategy miscarries. After trying several times to find a way to rest one button on a single block, A. resorts to another plan. She simply lays down a line of buttons on top of the blocks until she has two lines which match each other in extent. She has three buttons left over. A. lays one at each end of her structure and then hands the remaining button back to the experimenter.

In this account of children moving toward mastery of a new symbolic domain, it is possible to glimpse the continued influence of dramatizing and patterning styles. J. approaches the question of number in event-structure

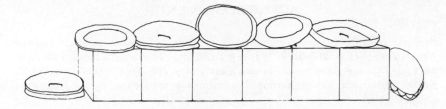

FIG. 7.5.   Patterner's response to the question, "Are there more blocks or buttons?"

terms, quickly inventing an imaginary situation in which the items to be counted are donuts and the arithmetic issues of "more" and "less" are given psychological significance. By contrast, as can be seen in Fig. 7.5, A. approaches counting or making equivalences largely in spatial or visual terms. She "solves" the problem the experimenter sets by creating a symmetrical display which combines the two quantities to be counted.

A major theme of this chapter has been to characterize a range of routes toward symbolization as "normal." However, without phases of "complementarity," style may become disability. It is possible that there exists a small minority of individuals who remain throughout their lives capable of only one approach to materials. The most limited of these individuals may resemble the autistic child (who appears capable only of dealing with object attributes) or the child with Down's syndrome (whose chief strengths lie in the interpersonal sphere). Less severely disturbed children are likely to be counted among the "learning disabled"—those who succeed with certain subject matters while struggling with others. The most successful of these "single-style individuals" have been able to reconstruct the world so that they can handle in their own way those materials which most normal individuals process quite differently: learning event-structure skills via attribute mapping, learning to read not by contextual clues but via a highly articulate memory for word shapes; recalling the format for stories through spatial imagery.

Based on our findings, it appears that effective symbolic development encompasses the ability to capture both events and attributes. If this is so, then a major educational challenge lies in learning to engineer bridges between the two domains where handicap or life circumstances prevent their natural construction.

ACKNOWLEDGMENTS

Preparation of this paper was supported by the Spencer Foundation and by Harvard Project Zero (NIE G-00-3-0169). We are grateful to the children and families whom we have been studying and to our research associates: Jennifer Shotwell, Ann Smith, Shelley Rubin, and Pat McKernon. Illustrations were prepared by Jen Silverman.

REFERENCES

Bayley, N. *Bayley scales of infant development.* New York: The Psychological Corporation, 1969.

Bloom, L., Lightbown, P., & Hood, L. Structure and variation in child language. *Monograph of the Society for Research in Child Development, 1975, 160.*

Escalona, S. *The roots of individuality: Normal patterns of development in infancy.* Chicago: Aldine, 1968.

Freud, S. The relation of the poet to day-dreaming. In E. Jones (Ed.) *The collected works of Sigmund Freud.* London: Hogarth Press, 1955.

Gardner, H., Wolf, D., & Smith, A. Artistic symbols in early childhood. *New York University Education Quarterly, 1975, 16,* 13–21.

Jennings, K. D. People versus object orientation, social behavior, and intellectual abilities in preschool children. *Developmental Psychology, 1975, 11,* 511–519.

Kagan, J., & Kogan, N. Individuality and cognitive performance. In P. Mussen (Ed.), *Carmichael's manual of child psychology (Vol. 1).* New York: Wiley, 1970.

McCarthy, D. *McCarthy scales of children's abilities.* New York: The Psychological Corporation, 1972.

Nelson, K. Structure and strategy in learning to talk. *Monograph of the Society for Research in Child Development, 1973, 149.*

Shotwell, J., Wolf, D., & Gardner, H. *Exploring early symbolization: Styles of achievement.* Paper presented at the Wenner-Gren symposium on early symbolization, Burg Wartenstein, Austria, July 1977.

Thomas, A., Chess, S., & Birch, H. *The origin of personality.* San Francisco: W. H. Freeman, 1970.

Uzgiris, I., & Hunt, J. McV. *Assessment in infancy: Ordinal scales of psychological development.* Chicago: University of Illinois Press, 1975.

Wechsler, D. *Wechsler intelligence scale for children.* New York: The Psychological Corporation, 1949.

Werner, H., & Kaplan, B. *Symbol formation.* New York: Wiley, 1963.

8 Development of Gesture

Sybil S. Barten
College at Purchase, Purchase, New York

Human beings use gesture as an alternative to speech under a wide variety of circumstances. Frequently gestures and facial expressions are the only mode of communication that is feasible, for example, in deaf people, foreigners, and persons working under noisy conditions. Gesture predominates when convention or religious commitment dictates against the use of words, as in the art form of mime and in silent orders of monks. When words might shock or frighten, it is possible to substitute conventionalized obscene and sacriligious gestures, many of which can be traced to Etruscan times (Röhrich, 1960). Hand gestures indicating the identity and location of animals alert fellow hunters against scaring away animals during the hunt. In addition to serving as a substitute for speech, gestures and facial expressions almost invariably accompany speech in everyday life and in ritualistic settings.

Among psychologists, ethologists, and sociologists there is great interest today in nonverbal communication. Research in this area has become more sophisticated as a result of advances in videotaping and recording technology. Anthropologists (see Hewes, 1973, 1976) have presented arguments for a gestural origin of language. Further, research demonstrating the capacity of chimpanzees for learning sign language has encouraged psychologists to look beyond speech in seeking to understand the foundations of language.

In view of the pervasiveness of gesture as well as its theoretical significance, it is remarkable that psychologists have given so little systematic attention to the development of gesture in children. Even though the importance of gesture as an early form of symbolization is recognized by developmental psychologists (Piaget, 1951; Werner & Kaplan, 1963), very few studies exist in the literature, and these have generally included only a small number of children (Anderson, 1972; Bates, Camaioni, & Volterra, 1975; Blurton-Jones, 1971; Brannigan & Humphries, 1972; Jancovic, Devoe, & Wiener, 1975; Kaplan, 1968; Klapper & Birch, 1969; Michael & Willis, 1968; Overton & Jackson, 1973).

Research in this area has been hampered, I believe, by the absence of a taxonomy of gesture. In the first part of this chapter, I shall attempt to categorize and describe the various types of gestures according to the communicative function served by the body movement, posture, or configuration. Such a taxonomy is a prerequisite for further theoretical discussion since generalizations pertaining to one type of gesture may not apply to another. In the second part, I shall present some ideas about processes involved in mastery of the gesture medium, using the development of depictive gesture as a paradigm.

A TAXONOMY OF GESTURE

Deictic Gesture

The earliest type of gesture to develop in infants would seem to be *pointing*, usually with the index finger and often accompanied by glancing at the addressee. Anderson (1972) claims that children never point *at* the mother—they point exclusively for the mother—and that this form of gesture is never directly imitated. Anderson believes that pointing serves to reduce fear: The child points at an anxiety-producing or unfamiliar sight and is relieved by the mother's absence of fear. Werner and Kaplan (1963) posit a more cognitive function when they speculate that pointing serves to isolate an object of reference from its context and that this indicative function distinguishes pointing from reaching.

Although pointing with the index finger seems so natural that it must be universal, there may indeed be some variation in the *form* taken by this gesture. LaBarre (1947) cites the case of Mary Buffalo, an 88-year-old Kiowa Indian, who responded to LaBarre's request for the location of an object by pointing with her lips, perhaps because her hands were occupied.[1]

---

[1]As Asch (1952) has argued, however, the old woman did not respond by orienting 45⁰ to the side of the object. Thus, the vectorial property of the deictic gesture—the imagined line from body part to object—is intrinsic to the gesture, whether it is performed by the index finger or some other organ.

One should distinguish between the function of the child's pointing and the child's response to the pointing of others. Anderson states that the first result of the mother's pointing is to draw attention to herself and that only after children are 2 years old do they begin to look in the direction of the mother's pointing hand rather than at the hand itself or at the mother's face.

Bates et al. (1975) claim that pointing undergoes a shift in function toward the end of the first year. Earlier pointing sequences involved in exploration and orienting toward novel events precede pointing for others, which Bates et al. feel involves seeking adult attention.

There is some evidence that pointing is an early mode of referring to objects. Hoemann (1974) found an age-related change in deaf children's way of communicating object concepts such as "leaf" and "teacher." The youngest children (age 6–7) referred to here-and-now objects by pointing at them and to absent objects by pointing to their usual locations (e.g., out the window, at the blackboard). In contrast, older deaf children created gestures that represented activities *by* or *upon* the objects (e.g., pretending to munch a carrot for "carrot" or to write on the blackboard for "teacher"). A similar developmental trend is indicated in Kaplan's (1968) finding that 4-year-olds are distinguished from 8-year-olds by their greater tendency to use deictic movements (i.e., pointing) in their representations of action sequences. Thus, the younger children would point inside their mouths to represent "brushing teeth."

Instrumental Gesture

Instrumental gestures are movements intended to regulate or change the behavior of others. These gestures have often been studied in the context of attachment and other forms of early social behavior. A very early form is the arms-raised gesture of toddlers wanting to be picked up. Carver (1975), analyzing one child's prelinguistic communication, noted that some gestures of this sort are already conventionalized by the age of 2. She describes the child patting a couch in order to make his mother sit by his side. Michael and Willis (1968) describe 12 common gestures in 4- to 7-year-old middle-class children. These gestures communicate commands such as "go away," "come here," "be quiet," etc. Instrumental gestures can be viewed as precursors to verbal commands, demands, and requests.

An intriguing methodological problem besets the investigator attempting to distinguish instrumental gestures from simple goal-directed action. How can one know whether a child intends his action to influence another person's behavior? Carver's observations suggest that what she terms "regulators" are generally accompanied by glances at the observer. Here, as in the other categories of gesture, the defining intention and function can be inferred only by taking other aspects of the context into account.

Expressive Gesture

This category comprises movements of the hands, face, and postures of the whole body that express (in the ethologists' terminology, "display") feelings and intentions. Observers of nonverbal communication have reported a multitude of expressive gestures, e.g., "ear flipping, " "hand in mouth," and "kneading feet," and have interpreted them as expressions of anxiety, affiliation, etc.

What is not clear from the ethological description is that expressive gestures emerge out of total organismic responses—of fear, anger, rage, uncertainty. Parts of these global responses are lifted out or decontextualized (Werner & Kaplan, 1963), so that, for example, the clenched fist can express anger, solidarity, or determination. Even though one part of the body is the focus of the expressive gesture, it is appropriate to view such gestures as an expression of the whole organism. Thus, understanding of expressive gestures occurs partly through empathy with the person who raises the clenched fist or who knits his brows in perplexity.

Enactive Gesture

Enactive gestures are movements that represent actions upon objects or actions performed with objects, for example, pretending to catch a fish, to ride a bicycle, or to comb one's hair. Klima and Bellugi (1975) point out that a large proportion of the signs of American Sign Language were originally more pantomimic and have become more stylized and arbitrary with time. As an example of what we would term an enactive gesture, they cite the rotary hand movement associated with manual coffee grinders, a vestigial form of which serves as the present sign for "coffee."

Studies by Kaplan (1968), Klapper and Birch (1969), and Overton and Jackson (1973) deal with children's developing ability to use their bodies to represent imagined action sequences on objects. For example, Kaplan asked her subjects to make believe they were using a pencil to write, cutting with scissors, or combing their hair. Younger children tend to use a body part to represent the object held, whereas older children are able to "leave a gap," that is, to perform actions upon (and with) totally imaginary objects. My own experience suggests that adults' responses parallel those of younger children. An adult told to "brush your hair" will frequently use a closed fist to represent the brush which passes over the hair.

Depictive Gesture

Depictive gestures are movements and configurations which represent an action or static property of the object itself. To use another example from American Sign Language, the sign for "bird" uses the fingers to represent the opening and closing of the beak of a bird, and the sign for "tree" uses the upright arm and moving hand to represent the trunk and swaying branches of a tree.

Depictive gestures come the closest—of all the forms of gesture—to being a visual medium external to the symbolizer. Piaget (1951) sees depictive gestures as the earliest type of symbolization, and he believes that they derive from the child's direct imitation of movements. Piaget's most cited example is that of his 1:4-month-old daughter, who slowly opened and closed her mouth to represent the analogous movements of a match box. Piaget also describes J., age 1:3, making her finger into the shape of her toy clown's foot and catching it in her dress just as the clown's foot had been caught (Piaget, 1951). As these two examples illustrate, depictive gestures may involve static as well as dynamic properties of the referents they represent.

Franklin (1973) has suggested that the younger child's representation of an *object* (e.g., hammer) is not fully differentiated from his representation of the *action* with the object (e.g., hammering), but as far as I know there have been no attempts to determine whether younger children would use the same gesture to represent "what a hammer looks like" and "what you do with a hammer." If Franklin is right, it would suggest an initial lack of differentiation between enactive and depictive gesture.

In a study of the development of depictive gesture, Gindes and Barten (1973) found marked differences between younger (mean age 46 months) and older (mean age 55 months) preschool children in their ability to represent nonconventional visual configurations. The children were shown two-dimensional configurations constructed from pipe cleaners and asked to "show what these look like: Use your hands, fingers, or any part of your body." (See Fig. 8.1.) The analysis of data for this study entailed construction of a rating scale consisting of seven levels of response. The assumption underlying the scale is that representation progresses from a diffuse, global state, through a state of differentiated but unrelated parts, and finally to a state in which the parts are integrated into a whole. The lowest category includes failure to respond and response in the wrong modality (e.g., a purely verbal description). The highest rating was assigned to gestures which adequately represented the number of parts, shapes, orientation, and organization of the stimuli. Intermediate levels of gestural depiction represented these properties to varying degrees. Thus, a rating of 4 was given when the gesture clearly depicted only one part of the configuration or when two parts were shown but in the wrong spatial relation.

Roth (1975) attempted to replicate this study with young deaf children in order to determine whether the absence of verbal language would influence capacity for depictive gesture. She found that the deaf children did not differ significantly from the hearing sample in level of gestural representation, but she did discover some qualitative differences between the two groups. These differences seemed to involve differences in the mastery of the gestural

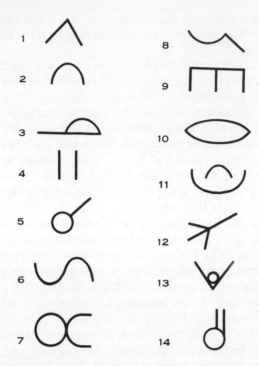

FIG. 8.1. Visual configurations used as stimuli for gestural depiction task.

medium. As a consequence of this finding, I have reexamined the gestures produced by the hearing children for other evidence that the development of gesture involves, in part, acquiring knowledge of the medium. In the next section of this chapter I shall present the results of this preliminary examination.

DEVELOPING MASTERY: DEPICTIVE GESTURE

Mastery of the gesture medium involves developing conceptions of the possibilities inherent in hands, fingers, and other parts of the body for use as symbolic vehicles. Mastery of the medium also includes knowledge or anticipation of how an addressee will look upon and understand the gesture produced. In the discussion that follows, it should become clear that many of the processes underlying mastery may apply not solely to depictive gesture but to other forms of gesture as well.

Isolating the Medium

The first requirement for gestural depiction is that the child must realize that the body or some part of the body must be used for the task. In most cases, the children tested in our sample were able to do something with their hands to represent the configurations. However, for at least 1 of the 14 stimuli, 11 of the 19 younger children and 5 of the 20 older children gave a verbal rather than a gestural response. Thus, they might say, "It's a lollipop," or "an *E*," etc.

The deaf children occasionally produced a response that might be construed as comparable to the hearing children's verbal descriptions: They would point to the mouth for configuration 10 and stick an index finger in the mouth (as if to depict a lollipop?) for configuration 5 (see Fig. 8.1). It is remarkable that the deaf children were generally able to differentiate between the perceptual appearance of the stimulus configuration and an object concept represented by the configuration. It would seem intuitively that this distinction is facilitated when two distinct media (gestures and words) are available to the child.

In addition to isolating the gesture medium from other modes of representation, the gesture itself must be separated from the external environment. In a few instances, children used the edge of the table to serve as the "base" of their symbols rather than forming a base with a part of their body.

Through the differentiation of gesture from other symbolic media and through detaching the gesture from reliance on the external environment, the child creates a medium of expression that is increasingly autonomous (Werner & Kaplan, 1963).

Creating a Static Symbol

Piaget asserts that a static image derives from the internalization of the ocular movements which are used in tracing the contours of an object. In our original study, eight younger children and six older children traced the stimulus configurations with their fingers, often directly on the stimulus and occasionally in the air. Since several of the figures resemble inverted letters of the alphabet, some of the children may have interpreted the task to be one of writing or copying. It is also possible, however, that tracing the stimulus reflects an inability to process the configurations as a whole.

Another aspect of creating a static symbol is detaching the gesture from the referent. Our instructions were to "use your fingers. . . to show what the thing (configuration) looks like." A few children responded to the task by placing their hands directly *on* the pipe-cleaner configuration, aligning their fingers with the stimuli. In some cases, children would "complete" the visual pattern, for example, by placing an index finger across the open curve in configuration 8.

These examples illustrate various ways in which young children have not yet realized certain generic features of the gesture medium: that it is external both to self and to referent and that they are implicitly being asked to create a symbol that is a visible and quasi-permanent equivalent of the referent.

Excluding Irrevelant Body Parts

There is a metasymbolic aspect to depictive gesture that is so obvious that it frequently escapes notice. Since only certain parts of the hand or body serve as the vehicle for a particular gesture, it is necessary somehow to set off the relevant parts from the rest of the body. In the case of graphic symbolism, when a drawing of a circle is used to represent a face, the sun, a wheel, or some other circular object, it is not necessary to indicate that some parts of the drawing should be considered the symbol and other parts are to be disregarded. In contrast, when thumb and index finger form a circle, the other fingers have to be taken out of the way, and it must be communicated that they are irrelevant to the gesture.

Our understanding of the mechanisms involved in highlighting relevant and excluding irrelevant parts of the body can at present only be intuitive. Perhaps the relative stiffness of the important parts plays a role. The orientation of the gestural product toward the observer would seem to be crucial as well.

The difficulty which we encountered in scoring gestures in the original study (Gindes & Barten, 1973) was sometimes related to the problem of not knowing what to look at within the total presentation. The developmental assessment of gesture is based in part on whether the child is able to construct a symbolic vehicle that stands out as a figure against the background of the rest of the body.

Explicit Representation

A closely related feature of mastery of the medium is the achievement of increasing explicitness in the formation of the gestural symbol. The child must learn to articulate the gesture clearly. Three degrees of explicitness are illustrated in the depictions of configuration 9, the sideways E, (in Fig. 8.2).[2] In a, the three line segments and the cross bar are all explicitly depicted. In b, we cannot be certain whether the cross bar is absent (since it is not explicitly presented) or whether it is implicit and "intended" in the line that forms the base of the three fingers. The same problem occurs in c in a more extreme form, where more than three fingers are extended. Does the child intend for only three fingers to "count" as the gesture, or is his perception of referent and symbol global and undifferentiated?

Knowing the Limitations of the Medium

The children whom we tested sometimes devoted a great deal of effort to modifying their hand positions in order to depict the stimulus adequately. For

---

[2]My thanks to Mary Ann Minster for drawing this figure.

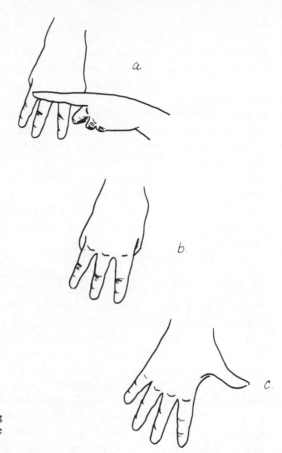

FIG. 8.2.   Gestures manifesting three degrees of explicitness in the representation of configuration 9.

example, one child attempted to bend his index finger back far enough with his middle finger so that configuration 6 could be depicted with only one hand. There are, however, limits to the modifiability and suitability of gesture as a symbolic medium. Certain symbols cannot physically be created, and the child must develop an awareness of what is possible and what is impossible.

Motor Organization

To produce a gesture, a child must have achieved the requisite level of motor organization and differentiation. One particular aspect of hand gestures which came to our attention through Roth's (1975) replication study was that deaf children produce significantly more bilaterally symmetrical, mirror-image gestures than do hearing children. By contrast, hearing children produce more gestures in which the two hands assume different configurations.

It seemed at first that the use of sign language could account for this symmetrization, since many signs in American Sign Language entail the symmetrical use of the two hands (Klima & Bellugi, 1975). For example, the sign for "same" requires that the two index fingers be placed side by side; the sign for "different" is two index fingers performing simultaneous outward arcs from an initially parallel position. However, only 4 children in Roth's sample of 20 were actively using sign language. Descriptions of the early stages of signing (Schlesinger & Meadow, 1972; Schlesinger, 1975) did suggest a possible explanation. Many "baby signs" are given symmetrically with two hands and only later are performed with one hand. Such duplicated signs are analogous to the hearing child's reduplicated early vocables and words. It also seemed plausible that the greater number of symmetrical gestures might reflect more primitive gestural-motor organization caused by neurological impairment in the deaf children, although this notion could not be substantiated.

To determine whether symmetrization of asymmetrical configurations is characteristic of an earlier stage of motor organization, I reexamined gestures given by our sample of hearing children. If symmetry reflects more primitive motor organization, younger hearing children should produce a larger proportion of symmetrical gestures than older children.

The most decisive comparison can be made for the 10 "complex" stimuli that require the child to use the hands asymmetrically or differently for an adequate representation of the stimulus. Thus, patterns 12, 11, and 3 are difficult if not impossible to depict unless the child uses the two hands differently to portray the separate components of the configuration. Table 8.1 presents the mean number of gestures using one hand, two hands symmetrically, and two hands asymmetrically. As can be seen from this table, there is a slight decrease with age in the number of one-handed gestures and a large increase in the number of two-hand different gestures. I also examined the children's dominant gestural mode, defined as the mode employed for at

TABLE 8.1
Mean Number of One-Handed (1H), Two-Handed
Symmetrical (2HS), and Two-Hand Different (2HD)
Gestures for the 10 Complex Stimuli

Group	N^a	Age (yrs.)	1H	2HS	2HD
Young	19	3:9	2.26	1.79	2.89
Old	21	4:7	1.30	1.15	5.45

[a]Some of the children's responses were not included in this analysis because they were purely verbal responses, failures to respond, tracing in the air, etc. Mean nonscorable responses for the young group = 3.1, for the old group = 2.1.

TABLE 8.2
Number of Younger and Older Children Whose
Dominant Gestural Mode Is One-Handed (1H), Two
Hands Symmetrical (2HS), and Two Hands Different
(2HD)

		Dominant Mode		
Group	N^a	1H	2HS	2HD
Young	19	4	2	7
Old	21	0	0	14

[a]Six younger and six older children manifested no dominant
response mode as defined (at least 5 of the 10 gestures using that
mode).

least 5, or 50%, of the 10 complex stimuli. Table 8.2 reveals that the older
children predominantly use their two hands differentially in depicting these
configurations.

This developmental trend is not surprising in view of the fact that under all
conditions it is more difficult to make our two hands perform different
actions simultaneously, for example, at the piano or in the game of rubbing
stomach and patting head at the same time. The strength of the obtained trend
within such a narrow age range is striking, however, and suggests that
significant motor-gestural differentiation may be occuring around the age of
4 and 5. In this connection, Bergès and Lézine (1965) report that 3-year-olds
have difficulty in direct imitation of bilaterally asymmetrical hand positions.

CONCLUSIONS

In this chapter I have presented a taxonomy of gestures as a prerequisite for
systematic empirical study of the development of gesture. This classification
into gestures differing in function suggests two possible forms that the
development of gesture might take: (1) development *within* a particular type
of gesture, for example, within expressive or depictive gesture, and (2)
differentiation of the types of gesture from one another, as when enactive and
depictive gesture become separate functions. The first type of analysis focuses
upon the ways in which the child achieves organization and differentiation
within a mode. The second deals with how the child distinguishes among
communicative intentions and makes such differentiation clear to others.

It is clear that the investigation of symbolic processes in children must
involve an examination of the developing knowledge of the medium itself,
including characteristics and limitations of that medium as a vehicle for
symbolization. Although depictive gesture was the basis for the analysis of

mastery of the gesture medium, it is assumed that many of the processes discussed apply to other forms of gesture as well.

REFERENCES

Anderson, J. W. Attachment behavior out of doors. In N. G. Blurton-Jones (Ed.), *Ethological studies of child behavior*. Cambridge: Cambridge University Press, 1972.

Asch, S. *Social psychology*, New York: Prentice-Hall, 1952.

Bates, E., Camaioni, L., & Volterra, V. The acquisition of performatives prior to speech. *Merrill-Palmer Quarterly*, 1975, *21*, 205–226.

Bergès, M. & Lézine, I. *The imitation of gestures*. London: Heinemann, 1965.

Blurton-Jones, N. G. *Nonverbal communication*. Oxford: Oxford University Press, 1971.

Brannigan, C. R., & Humphries, D. A. Human non-verbal behavior, a means of communication. In N. G. Blurton-Jones (Ed.), *Ethological studies of child behavior*. Cambridge: Cambridge University Press, 1972.

Carver, J. *An observational study of a two-year-old child's nonverbal methods of communication*. Unpublished senior thesis, State University of New York, College at Purchase, 1975.

Franklin, M. B. Non-verbal representation in young children: A cognitive perspective. *Young Children*, 1973, *11*, 33–53.

Gindes, M., & Barten, S. *The development of verbal and nonverbal representation in children*. Paper presented at the Eastern Psychological Association, Washington, D.C., May 1973.

Hewes, G. W. Primate communication and the gestural origins of language. *Current Anthropology*, 1973, *14*, No. 1–2, 5–12.

Hewes, G. W. The current status of the gestural theory of language origin. In S. R. Harnad, H. D. Steklis, & J. Lancaster (Eds.) *Origins and evolution of language and speech* (Vol. 280), Annals of the New York Academy of Sciences, New York, 1976, 482–504.

Hoemann, H. W. *The communicative behavior of preverbal deaf children*. Paper presented at the Eastern Psychological Association, Philadelphia, April 1974.

Jancovic, M., Devoe, S., & Wiener, M. Age-related changes in hand and arm movements as nonverbal communication: Some conceptualizations and an empirical exploration. *Child Development*, 1975, *46*, 922–928.

Kaplan, E. *Gestural representation of implement usage: An organismic-developmental study*. Unpublished Ph.D. dissertation, Clark University, Worcester, Mass., 1968.

Klapper, Z., & Birch, H. G. Perceptual and action equivalence to objects and photographs in children. *Perceptual and Motor Skills*, 1969, *29*, 763–771.

Klima, E. S., & Bellugi, U. Perception and production in a visually based language. In D. Aaronson & R. W. Rieber, (Eds.), *Developmental psycholinguistics and communication disorders* (Vol. 263). Annals of the New York Academy of Sciences, New York, 1975, 225–235.

LaBarre, W. The cultural basis of emotions and gestures. *Journal of Personality*, 1947, *16*, 49–68.

Michael, G., & Willis, F. Development of gestures as a function of social class, education, and sex. *Psychological Record*, 1968, *18*, 515–519.

Overton, W. F., & Jackson, J. P. The representation of imagined objects in action sequences: A developmental study. *Child Development*, 1973, *44*, 309–314.

Piaget, J. *Play, dreams and imitation in childhood*. London: Heinemann, 1951.

Röhrich, L. Gebärdensprache und Sprachgebärde. In W. D. Hand & G. O. Arlt (Eds.), *Humaniora: Essays in Literature, Folklore, bibliography honoring Archer Taylor*. Locust Valley, New York: Augustin, 1960, 121–149.

Roth, J. C. M. *The development of nonverbal representation in deaf children.* Unpublished senior thesis, State University of New York, College at Purchase, 1975.

Schlesinger, H. S. The effects of deafness on development in childhood: An Eriksonian perspective. In L. S. Liben (Chair) *Theoretical and practical implications of research on the development of deaf children.* Symposium presented at the meeting of the Society for Research on Child Development, Denver, April 1975.

Schlesinger, H. S., & Meadow, K. P. *Sound and sign: Childhood deafness and mental health.* Berkeley: University of California Press, 1972.

Werner, H., & Kaplan, B. *Symbol formation: An organismic-developmental approach to language and the expression of thought.* New York: Wiley, 1963.

9 Copying and Inventing: Similarities and Contrasts in Process and Performance

Edna Shapiro
Bank Street College of Education

WHAT DOES COPYING INVOLVE?

Watch a 5-year-old try to copy a drawing of a diamond: The child starts off ∧; then, in beginning to make the lower portion, the line wavers. Pause. The child looks at the model again and then back at the partially drawn figure; hand and pencil make a line that wobbles erratically down the page. Another line from the same starting point is attempted, but it too dribbles off. Just before trying to copy the diamond, this child has drawn a perfectly acceptable square (with four neat corners) sitting firmly on its base. Why is drawing the diamond so much more difficult? Of course, psychologists are not so surprised as the children since we expect developmental progression and know that on the Stanford-Binet the 3-year-old is expected to draw a passable circle, the 5-year-old a square, and the 7-year-old a diamond. But why it should take 2 years to be able to depict a four-sided figure turned on one of its corners is a question that has intrigued psychologists for a long time and still has no satisfactory answer.

If we watch an adult or an older child, say a 10-year-old, copy a two-dimensional figure such as a diamond, we see a series of smooth, well-regulated actions leading to a predictable result—a copy that closely resembles the original. The performance skills involved in successful completion of this task look almost effortless. The integration of perceptual information, monitoring of hand movements, and feedback from the look of the line on the page all seem automatic. As with many other apparently' routine sets of skills, observation of the behavior before these skills have become routinized, like watching a slow-motion replay, can help the observer to disentangle the different competences involved and makes possible a more fine-grained analysis of the component skills.

Copying is of theoretical interest because it offers a paradigm of the transformation of perceptual information into overt action. Yet such a statement belies the complexity of the processes involved and can be more obscuring than clarifying. The idea of matching to a standard has often dictated the terms in which copying has been assessed; that is, the investigator (or tester) has looked for the adequacy of the match, the correspondence between copy and model. My purpose is to reappraise what is involved in copying; to look at copying behavior in terms not only of the adequacy of the match but also in terms of the requirements of the task and the processes and capacities needed for competent performance. As soon as we begin to look at copying in this way, we see that it is not necessarily automatic or a rote performance. In fact, the actions and the sequencing of actions often have to be thought out and invented on the spot. Copying and inventing, then, may not always be at opposite ends of a continuum; in certain circumstances there is overlap in the processes that determine action.

Copying—especially drawing simple forms with a model present—has been studied by psychologists of different persuasions, and an analysis of copying pulls strands from many sources. The investigation of "pictorial space" and the abstraction of shape has been a long-standing interest of Piaget and Inhelder (1956, 1969); Vereeken (1961) has formulated levels of the development of what he terms "constructive-praxic" behavior, including drawing and copying spatial arrangements; copying has served as a means for studying "perceptually directed action" (Birch & Lefford, 1967); the action sequences involved in copying figures have been analyzed by Jacqueline Goodnow and her colleagues (Bernbaum, Goodnow, & Lehman, 1974; Goodnow & Levine, 1973); Olson (1970) has taken the child's acquisition of diagonality, as evidenced by the ability to copy a diagonal, as a paradigm of cognitive development; Maccoby and Bee (1965, 1968) have offered a hypothesis to account for some of the difficulties that seem to be inherent in certain copying behaviors; and, most recently, Farnham-Diggory and Simon (1975), studying eye movements and drawing sequences, have applied an information-processing analysis to copying. Many different variables that influence copying behavior have been described, and different explanatory concepts have been offered to account for the data. However, the processes involved as well as the interrelationships among variables remain confusing.

Certain characteristics of copying and "free" or "spontaneous" drawing follow from the limitations and particularities of the medium—the sharpness or softness of the pencil, the thickness of the crayon line, the smoothness of the marker, the absorptiveness of the paper. Further constraints are imposed by the nature of the intent. Early scribbling usually has an undirected intent. When a young child draws a pattern of lines and then calls out, "It's a ladder," we assume that the form was produced without the intent to create a ladder, that the action involved in the drawing was action per se; meaning is added on but did not necessarily generate the activity. Luquet (1927), in his early studies of children's drawings, called this "fortuitous realism"—fortuitous in that the meaning of the scribble is discovered in the course of creating it. Piaget and Inhelder (1969), building on Luquet's analysis, consider drawing as "a form of the semiotic function... halfway between symbolic play and the mental image. It is like symbolic play in its functional pleasure..., and like the mental image in its effort at imitating the real" (p. 63).

Copying clearly requires accommodation to the real. The directive to make a drawing "just like this one" necessarily limits the drawer's options. Yet most children will accept the task as reasonable and potentially enjoyable and proceed to try it. When children cannot make an adequate copy of a complex figure, or of a diamond, they are often perfectly aware of the discrepancy between their effort and the model and react to that discrepancy sometimes with amazement, annoyance, or anger. The frustration that derives from the perceived discrepancy between the product and the intent points to the problem-solving aspects of the copying task. A problem is presented that has to be solved; strategies have to be worked out. Copying is not a matter of triggering a set of predetermined actions; the person is not a Xerox machine. Franklin (1973) emphasizes the importance of intentionality, the intention to make or to let one aspect of experience stand for another in a particular kind of way, and considers it the distinctive orientation that is the hallmark of representational functioning. The intent to create is present in pattern copying, as it is in pattern invention. But in copying the intent is for one-to-one correspondence, an equivalence of formal properties.

Intentionality can be inferred, but the direction of the intent is often more difficult to determine since young children often change the conception of what is to be drawn as the drawing proceeds. Some of these changes occur because the child cannot fulfill the original intent. While this may lead to frustration or giving up the task, it may, on the other hand, sometimes lead to creative expression, a kind of bravado performance that obscures the inability to carry out the mimetic intent.

Representation involves the construction of correspondences between two aspects of experience; certain properties of what is being signified— properties of shape, texture, feeling tone, and color—must be preserved in the representation. But there are also dissimilarities between the two: The drawing is not the object, the clay form is not a cat, and the gesture is not the same as the statement. In copying there is necessarily close correspondence between what is being copied and the product, but in neither case can there be identity. As Arnheim (1954) has phrased it; "Representation never produces a replica of the object but its structural equivalent in a given medium" (p. 162). This basic principle applies to copying as well as to symbolic representation.

It is essential not only to compare the model and the end product but also and most important to differentiate the particular conditions and relations between model and copy, since variation in these (relations, conditions) will determine the processes that are required to produce the end product.

What is involved in copying depends, for example, on whether the model is to be copied with or without observation of the steps that led to making it. The task is considerably more difficult when the model is presented as a finished product, a fait accompli. Further, the task of copying has to be differentiated in terms of whether the model and the copy (or new product) are in the same medium or in different media.

The copier has the greatest amount of information available when the copy is to be made in the same medium as the original model and the steps leading to the end result have been observed. The copier has to reproduce the actions he or she has observed, often in the proper sequence, in order to achieve the desired result. But common sense will confirm that it doesn't always help merely to watch a more skillful performer. Adults as well as children can analyze and "appreciate" skill and artistry without thereby being able to duplicate it. It is one thing to be able to analyze and another to be able to do. (The balletomane does not become a dancer.) Copying (like all forms of imitation) requires perceptual differentiation of the component parts and an awareness of their relationships as well as mastery of the component activities and the ability to put them together in sequence and relationship that will yield the desired result. The whole and the parts and the interrelationships among them must be apprehended.

But copying a model in the same medium requires familiarity with and expertise in the medium as well as differentiated perception of the formal properties of the model. If either one's perception of the formal characteristics of the model or one's competence in the medium is inadequate, then the steps to achieving the final result exemplified by the model need to be reinvented by the copier. Thus, 5-year-old Dav, one of Piaget and Inhelder's (1956) subjects, trying to draw the lower half of the diamond, said, "It must be like the top half but I can't get it" (p. 72).

Another layer of difficulty is introduced when the model is to be reproduced in a medium different from that of the original; then a greater number of transformations of the formal properties of the model is required to yield structural equivalents in the new medium. On the other hand, the ease or difficulty of making such transformations will vary depending on the nature of the media. It should be easier, for instance, to copy a drawn linear figure with rods than to draw a copy, since in constructing with rods, the component units of the figure are given in the structure of the rods.

Translation from a three-dimensional model to a two-dimensional medium, as in "copying from nature," necessarily involves multiple transformations. But so does creating a likeness in three dimensions. Furthermore, one needs to understand the possibilities and the conventions of the medium. Very young children making an image of the human figure in play dough may treat the three-dimensional medium as if it were two dimensional, that is, scratch the surface and outline the figure with thin strips of play dough (Golomb, 1972). In this instance, lack of familiarity with three-dimensional media as well as a certain amount of facility in the graphic medium have taken precedence over the awareness of the three-dimensionality of the human form and the three-dimensionality of the stuff they are working with. Such responses highlight the power of the medium and the individual's need to experiment with its possibilities and also remind us that there are many kinds of correspondence between model and product.

In sum, the processes involved in copying are processes that have to do with perceiving, determining, and constructing equivalences—forms in the new product that correspond in some ways to those in the model. Even when the new product is intended to be isomorphic with the model, is intended to be a "faithful" copy, processes of perceptual analysis and integration, strategies for constructing equivalences, and the performatory skills and knowledge of the medium necessary for enacting them are called into play. It is crucial to keep in mind that these processes interact at a tacit rather than an explicit level of understanding. One is not explicitly aware of what one is doing. Further, evidence from diverse sources suggests that these capacities do not develop simultaneously.

DISCREPANCIES BETWEEN PERCEIVING
AND PERFORMING

It is generally agreed that there is an orderly progression from discrimination to recognition to production; that is, one must be able to discriminate what Eleanor Gibson has called the distinguishing features of a stimulus before one can recognize it, and, in turn, one must be able to recognize a stimulus before one can produce it (cf. Gibson, 1967). Copying, since it depends on the translation of perception and perceptual information into action, comes under this rubric. But competence in perception is not a sufficient condition for competence in production.

As others have pointed out (Maccoby, 1968; Maccoby & Bee, 1965), it is well known that children can make perceptual discriminations that they are not able to produce in their own behavior. This lag between discrimination or perception and performance has been studied in hearing and speech as well as in visual perception and drawing. Children can understand words that they are often unable to articulate. For instance, Berko and Brown (1960) note that children may articulate particular sounds incorrectly, although they are able to discriminate the same sounds accurately when they are spoken by others. (A common instance is the substitution of an initial *w* for an initial *r* sound, as in run/wun or ring/wing.)

Similarly, children are able to recognize visual forms that they are often unable to draw. Fantz (1958), for example, has shown that very young infants are able to discriminate among different forms; the ability to *produce* a simple circular shape takes several years of development. While the development from early babbling to speech and from neonatal discrimination to drawing obviously involves massive changes in perceptual capacity and in the voluntary control of motor skills, at later stages the lag between perception and performance is not simply a matter of immature motor skills. As Maccoby (1968) says, with respect to the lag between hearing and speech, "The mere presence of a component in the repertoire of sounds a child has been known to make... is no guarantee that he can execute this sound in its proper speech context, even though he has discriminated the components in the model's performance" (p. 163). The separate components of the diamond figure may appear in the drawings of children who cannot draw a fair copy of a diamond; furthermore, the motor skills involved in constructing diamonds do not appear to be so different from those involved in drawing squares or triangles. In addition, young children are able to make better copies of triangles and diamonds when tracing them, or connecting dots that define the angles, than when they are drawing freehand (Birch & Lefford, 1967). Thus, the ability to discriminate and the component performance skills may be present in the child's repertoire, yet the child may not be able to perform a particular copying task that depends on those skills. Goodnow (1972) describes performance as "selection from a repertoire." But once we have ascertained that the skills are present, we know very little about the rules that govern selection and even less about rules for combining and integrating separate skills.

When we speak of discrepancies among the processes of discrimination, recognition, and re-creation, we have to look more closely at what is involved in each of these types of activities. Activity is the key word. Perception is not merely passive registration but a sequence of actions. And drawing "a form like that one" is a shorthand expression for a set of performatory acts requiring, at the least, coordination of eye and hand, monitoring of hand movements, as well as cognitive strategies that determine the content, sequence, and style of the performatory acts.

The perceptual activity and the performatory acts are intimately related. Piaget and Inhelder (1956) say that

> the drawing, like the mental image, is not simply an extension of ordinary perception but is rather the combination of the movements, anticipations, reconstructions, comparisons, and so on, that accompany perception, and which we have called perceptual activity. (p. 33)

They are well aware that drawing is not simply a reflection of perceptual activity. In discussing the fact that it may take 2 years to move from copying a square to copying a diamond, they remark that "all that is needed is to shorten the diagonal of an oblique square"—an analysis that seems to be excessively intellectualistic. It is unlikely that, for children and adults who can make an adequate copy of a diamond, the competence can be conceptualized in these terms. Nevertheless, their fundamental proposition is that the abstraction of form, the development of representational space, is built up not only from direct perception of objects but on the basis of the coordination of the child's actions upon objects. Experience with forms in many different perspectives and contexts is therefore the sine qua non for the construction of representational space.

Thus, on the one hand, there is reason to anticipate close correspondence between perceptual and performatory activities, while, on the other hand, there is clear evidence of discrepancy. How can we account for the lag between the discrimination of shapes and their depiction?

Maccoby and Bee (1965) have offered "some speculations concerning the lag between perceiving and performing" and suggest a solution which they call the "number of attributes" hypothesis: "to reproduce a figure, the subject must make use of more attributes of the model than are required for most perceptual discriminations of this same model from other figures" (p. 375). To take into account Arnheim's observations as well as developmental trends in perception, Maccoby (1968) has revised the formulation to say that holistic perception suffices for the discrimination of (simple geometric) form but is not enough for making a copy. Even this version, however, makes the child's ability to fractionate the stimulus the fundamental competence. Goodson, working with 3- to 5-year-olds, contrasted the effects of training in perceptual discrimination with training in actually making the movements required for copying triangles and diamonds. Focusing on more careful discrimination of the attributes of the stimuli led to greater improvement in drawing than did training and practice in motor performance (reported in Maccoby, 1968). But the fundamental issue in focusing on attributes remains the question of how they are to be defined. Maccoby and Bee, like many researchers, define attributes from the point of view of the adult analyzer. As Olson (1968) also has pointed out, this is the basic "psychologists' fallacy": "Attributes are assumed to be preexistent and it remains for the mind simply to link them up" (p. 172). Further, it is likely that an important part of perceptual development consists in the redefintion of attributes and shifts in the nature and generality of dimensional characteristics. In Birch and Lefford's study and in our own work (Shapiro, 1977) there is no unequivocal relation between young children's ability to analyze the components of a stimulus figure such as a triangle or diamond and their capability in drawing it. Nor does the ability to recognize different forms give clear baseline data for the ability to depict them.

In our research, we showed children of different ages a set of geometric forms and asked them to identify them: The designs were displayed on a large card, and each child was shown each design drawn (in the same size) on a smaller card and was asked to locate that design on the large card. The children, aged 4 through 9, made very few errors, and, as expected, the younger children made more errors. The errors make sense: More similar stimuli such as the " + " and the " × " are confused with each other, as are the triangle and the upside-down triangle. The major source of error (approximately half of all errors) is the confusion of two figures: a square with a diagonal going from upper left to lower right and a square with a diagonal going from upper right to lower left. Most of the errors that older children make are made on these diagonals. (This too makes sense: It is well established that oblique lines present special problems in discrimination. We locate ourselves, move, and act on objects in terms of vertical and horizontal coordinates. Further, we have no names, no verbal tags, to differentiate these two diagonals.)

But then, when we asked the children to copy a square with a diagonal, many of those who confused the stimuli in the recognition task made adequate copies; only a few reversed the direction of the diagonal in their drawings (6 of 120). Later, we asked the children to construct a square with a diagonal out of rods and to copy a diagonal made of checkers on a checkerboard. The child who confuses the direction of the diagonal in the recognition task often can make an accurate construction or copy. In this case, then, discrimination errors do not necessarily lead to or predict errors of production. On the contrary, competence in production can be more adequate than competence in perceptual discrimination. Thus it seems that the so-called lag can be reversed. As so often happens in psychological research, the particular measure used determines the outcome. What seems to be critical are the demands of the tasks. One can say that the discrimination task is perhaps too easy for the older children, and consequently they don't give their full attention to it. The drawing task, although far from difficult for 8- or 9-year-olds, does require closer self-monitoring. Perhaps more significant, however, is the fact that perceptual activity and performatory activity require different kinds of information.

Performance, moreover, depends not only on perceptual information and performance skills but on adequate ways of representing the information in the chosen medium. The development of a system of representation is the crucial intermediary between perceptual and performatory activities. This should not be taken to mean that performance mirrors intellectual development. While the use of children's drawings of the human figure as an index of intellectual development is based on this assumption (cf. Harris, 1963), I doubt if anyone seriously believes that young children either perceive or conceive of human beings as rounded blobs with appendages stuck on. Still there can be little doubt that children's level of cognitive (and affective) development does underlie their ability to make copies, to imitate, and to create. Although the product cannot be read off as a reflection of knowledge, conceptual understanding can be said to set a lower limit on what can be intentionally depicted. Lindstrom, in her book on children's art (1967), includes a series of San Francisco children's depictions of the Golden Gate Bridge. In this sequence we see in the painting of the youngest child a clearly recognizable span across water and the rudimentary rendition of the towers, cables, and piers of the bridge. Some or all of the component structural features are rendered with more or less skill in the children's paintings. There is a notable progression from the decorative to the functional, from registering the fact of the presence of, say, the towers to their integration into the structural design. The final painting in the sequence shows a bridge hung by cables which are held by towers rising vertically from a foundation. Depicting these functional connections requires more than "seeing" the bridge. The gradual integration of the necessary structural relations depends on developing a means of representation which feeds back to differentiation of perception and to experience in the medium and can then be reflected in the child's depiction.

Pitting perception against performance is not a profitable exercise. There is an interplay between differentiated perception and skilled performance in the medium one is working in. One can "know" what one wants to do and still not be able to transform the knowledge and intent into action. Adults, too, show a lag between perception and performance, and, as noted earlier, merely observing, even very careful observing, doesn't necessarily lead to skilled performance. Differentiation of perception and the selection, utilization, and organization from a repertoire of performance skills are informed by a system of representation, a system that governs expression, the making of a tangible product in a particular medium. Each—the fineness and comprehensiveness of perceptual activity, the range and skill of performance, and the conceptual validity and breadth of the representational scheme—can inform or can constrain the other. But it seems likely that the processes involved in the attempt to reproduce a given end must nourish the perception and appreciation of the original. The effort of trying to match one's performance to a given standard may in fact have a salutary effect—the sharpening of perceptual as well as of performance skills.

COPYING AND CREATING

Both Western culture and developmental theory place a high premium on creativity and inventiveness; consequently, copying, repeating what has already been done, is generally derogated. True, there are certain circumstances in which inventiveness is not encouraged, although a high level of performance skill may be called for. Classical dancers and musicans, for instance, are characteristically supposed to give true but not necessarily creative performances. Nevertheless, we reserve our highest accolades for those who develop personal interpretations of the works they perform, for those who go beyond technical facility. In this context, then, copying, or matching one's performance to a given standard, is seen not as an end point but as an intermediate stage en route to creative expression.

We focus on individual creative expression and on the product. Other cultures and other eras have taken different perspectives on the significance of what is made and who made it, the steps and processes involved in the making, and the uniqueness or originality of the product.

Where objects are made for use, there is no need to signify who the maker was; we taught the Eskimo and Indian makers of fetishes, jewelry, masks, and pots to sign their work. When these objects were made in the nexus of the ceremonial life of an intact culture, their makers may have been known to all, but the act of signing, signifiying a special creative relationship to the object, was not considered necessary.

Where myth and symbol retain their potency, certain forms of symbolic expression can carry such inherent power that their depiction alone, without variation or conscious personalization, has ritual or magical significance. The form itself is potent, and, in the proper context, repetition can signify participation in and invocation of that power.

I do not mean to suggest that the child's copying of a geometric form is analogous to the Navajo healer strewing the sands for ritual designs that carry curative powers. What I have been arguing is that our culturally and theoretically supported valuing of individual uniqueness and creativity have possibly led to an exaggeration of the distance between copying and inventing. There is perhaps an analogue here to the dichotomization of convergent and divergent thinking. Both are treated as antipodal. Yet some convergent thinking requires creative problem solving; some divergent thinking comes down to the application of already-tested approaches. Similarly, under certain circumstances, copying requires invention of means to achieve a given end; all inventions are not necessarily unique or powerful.

REFERENCES

Arnheim, R. *Art and visual perception.* Berkeley: University of California Press, 1954.

Berko, J., & Brown, R. Psycholinguistic research methods. In P. Mussen (Ed.), *Handbook of research methods in child development.* New York: Wiley, 1960.

Bernbam, M., Goodnow, J. & Lehman, E. Relationships among perceptual-motor tasks: tracing and copying. *J. of Educational Psychology,* 1974, *66,* 731–735.

Birch, H. G., & Lefford, A. Visual differentiation, intersensory integration, and voluntary control. *Monographs of the Society for Research in Child Development,* 1967, *32,* (110).

Fantz, R. L. Pattern vision in young infants. *Psychological Record,* 1958, *8,* 43–47.

S., & Simon, E. *Information processing analysis of eye-hand coordinations during pattern drawing.* Paper given at meeting of the Society for Research opment, Denver, March 1975.

Non-verbal representation in young children: A cognitive perspective. *Young 3, 29,* 33–53.

rinciples of perceptual learning and development. New York: Appleton-Century-

volution of the human figure in a three-dimensional medium. *Developmental Psychology,* 1972, *6,* 385–391.

Goodnow, J. J. Rules and repertoires, rituals and tricks of the trade: Social and informational aspects to cognitive and representational development. In S. Farnham-Diggory (Ed.), *Information processing in children.* New York: Academic Press, 1972.

Goodnow, J. J. & Levine, R. A. "The grammar of action": sequence and syntax in children's copying. *Cognitive Psychology,* 1973, *4,* 82–98.

Harris, D. B. *Children's drawings as measures of intellectual maturity: A revision of the Goodenough Draw-A-Man Test.* New York: Harcourt, Brace & World, 1963.

Lindstrom, M. *Children's art.* Berkeley: University of California Press, 1967.

Luquet, G. H. *Le dessin enfantin.* Paris: Alcan, 1927.

Maccoby, E. E. What copying requires. *Ontario Journal of Educational Research,* 1968, *10,* 163–170.

Maccoby, E. E., & Bee, H. Some speculations concerning the lag between perceiving and performing. *Child Development,* 1965, *36,* 367–377.

Olson, D. R. From perceiving to performing the diagonal. *Ontario Journal of Educational Research,* 1968, *10,* 171–180.

Olson, D. R. *Cognitive development: The child's acquisition of diagonality.* New York: Academic Press, 1970.

Piaget, J., & Inhelder, B. *The child's conception of space.* London: Routledge & Kegan Paul, 1956 (New York: Norton, 1967).

Piaget, J., & Inhelder, B. *The psychology of the child.* New York: Basic Books, 1969.

Shapiro, E. *Discrepancies among measures of performance: An analysis of pattern-copying* (Final Report). New York: Bank Street College of Education, 1977.

Vereeken, P. *Spatial development: Constructive praxia from birth to the age of seven.* Groningen, The Netherlands: Wolters, 1961.

III LANGUAGE

10 The Child's First Terms of Reference

Jeremy M. Anglin
University of Waterloo
Waterloo, Ontario, Canada

Common nouns are generalizations in that they refer not to one but rather to a group of objects. When we use a name to refer to an object whether consciously or unconsciously we place that object in a category or class of objects which share the same category label. The word *dog* refers to collies, terriers, poodles, and several other kinds of dogs, just as the word *flower* refers to roses, tulips, carnations, and several other kinds of flowers. A given object can be named in several different ways, and each name serves to classify that object at a certain level of generality. This flower might be called a *rose*, a *flower*, or a *plant*, and each of these terms classifies the object at increasingly generic levels. Thus the common nouns of a natural language constitute a conceptual system in which the concepts include as instances all of the objects that happen to be labeled by the same name in that language.[1] The research to be described below is based on a scientific investigation of the acquisition by children of this conceptual system, their first terms of reference.

To understand the nature of the child's first terms of reference two fundamental questions must be distinguished at the outset: (1) What is the order of acquisition of category labels, and, in particular, what are the child's first terms of reference? (2) How do the meanings of these terms of reference change as the child grows older? It is important to separate these two questions clearly, for even though a child may have a particular word in his vocabulary, it cannot be assumed that that word has the same meaning for him as it does for an adult. In this chapter I shall describe research related to

---

[1]Throughout this chapter, when a particular word is being discussed, italics are used (e.g., *dog*); when a particular concept is being discussed, small capital letters are used (e.g., DOG).

each of these questions in turn, and then I shall briefly formulate some conclusions.

THE ORDER OF ACQUISITION OF CATEGORY LABELS

In thinking about the possible determinants of the order of acquisition of category labels I have found it useful, if somewhat simplistic, to distinguish between horizontal development and vertical development. By horizontal development I mean the acquisition of category labels which categorize the world at roughly the same level of generality. It will come as no surprise that the child is better able to name correctly an apple than a persimmon or a dog than a wombat. Such results are hardly startling, and they suggest simply that the child will learn category labels first for objects which are familiar to him, salient in his world, and important in his transactions with it and only later will he learn names for less familiar, less salient, and less important objects.

But what about vertical development by which I mean the acquisition of category labels at different levels of generality. As noted above, any object can be named in several different equally valid ways. The child may want a term to refer to his pet collie, but the English language, in fact, contains several possible names at different levels of generality, for example, *Lassie, collie, dog, mammal, animal, being, thing,* and *entity.* Is it possible to predict the order of acquisition of such hierarchically related category labels?

In his recent path-breaking book on language development Brown (1973) has dealt at length with a related problem: how to predict the order in which the child will acquire various grammatical morphemes. He has concluded that while frequency of occurrence in parental speech is not a good predictor, a metric of semantic complexity (as well as one of grammatical complexity) is predictive of their order of acquisition (see also H. Clark, 1973; Slobin, 1971). Is it possible that there exists a definition of semantic complexity for English nomenclature which might allow us to predict the order in which the child will acquire terms of reference at different levels of generality? What are the semantic relationships among category labels which can be ordered along a specific to general dimension such that the category denoted by one word is a proper subset of the category denoted by another word? Consider, for example, the terms *collie, dog,* and *animal.* Is there some sense in which one of these terms might be considered to be semantically more complex than the others, and might this metric of semantic complexity be a predictor of the order of acquisition of such category labels?

Philosophers and psychologists have often distinguished between the extension of a word and the intension of that word (see, for example, Brown, 1958a; Goodman, 1972; Inhelder & Piaget, 1969). Roughly, extension refers to the group of objects denoted by the word, whereas intension refers to the properties which define the word. For example, the extension of the word *animal* is the set of dogs, cats, birds, fish, insects, etc., which are its referents. The intension of the word *animal* is the set of properties *lives, breathes, digests, reproduces, is capable of spontaneous motion*, etc., which constitute the defining properties of the class of ANIMALS. It is possible to postulate a metric of semantic complexity for nested category labels defined either in terms of extension or in terms of intension.

Consider first a definition of semantic complexity in terms of extension. Semantic complexity might be defined in terms of extension such that a term that refers to a set of objects is semantically more complex than a term which refers to only a subset of those objects. According to this definition, the more diversity in the reference class of a given category label the more semantically complex it is. If semantic complexity were defined in this way and if the resulting metric were the sole predictor of the order of acquisition of category labels such that simple terms are acquired before complex terms, then the order would be *collie* first, *dog* second, and *animal* third in this particular hierarchy of terms.

Consider now a definition of semantic complexity in terms of intension, that is, the set of properties that define the word. It is the case that for nested category labels every property which is true for all instances of the superordinate term is also true for all instances of the subordinate term. For example, the properties *live, breathe, digest*, etc., which are the defining properties of the class of ANIMALS are also true of the class of DOGS. However, there are certain properties which are true for all instances denoted by the subordinate term which are not true for all instances denoted by the superordinate term. For example, *is a mammal* is a predicate which applies to all dogs but not to all animals, and *has four legs, has fur, barks*, etc., are predicates which apply to virtually all dogs but by no means to all animals. If semantic complexity were defined solely in terms of a word's intension such that a term defined by a set of properties is semantically simpler than a term defined by those properties *and* other properties as well, then according to this definition of semantic complexity *animal* would be simpler than *dog*, which would be simpler than *collie*. If this definition of semantic complexity were the sole predictor of the order of acquisition of category labels such that simpler terms are acquired before more complex terms, then the order would be *animal* first, *dog* second, and *collie* third for this particular hierarchy of terms.

As a matter of fact, neither of the aforementioned definitions of semantic complexity proves to be predictive of the order of acquisition of nested category labels. In a number of studies in which we tested the child's ability to both produce and comprehend terms of reference we found that children often begin by learning terms at some intermediate level of generality and beyond that learn both more specific or differentiated terms and more general or abstract terms. For example, a typical child learns *dog* before he learns *collie* or *animal,* learns *flower* before he learns *rose* or *plant*, and learns *car* before he learns either *Volkswagen* or *vehicle.* In one set of hierarchically related terms which we have studied children do seem to acquire first the most specific word in the set. Thus most children gave evidence of having acquired *apple* before *fruit* or *food.* However, even though we did not test the child's ability to produce or comprehend a term such as *McIntosh*, it is safe to assume that such a term would not be in the child's vocabulary before the term *apple.* In another set children do seem to acquire first the most general word in that set. Specifically, many children gave evidence of having acquired the term *money* before either *dime* or *coin.* Again, however, it is safe to assume that had we tested for the more general term *currency* children would not have given evidence of control over this word before *money.*

Thus there is neither a unidirectional specific to general progression nor a unidirectional general to specific progression in vocabulary development, which means that neither of the definitions of semantic complexity outlined above provides a good predictor of the order of acquisition of category labels. There is still, of course, the possibility that some alternative definition of semantic complexity, possibly one that acknowledges the existence of "natural kinds," is predictive (cf. Rosch, Mervis, Gray, Johnson, & Boyes-Braem, 1976), although at the moment I am somewhat doubtful of this intriguing possibility.

What does appear to be a good predictor are various measures of frequency of occurrence and in particular the frequency of occurrence of the words in child speech according to Rinsland (1945). Specifically, words which have a high frequency of occurrence among first-grade children (Rinsland, 1945) are likely to be acquired before words which have a low frequency of occurrence. Rinsland (1945) proves to be predictive of the order of acquisition of terms of reference both within and across hierarchies, which means that it is predictive of both vertical and horizontal development.

To argue that there is a high correlation between the frequency of occurrence of words in child speech and the order of acquisition of those words is not, of course, equivalent to explaining the order of acquisition of those words. For one thing, we lack a clear understanding of exactly why some words occur more frequently than others. Nonetheless, identification of frequency of occurrence as a predictor of the order in which words are acquired gives us a clear hypothesis as to which words are the first to be acquired by English-speaking children and which words are acquired only later. Specifically, according to this hypothesis, among the first category labels to be acquired by children are those occurring most frequently in Rinsland (1945). We thought that by examining the most frequently occurring category labels in Rinsland we might be able to make some progress toward discerning the origins of the child's first verbal concepts.

As a first step in this direction we took from Rinsland (1945) the 275 most frequently occurring names of objects listed for Grade 1 and sorted them into semantic categories on the basis of similarity of meaning (cf. Anglin, 1970; Miller, 1967, 1969, 1972). Elizabeth Smith and I took turns sorting these words into semantic categories until we finally agreed on a single classification scheme. For comparison we also sorted the 275 most frequently occurring names of objects according to two frequency of occurrence tables: (1) the General Count in Thorndike and Lorge (1944) and (2) Howes (1966). These frequency of occurrence norms are based on material written and spoken, respectively, by adults.

The majority of the words from Rinsland (i.e., more than 60%) fell into seven categories: (1) animals; (2) people; (3) food; (4) toys, games, and sports; (5) body parts; (6) clothing; and (7) furniture and house parts. These categories accord well with classification of the nouns in the child's early spontaneous vocabulary (see, for example, Nelson, 1973b, pp. 29–34). A lot of the most frequently occurring words in Rinsland were the same as the most frequently occurring words taken from the adult counts. Nonetheless, there were differences. For example, the list for children contained many more words in certain domains (e.g., animals, toys) than did the lists for adults. On the other hand, the list for children contained far fewer terms for other domains than the lists for adults (e.g., geographic terms, buildings). The distribution of words in the people category was especially interesting. The list for children included more kin terms than the lists for adults. Notably lacking among the kin terms in the child's list, however, were the terms *wife* and *husband*, both present in both lists for adults. Apart from kin terms other kinds of terms for people (nonkin descriptions, occupations, groups, and proper names) were more frequent in the lists for adults than in the list for children.

As a first approximation both the distribution of the most frequently occurring words in the list for children and the differences between this list and the lists for adults suggest that the most frequently occurring terms of reference for children are labels for objects which are likely to be important to them in their day-to-day commerce with the world or salient in their environment. Many of the categories which include the greatest number of terms in the children's list cover basic activities which are presumably important to the child in his early years (e.g., social interaction [people], eating [food], play [toys], dressing [clothing], etc.). Moreover, it seems reasonable that, since children do not normally work for a living or travel as much as adults, they would not have as much use for occupational terms or geographical terms as would adults. Thus many of the words in the child's list seem to be consistent with the notion that these words denote objects that serve important functions in the child's life. Not all of these terms, of course, fit neatly into an interpretation of function or utility. For example, it is not clear what function animals serve in the life of a child, and yet there are more animal terms in the list for children than any other single category. Yet animals may be very salient in the child's environment because he will often encounter them as household pets or as toys or as pictures in children's books and so on. Thus if the hypothesis is correct, that the category labels occurring most frequently in Rinsland are, in fact, among the child's first terms of reference, then it would appear that the child first learns terms for objects which he will interact with or which are salient in his environment.

These conclusions are considerably strengthened and amplified by the recent work of Nelson (1973b). In an extensive study of the first words acquired by children between the ages of 1 and 2 she found that most category labels refer either to objects which the child can act upon (e.g., shoes, toys, food, etc.) or to things which are likely to change in his environment (e.g., dogs, cars, etc.). She emphasizes the point that the child seldom learns terms for objects which are simply there such as houses, walls, or tables. Thus Nelson's work confirms the conjectures outlined above and pinpoints the somewhat vague notion of salience by identifying it with movement and change.

This discussion suggests a solution, although admittedly not a very surprising one, to the problem of horizontal development. The child will learn first names of objects which he is likely to act upon or which are salient in his world (where important determinants of salience are movement and change) and only later will he learn names for objects which he does not act upon and objects which are less salient. However, it does not solve the problem of vertical development, the problem of at what level of generality the child will first categorize the useful and salient objects in his world.

At this point it is necessary to bring to this discussion a consideration of the source of the child's first terms of reference. Children learn the names of objects from other members of their linguistic community and in their early preschool years from their mothers in particular. In a study which we conducted in which adults were asked to name pictures of objects it was found that they would often produce quite specific names such as *Volkswagen, collie,* and *rose.* Children, however, when asked to name the same pictures usually produced somewhat more general and less discriminating responses such as *car, dog,* and *flower.* The difference between the names used by children and by adults raises the question of why it is that the child does not learn the specific names which adults seem to use when they name objects. Is it possible that mothers tailor their naming practices for their children in a way which accords with the character of the child's early vocabulary? This possibility, which had been suggested earlier by Brown (1958b), was the subject of two experiments. Mothers were asked to name pictures of objects for their 2-year-old children and for another adult, the experimenter. When mothers named objects for the experimenter they often gave very specific names (e.g., *Volkswagen, collie, pigeon*, etc.). However, when mothers named objects for their children they often tailored their naming practices, providing the child with less specific but more frequently occurring terms of reference (e.g., *car, dog, bird*, etc.). Whenever there was a difference in the way in which mothers named objects for adults and for their children it almost always appeared to be in the direction of the less specific but more frequently occurring term for the child. When naming objects for her child a mother will often supply him with vocabulary at an intermediate level of generality, the same level of generality at which our other experiments suggest that the child first learns to categorize objects. Thus children's first terms of reference are in fact consistent with the way in which mothers name objects for them.

Why will a mother choose this intermediate level of generality when naming objects for her child? At the moment I favor an explanation suggested by Brown in his brilliant paper "How Shall a Thing Be Called?" (1958b) and elaborated in Chapter 7 in his text *Social Psychology* (1965). Brown argued that a mother will provide children with names that will categorize objects at their "usual level of utility" (1958b), which he later defined as their "level of probable non-linguistic equivalence" (1965). The objects named by the same common noun are linguistically equivalent because the same name applies to each of them. These objects are also "non-linguistically equivalent" or "behaviorally equivalent" in some degree because behavior which is appropriate to one of the objects named by a word will also be appropriate to all of the other objects named by that word. Some words may group together things which are more behaviorally equivalent than the objects grouped together by other words. For example, *rain* has a higher degree of behavioral equivalence than *weather*, for there are many behaviors appropriate to and only to rain—we use an umbrella when walking in it, we avoid stepping in puddles, we wear rubber boots, etc.—but few behaviors exclusively appropriate to (and only to) weather since *weather* refers to all prevailing atmospheric conditions (sunny, rainy, snowy, windy, muggy, hot, foggy, etc.), each of which requires a different set of behaviors. Or, to take another example, *flower* has a higher degree of behavioral equivalence than either *tulip* or *plant* since there are certain behaviors which are appropriate to flowers—you can smell them, you can but perhaps should not pick them, etc.—which are not appropriate to all plants (you don't smell or pick trees) or exclusively appropriate to tulips. When a mother names an object for her child it is quite possible that she will choose a name that will categorize it with other objects which will be behaviorally equivalent to it for the child.

As a partial test of this speculation, after explaining to a group of adults what was meant by behavioral equivalence, we asked them to rate the terms within a set of hierarchies of nested category labels for their degree of behavioral equivalence for the 2-year-old child. These sets of terms were the same ones mentioned earlier for which we had previously determined the order of acquisition in children. The result of the study was that in seven of eight hierarchies the adult judges rated the term which children had previously been shown to acquire first as being most behaviorally equivalent for the 2-year-old child. Thus the adults rated *car* as being more behaviorally equivalent than either *Volkswagen* or *vehicle, dog* as being more behaviorally equivalent than *collie* or *animal, flower* as more behaviorally equivalent than *rose* or *plant, money* as more behaviorally equivalent (for the 2-year-old child) than *dime* or *coin*, and *apple* as being more behaviorally equivalent than *fruit* or *food*. Adult ratings of behavioral equivalence of these terms of reference proved to be more consistent with their order of acquisition than a variety of other dimensions along which we have asked adults to scale them. While this is not a definitive study, it is consistent with the hypothesis outlined above, that mothers will initially label objects with names, and that therefore children will initially learn names, which classify the world into groups of things which will be behaviorally equivalent for the child.

Thus the functions served by objects are implicated in both horizontal and in vertical development (see also Brown, 1958b, 1965; Nelson, 1973a, 1973b, 1974). The child will learn the names of objects with which he interacts in his commerce with the world whether the interaction fulfills basic needs such as eating food or whether the interaction is less intimately related to survival such as playing with toys or simply looking at salient objects. Moreover, because of the ways in which parents name these objects for him he will initially learn terms often at some intermediate level of generality, which classify them in maximally useful ways in the sense that they group together objects which he should behave toward similarly.

DEVELOPMENTAL CHANGES IN THE MEANING OF TERMS OF REFERENCE

The vocabulary of a child cannot be taken as a direct measure of his conceptual categories for it cannot be assumed that when he has a word in his vocabulary that it has the same meaning for him as it does for an adult or that he applies it to the same range of referents as adults do. In our work on the meaning of the child's first terms of reference we have concentrated, although not exclusively, on the extension of the child's category labels rather than on their intension. It is with the extension of their terms of reference that I shall be primarily concerned below.

In trying to conceptualize the relationship between the extension of a child's term as compared with the corresponding adult term one can imagine several possibilities:

1. *Underextension*: The child may use the term to apply only to a subset of the objects included in the corresponding adult concept. For example, the child might include only quadrupeds in his concept of ANIMAL.

2. *Overextension*: The child might use the term to apply to a broader range of referents than the adult does. For example, he may initially apply the term *dog* to all quadrupeds.

3. *Overlap:* The child might use the term to apply to some of the same objects that an adult does, not apply it to some objects covered by the adult term, and apply it to some objects not encompassed by that adult term. For example, the child might apply the term *flower* to most flowers but not to roses and daisies and, in addition, might apply the term to other kinds of plants.

4. *Nonoverlap:* The child might use the term to apply to a completely different range of referents from the range of referents denoted by the adult term. This particular relation would seem to be unlikely but would prevail, for example, if the child used the term *dog* to apply only to cats.

5. The child might not use the word to apply to any referent. This is the case for terms which have not yet entered the child's vocabulary. For example, he may never use the term *philodendron* to refer to anything.

6. The child might use a word which does not exist in the adult vocabulary to apply to some range of referents. For example, the child might use a word such as *psee* to apply to flowers, trees, and other forms of vegetation.

7. *Concordance:* The child might use the term to apply to exactly the same range of referents as is encompassed by the adult term. For example, the child might use the term *person* to apply to exactly the same set of featherless bipeds as the adult does. This relation of concordance represents the end state toward which development progresses.

The psychological literature on the subject has often characterized the relation as one of overextension—the child is portrayed as using a term of reference to apply to a broader range of objects than the adult does (see, for example, Brown, 1958b, and E. V. Clark, 1973). The corresponding developmental process is therefore viewed as differentiation or delimitation; the child who begins with overly general categories gradually narrows them down until they focus on the same range of referents as are encompassed by the adult term.

Many of the advocates of this point of view offer as the primary source of evidence for their hypothesis that the child's early concepts are overly general the results of diary studies in which the words used by the child are recorded along with the contexts in which they are used (see, for example, Chamberlain

& Chamberlain, 1904; Leopold, 1939, 1948; Moore, 1896; Stern, 1924). E. V. Clark (1973) has recently written a valuable review of the diary literature, although I disagree with her theoretical position. The point stressed by Clark and by others is that the child often overextends a term to objects which are not included in the adult category. For example, children have been observed to use the term *papa* to apply to men other than their fathers (Moore, 1896), the term *bottle* to apply to various glass containers (Leopold, 1939), the term *dog* to apply to various animals (Stern, 1924), and so on. Clark has argued that overextension is language independent and universal. Furthermore, she argues that the determinant of overextension is perceptual similarity between the object evoking the overextension and the instances of the class denoted by the term. According to Clark, the child narrows down the meaning of an originally overextended term as he adds new and increasingly specific semantic features to the word, as new words are introduced into his vocabulary to take over subareas of the semantic domain.

Undoubtedly there are instances of overgeneralization in the child's early use of words. However, the evidence from diaries is systematically biased to show overextension only and, because of the way it is collected and interpreted, cannot reveal underextension if it occurs. Consider the way these data are collected in terms of a specific example:

Referent	Name	Error
Collie	*Dog*	No error
Cat	*Dog*	Overextension
Poodle	—	— (not recorded)

If in the presence of a collie the child uses the word *dog,* he is using the term as an adult would and is therefore considered to be correct. Now suppose that in the presence of a cat the child says *dog.* This is counted as an overextension because the child is referring to an object by means of a term that is more restricted in adult use. (Notice that if the word *cat* is in the child's vocabulary, then this could be considered to be an example of underextension of the word *cat,* although it is not recorded as such.) Now suppose the same child sees a poodle but does not realize that this particular creature is an instance of the concept DOG. Either the child will not call it anything in which case nothing will be recorded in the diary, or he will name it with some inappropriate term in which case his response will be recorded but will be viewed as a case of overgeneralization of the inappropriate term. In other words, the child either uses a word appropriately or he does not. Whenever he uses the word appropriately his response is counted as correct. Whenever he does not use the word appropriately his response is counted as incorrect and an instance of overextension. In this way diary studies are systematically biased to show overextension and to suggest differentiation (narrowing down categories) as the developmental process. They cannot show underextension, and therefore they cannot reveal the process of generalization (filling out categories) if it occurs in the development of verbal concepts. It is possible, therefore, that overgeneralization is like the tip of an iceberg, the most visible but neither the only nor necessarily the most prevalent component of the child's early referential problems.

The possibility that the young child might undergeneralize as well as overgeneralize his first terms of reference has by now been pointed out by a number of authors (see, for example, Bloom, 1973; Nelson, 1973b, 1974). Over the last few years my colleagues and I have conducted a series of studies examining the tendency of children to overextend and underextend their first terms of reference. We have found that children do in fact make both kinds of responses. Indeed, in one study in which we attempted to create an equal opportunity for both kinds of responses we found that children made about twice as many underextensions as overextensions. It is not my intention, however, to argue that the child's propensity to make one kind of response is greater than his propensity to make another. Rather my position is that he in fact makes both and that the task for a psychologist is to discern and to try to understand the conditions under which he will make either. Our work has suggested that whether the child will overgeneralize or undergeneralize a given term of reference depends on at least the following three factors: (1) the particular child in question, (2) the particular terms of reference being investigated, and (3) the nature of the instances and noninstances of the concept being tested.

With respect to the child in question, some children will overextend certain terms, whereas others will underextend those same terms; others will both overextend and underextend them, while still others will do neither much relative to adult standards.

With respect to the word being investigated, certain verbal concepts are usually overgeneralized by children, whereas others are usually under-generalized. For example, the preschool child's concept of FLOWER often extends beyond the adult's concept of FLOWER since the child often includes several other kinds of plants (e.g., elephant's ear, philodendron, cactus, etc.) in the category FLOWER. On the other hand, the child's concept of PLANT is often less general than the adult's concept of PLANT since the child will often not include certain kinds of plants (such as trees and sometimes flowers) in the category PLANT. Thus the concept FLOWER usually becomes more restricted with development, whereas the concept PLANT usually becomes more general.

We have conducted a number of studies in an attempt to discern the nature of the noninstances of a verbal concept which are likely to produce overextensions and the nature of the instances of a verbal concept which are likely to produce underextensions. With respect to overextensions our earlier work had suggested that three attributes of noninstances might be important in enticing the child to make such responses: (1) perceptual similarity—the noninstance is perceptually similar to an instance of the concept; (2) association through contiguity—the noninstance has been seen in the presence of an instance of the concept; and (3) functional similarity—the noninstance serves the same function for the child as an instance of the concept. In further studies we had adult judges rate various pictures with respect to these three dimensions for various concepts and then tested children to see which of these pictures were most likely to produce overextensions. Stimuli rated as "perceptually similar" to instances of a concept (e.g., balloon to APPLE) produced by far the most overextensions; stimuli rated as "likely to be contiguous" to an instance of a concept (e.g., saddle to HORSE) produced some overextensions; stimuli rated as "serving the same function" as an instance of the concept (e.g., sled to CAR) produced virtually no overextensions unless they were also rated as being "perceptually similar" or "contiguous." (It should be noted here, however, that it was extremely difficult for us to find pictures of objects which adults rated as being functionally similar to an instance of a concept but not perceptually similar. For example, a truck was rated as being functionally similar to CAR but also perceptually similar as well as likely to be seen in the presence of cars.)

With respect to underextensions, our earlier work had suggested that two factors may play a role in enticing the child to make such responses. First it seemed that children would often not count as instances those which intuitively did not seem to be typical examples or "central" instances (cf. Rosch, 1973, 1975) of the concept being tested. Second, children sometimes seemed to exclude familiar instances from general concepts which often seemed to be the result of their having another name for that instance ("That's a tree, not a plant"), which suggested that they did not fully appreciate that a single object can belong to more than one category at once or, to put it another way, that a given object has several equally valid names (cf. Inhelder & Piaget, 1969). Therefore, in a further study we asked adult judges to rate various pictures of objects along the two dimensions of centrality to a given concept and familiarity. On the basis of the adult ratings we chose four different kinds of instances (central-familiar, central-unfamiliar, peripheral-familiar, and peripheral-unfamiliar) for the four concepts (ANIMAL, FOOD, CLOTHING, and BIRD). We then showed these pictures to children, asking them, "Is this an animal?," "Is this food?," etc., depending on which picture was shown. The results showed that children almost always included instances which had been judged by adults as central to a concept whether they were familiar (horse to ANIMAL) or unfamiliar (aardvark to ANIMAL), whereas they often failed to include instances which had been judged by adults as being peripheral, whether familiar (butterfly to ANIMAL) or unfamiliar (centipede to ANIMAL). Although the effect was not so strong, children significantly more often excluded familiar instances from concepts than unfamiliar instances, which often seemed to be a result of the fact that they knew a dominant name for a familiar instance ("That's a butterfly, not an animal") which they did not know for unfamiliar instances (e.g., centipede).

I would like to discuss one other feature of this study. Before we tested the children on the pictures we asked them to define the concepts ANIMAL, FOOD, CLOTHING, and BIRD, which were the concepts we then tested in the main experiment. The definitions provided by the children for these terms were structurally different from those provided by a group of adults whom we also tested in this study. Children usually either listed instances of the concept (e.g., ANIMAL—"lion, tiger, dog"; FOOD—"carrots") or described the function of instances of the concept (FOOD—"to eat"; CLOTHING—"you wear it on you") or described an action of instances of the concept (BIRD—"it flies"). Adults almost always defined these concepts in terms of a superordinate class and a set of defining attributes (e.g., "an animal is a living creature that moves."). These differences are consistent with the findings of other studies of children's definitions (e.g., Feifel & Lorge, 1950). Moreover, the definitions provided by a child were often inconsistent with his performance in the extension study. That is, the child would often include instances in or exclude instances from a given concept in a way that violated the definition that he had earlier provided. For example, when asked to define *food* one child responded "eat it" but in the classification task said that edible objects such as a piece of bread, a lollipop, and ketchup were not *food*.

Children gave little evidence of relying on definitions at all in the extension study, and we felt that had we not asked the child for a definition of these terms he would not have attempted to formulate verbal criteria at all in the classification task. The classifications provided by adults, on the other hand, were for the most part consistent with the definitions that they had given for the various concepts. Moreover, on those few occasions where adults were inconsistent they would often point out the discrepancy, suggesting that they were keeping their definitions in mind in the classification task. For example, one adult had defined a bird as "a kind of animal that flies and has feathers" and then when shown a picture of a penquin and asked if it was a *bird* he answered that it was but pointed out that he was being inconsistent with his previous definition and that his definition should be changed since not all birds fly.

Thus children do not seem to consciously verbalize criterial attributes in assigning objects to categories, whereas adults often do. How, then, do children identify objects as instances of categories? Although I think the terms are problematic (see Goodman, 1968; Schwartz, 1968), the findings noted above and indeed most of the studies described in the latter half of this chapter seem consistent with the notion advanced by other authors that the child's concepts are stored "iconically" whereas the adult's concepts are stored "symbolically" as well as iconically, (see Bruner, Olver, & Greenfield, 1966, and especially Posner, 1973, Chapters 3 and 4; also see Piaget, 1962, pp. 213–291). Our results on the underextension responses made by children bear some affinity to the recent work on the formation of schemas or prototypes in adults (see, for example Franks & Bransford, 1971; Posner, 1969; Posner & Keele, 1968, 1970; Reed, 1972; see also Rosch, 1973, 1975). These studies have suggested that when presented with a series of instances of a given concept subjects tend to form a schema or a prototype which is an internal representation of the central tendency of the instances presented. Subjects appear to store in memory a prototype along with information about the individual instances of a concept and some notion of the breadth or "tightness" of the concept which they can later employ when identifying instances of that concept. Posner (1973), in reviewing the work on the formation of prototypes, argues that it is a relatively primitive process performed by animals as well as by humans and does not require deliberately analyzing a concept into a set of attributes or features, which he argues is a more advanced process.

Our findings concerning underextension and overextension in children suggest that their first concepts may be stored in terms of a prototype as well. The fact that children will usually include instances rated as central to concepts whereas they will often not include instances rated as peripheral is consistent with such an argument. The fact that children's overextensions are predominantly to noninstances which are perceptually similar to instances of a given concept is consistent with the notion that at least part of what is stored may be the typical form of the instances of a given concept, that is, a prototype. And the fact that children do not seem to attempt to analyze a concept consciously into its criterial attributes when identifying instances of that concept suggests that they are probably relying on some more primitive process in their classification which may well involve a prototype or schema. These findings, while consistent with the notion that children store a prototype or schema of the instances of a concept, might only indicate that they store images of specific instances of that concept which they have seen before. However, one of our most intriguing findings is that young children almost invariably recognize totally unfamiliar objects as instances of a concept provided they are central to that concept. For example, 20 out of 20 children in the underextension study identified a wombat and an aardvark as *animals* even though they had never seen a wombat or an aardvark before. Such a finding is similar to the findings of Posner and Keele (1968, 1970), Franks and Bransford (1971), and others that subjects will recognize a prototype as an instance of a concept or pattern even though they have never seen it before and suggests that part of what is stored may be a prototype rather than just specific examples. I am not arguing that a prototype is the only mental structure by means of which children represent concepts. For example, there is evidence that they also store information about individual instances of the concept and about the functions and the actions of instances of the concept. But I am advancing the hypothesis that one important component of the child's representation of his first concepts is a prototype or schema which represents the central tendency of the instances of the concept to which he has been exposed.

CONCLUSIONS

If the arguments presented above are well founded, this work has a number of implications for a theory of the development of the symbolic system known technically as English nomenclature.

1. The functions of objects will determine the order in which the child will learn names for those objects. Specifically, many of the category labels the child will first learn will be names of objects with which he will interact in his daily activities. These activities will include biologically basic endeavors such as eating food but also other activities not so intimately related to survival such as playing with toys and simply paying attention to objects which move and change in interesting ways in his environment. Moreover, the terms he will initially learn from his parents to name these objects will categorize them in maximally useful ways in the sense that these terms will group together objects which the child should behave toward in the same way.

2. From an early age these concepts will be represented in terms of their typical form, possibly in terms of a prototype. In addition to information about typical form the child will also store other information about a concept such as its name, its individual instances, their functions, and their actions. The child is unlikely, however, to consciously analyze or decompose a concept into a set of criterial attributes or features.

3. For the adult the names of objects constitute an organized system of interrelated concepts. For example, he appreciates the hierarchical relations among verbal concepts (see, for example, Bower, Clark, Lesgold, & Winzenz, 1969; Collins & Quillian, 1969, 1972; Mandler, 1967; Miller, 1967, 1969) so that he knows, for instance, that OAKS are TREES and that TREES are PLANTS. Preschool children, however, have not organized their verbal concepts into such a system, at least not consciously. For example, in the classification tasks described above they often failed to realize that the objects they called *trees* are also called *plants,* and in attempting to define concepts they usually failed to assign those concepts to superordinate classes, which adults almost always

did. The absence of a hierarchical system of interrelated concepts is a striking feature of the child's semantic memory. The evidence (cf. Anglin, 1970; Bruner & Olver, 1973; Vygotsky, 1962) indicates that such a system develops only gradually after the child has gone to school.

ACKNOWLEDGMENTS

This chapter was presented at a conference, Symbolization and the Young Child, held at Wheelock College, Boston, Massachusetts, November 1975. It is a revised version of a paper entitled "Les Premiers Termes de Référence de l'Enfant," published in French in the *Special Issue of the Bulletin de Psychologie on Semantic Memory* edited by S. Ehrlich and E. Tulving, 1976. The research described all too briefly in this chapter has been presented in detail in a recent book (Anglin, 1977). I would like to thank the following people for their assistance in carrying out the studies on which this paper is based: Maryellen Ruvolo, Marvin Cohen, Ruth Berger, Kay Tolbert, Joy Skon, Yvette Sheline, David Rubin, Janet Zeller, and, especially, Elizabeth Smith. The research was supported in part by a grant, Grant No. OEG1-71-111(508), from the Office of Education to the author.

REFERENCES

Anglin, J. M. *The growth of word meaning.* Cambridge, Mass.: The M. I. T. Press, 1970.
Anglin, J. M. *Word, object, and conceptual development.* New York: Norton, 1977.
Bloom, L. M. *One word at a time.* The Hague: Mouton, 1973.
Bower, G. H., Clark, M. C., Lesgold, A. M., & Winzenz, D. Hierarchical retrieval schemes in recall of categorized word lists. *Journal of Verbal Learning and Verbal Behavior,* 1969, *8,* 323–343.
Brown, R., *Words and things.* Glencoe, Ill.: Free Press, 1958. (a)
Brown, R. How shall a thing be called? *Psychological Review,* 1958, *65,* 14–21. (b)
Brown, R. *Social psychology.* New York: The Free Press, 1965.
Brown, R. *A first language: The early stages.* Cambridge, Mass.: Harvard University Press, 1973.
Bruner, J. S., & Olver, R. R. Development of equivalence transformations in children. In J. S. Bruner, *Beyond the information given* J. M. Anglin (Ed.) New York: Norton, 1973.
Bruner, J. S., & Olver, R. R., & Greenfield, P.M. *Studies in cognitive growth.* New York: Wiley, 1966.
Chamberlain, A. F., & Chamberlain, J. C. Studies of a child (I and II). *Pedagogical Seminary,* 1904, *11,*(3, 4), 264–292, 452–484.
Clark, E. V. What's in a word? On the child's acquisition of semantics in his first language. In T. E. Moore (Ed.), *Cognitive development and the acquisition of language.* New York: Academic Press, 1973.
Clark, H. Space, time, semantics and the child. In T. E. Moore (Ed.), *Cognitive development and the acquisition of language.* New York: Academic Press, 1973.
Collins, A. M., & Quillian, M. R. Retrieval time from semantic memory. *Journal of Verbal Learning and Verbal Behavior,* 1969, *8,*(2), 240–247.

Collins, A. M., & Quillian, M. R. How to make a language user. In E. Tulving & W. Donaldson (Eds.), *Organization of memory.* New York: Academic Press, 1972.

Feifel, H., & Lorge, I. Qualitative differences in the vocabulary responses of children. *Journal of Educational Psychology,* 1950, *41,* 1–18.

Franks, J. J., & Bransford, J. D. Abstraction of visual patterns. *Journal of Experimental Psychology,* 1971, *90,* 65–74.

Goodman, N. *Languages of art: An approach to a theory of symbols.* New York: Bobbs-Merrill, 1968.

Goodman, N. On likeness of meaning. In N. Goodman (Ed.) *Problems and projects.* New York: Bobbs-Merrill, 1972.

Howes, D. H. A word count of spoken English. *Journal of verbal learning and verbal behavior,* 1966, *5,* 572–604.

Inhelder, B., & Piaget, J. *The early growth of logic in the child.* New York: Norton, 1969.

Leopold, W. F. *Speech development of a bilingual child: A linguist's record* (Vol. I). Evanston, Ill.: Northwestern University Press, 1939.

Leopold, W. F. Semantic learning in infant language. *Word,* 1948, *4,*(3), 173–180.

Mandler, G. Organization and memory. In K. W. Spence & J. T. Spence (Eds.), *The Psychology of learning and motivation* (Vol. I). New York: Academic Press, 1967.

Miller, G. A. Psycholinguistic approaches to the study of communication. In D. L. Arm (Ed.), *Journeys in science: Small steps—Great strides.* Albuquerque: University of New Mexico Press, 1967.

Miller, G. A. A psychological method to investigate verbal concepts. *Journal of Mathematical Psychology,* 1969, *6,* 169–191.

Miller, G. A. English verbs of motion: A case study in semantics and lexical memory. In A. W. Melton and E. Martin (Eds.), *Coding processes in human memory.* Washington, D.C.: Winston, 1972.

Moore, K. C. The mental development of a child. *Psychological Review Monograph Supplements,* 1896, *1*(3).

Nelson, K. Some evidence for the cognitive primacy of categorization and its functional basis. *Merrill-Palmer Quarterly of Behavior and Development,* 1973, *19,* 21–39. (a)

Nelson, K. Structure and strategy in learning to talk. *Society for Research in Child Development Monographs,* 1973, *38*(1-2 serial no. 149). (b)

Nelson, K. Concept, word and sentence: Interrelations in acquisition and development. *Psychological Review,* 1974, *81,* 267–285.

Piaget, J. *Play, dreams and imitation.* New York: Norton, 1962.

Posner, M. I. Abstraction and the process of recognition. In G. H. Bower & J. T. Spence (Eds.), *The psychology of learning and motivation* (Vol. 3), New York: Academic Press, 1969.

Posner, M. I. *Cognition: An introduction.* Glenview, Ill.: Scott, Foresman, 1973.

Posner, M. I., & Keele, S. W. On the genesis of abstract ideas. *Journal of Experimental Psychology,* 1968, *77,* 353–363.

Posner, M. I., & Keele, S. W. Retention of abstract ideas, *Journal of Experimental Psychology,* 1970, *83,* 304–308.

Reed, S. K. Pattern recognition and categorization. *Cognitive Psychology,* 1972, *3,* 382–407.

Rinsland, H. D. *A basic vocabulary of elementary school children.* New York: Macmillan, 1945.

Rosch, E. H. On the internal structure of perceptual and semantic categories. In T. E. Moore (Ed.), *Cognitive development and the acquisition of language.* New York: Academic Press, 1973.

Rosch, E. H. Universals and cultural specifics in human categorization. In R. Brislin, S. Bochner, & W. Lonner (Eds.), *Cross-cultural perspectives on learning.* New York: Sage-Halsted Press, 1975.

Rosch, E. H., Mervis, C. B., Gray, W., Johnson, D. M., & Boyes-Braem, P. Basic objects in natural categories. *Cognitive Psychology,* 1976, *8,* 382–439.

Schwartz, R. Review of *Studies in cognitive growth* by J. S. Bruner et al. *Journal of Philosophy,* 1968, *65,* 172–179.

Slobin, D. I. Developmental psycholinguistics. In W. O. Dingwall (Ed.), *A survey of linguistic science.* College Park, Md.: University of Maryland, Linguistics Program, 1971.

Stern, W. *The psychology of early childhood.* New York: Holt, 1924.

Thorndike, E. L., & Lorge, I. *The teacher's word book of 30,000 Words.* New York: Columbia University, Bureau of Publications, Teachers College, 1944.

Vygotsky, L. S. *Thought and language.* (E. Hanfmann and G. Vakar, Trans.). Cambridge, Mass.: The M. I. T. Press, 1962.

11 Learning To Use Language in Two Modes

James Britton
University of London, London, England

INTRODUCTION

In 1962, quite unaware that I was putting forward a notion that had been proposed 25 years earlier, I suggested that *gossip* and not *the anecdote* ("Have you heard this one?") was the essential spoken counterpart of what we know as *literature*. "The distinction that matters, it seems to me, is not whether the events recounted are true or fictional, but whether we recount them (or listen to them) as *spectators* or as *participants;* and whenever we play the role of spectator of human affairs I suggest we are in the position of literature" (Britton, 1963).

Four years later I prepared a paper on "Response to Literature" for the Dartmouth Anglo-American Seminar on the Teaching of English. After roughly defining literature as "a particular kind of utterance—an utterance that a writer has 'constructed' not for use but for his own satisfaction," I went on: "Sapir pointed out long ago that man, unlike the zoological animals, does not handle reality by direct and *ad hoc* means but via a symbolic representation of the world as he has experienced it. Given this, two courses are open to a man: he may operate in the real world by means of his representation, or he may operate *directly upon the representation itself—* improvising upon it in any way that pleases him (that allays his anxieties, for example, or sweetens his disappointments, or whets his appetite, or flatters his ego). We all use language in both these ways, to get things done in the outer world and to manipulate the inner world. Action and decision belong to the former use; freedom from them in the latter enables us to attend to other things—to the forms of language, the patterns of events, the feelings. We take up as it were the role of spectators: spectators of our own past lives, our imagined futures, other men's lives, impossible events. When we *speak* this *language,* the nearest name I can give it is 'gossip'; when we *write* it, it is literature" (Squire, 1968).

My paper was discussed by a Dartmouth working party under the chairmanship of D. W. Harding, the English psychologist. It was then that I discovered that Harding's own article, "The Role of the Onlooker," published in *Scrutiny* in 1937, had formulated this same distinction and associated "gossip" with the novel as two forms in which we take up the role of spectator of recounted or symbolically represented events. He drew the important conclusion that "if we could obliterate the effects on a man of all the occasions when he was 'merely a spectator' it would be profoundly to alter his character and outlook" (Harding, 1937).

It is the nature of the distinction between the roles of participant and spectator as they are reflected in young children's uses of language that I want to explore here.

WHY WRITE (WHEN YOU CAN SPEAK)?

Since young children's talk rapidly becomes a fluid and flexible instrument adapted to many purposes, it may be helpful, in attempting to establish a distinction among its uses, to look first at their writing. I have known a number of children who have taught themselves to write, that is, who have learned to write without the help of deliberate teaching. Their first writings in all these cases have been stories. Usually they have begun by composing stories for someone else to write down; sometimes at this stage they do "pretend writing," and by processes I cannot explain there comes a day when, hey presto, they are writing their own stories for themselves. Thus, one child produced six tiny closely filled pages of the following sort before she was 4:

⸺ a ⸺ ⸺ the ⸺ and ⸺ ⸺ a ⸺

and the following clearly decipherable effort before she was 6:

> once theire was a little lizrd that lived in a pond. And one day a boy was fishing in the pond and he caught the little lizard he put it in his hand. he then put it back in the pond. he rushed back home....

It is typical of these early attempts at writing that they constitute storybooks. We might conjecture that their introduction to the written language as listeners has convinced these children that writing exists to record stories and that any intention to write on their part is conceived of as one of adding their own stories to the world's stock of children's storybooks.

I read the story one 4-year-old had dictated to his mother, and it contained the sentence "The king went sadly home for he had nowhere else to go." I was interested in the use of "for" to mean "because"; it was clearly a form that his parents did not use in speech: The boy had already internalized this item of the written language from listening to fairy stories.

When children learn to write in this way I believe they have at some point to make what amounts to a fresh start in acquiring mastery of writing. Before they come to use writing to cover a range of the purposes for which they already use speech, they have to sever its exclusive link with the language of stories and establish a more general connection between their speech and their writing. Their total language resources up to this point, with a very few exceptions such as the one I quoted above, have been recruited in the spoken mode; they need now to tap those resources for use in the new mode, that of writing. William, a 6-year-old American boy in whose family I once stayed, had gone through the stages of dictating stories and then writing his own. One morning I was sleeping in after a very heavy day, and the family was committed to keeping quiet; when the time came for William to get ready for school, he found a scrap of paper and wrote on it, "Ples ti my shos"—the first time his parents had seen him use the written language as a substitute for everyday speech. As a first move toward the distinction I want to make in this chapter, I would distinguish between storytelling language and the use of language *to get things done*—whether it be the tying of shoes or anything else.

Why should stories so appeal to children that they may identify the value of writing with the writing of stories? It seems reasonable to suppose that they are enticed by the freedom stories allow them—freedom to improvise upon what seems to them the "real world" and so construct temporary worlds in which *anything may happen*. They may use that freedom to portray the fulfillment of quite realistic desires on the one hand or to project extravagant fancies on the other. The 6-year-old who wrote

> One day a girl was very exceited her name was Sivveia and she was 15. She was ecieted becuase she was going to have a horse the next week. As the day's came nearer Silveia got more and more excieted and the day before it arrived her mother bought her some Jodphers and the next day it came.

was the girl who a few months earlier had written the story of the little lizard that lived in a pond. Here is the rest of that story:

> When he had told his Mother about it she said there is a dragon burning the flowers in our garden Oh said the boy I will kill it Oh dont said the Mother I will tonight and so he got his brother to help him. They waited till darkness At last Leyew that was boys name and his brother saw the Dragon with slashing sword his brother ran to the dragon ROAR went Dragon the brother was frightened then it was Lewews turn he went up to the dragon will you be my

Mathter said the Dragon yes said Leyew then the Dragon said bring me your brother and I will warm you both. Were is my brother said Leyew up a tree said the Dragon Oh thanc you But dont over warm us you shall thrust me all right I will go and bring him did you know that you ruscued me once when I was a Baby Lizard and now I am a big monster animal sobbed the Dragon. We will keep you said chage that was the brother's name so in the morning they told thier Mother all abuot it and now wath the children like best is riding the Dragon.

There is a continuum in the children's writings from the autobiographical narrative to the fictional—as indeed there is in the stories that concern us as adults. We embroider the events of our lives as we recount them, and even our nightmares are rooted in our life experiences.

PLAY AND PERFORMANCE IN CHILDREN'S SPEECH

Patricia at 9 wrote a story called "A Snow Day." It tells of a very old lady and man who lived in a very old cottage, a cottage that was always getting covered up in snow. "And if they was in it they could't get out but if they were not in it they couldn't get in." They arranged to move to a better home, but on the morning of the move the old lady woke to find there had been a snowfall and "the snow was three miles higher than her house and all her pipes had burst, and her house was flooded out. But one room wasn't and the woman and the man flooded the other room out with their tears." This playful turn in the way events are handled is echoed in much of the speech of young children. It is a characteristic part of the pleasure they find in speaking. If we are to believe Michael Oakeshott (1959), all early speech is speaking for the pleasure of it:

> Everybody's young days are a dream, a delightful insanity, a miraculous confusion of poetry and practical activity in which nothing has a fixed shape and nothing has a fixed price. "Fact" and "not fact" are still indistinct. To act is to make a bargain with events; there are obscure longings, there are desires and choices, but their objects are imperfectly discerned; everything is "what it turns out to be." And to speak is to make images. For, although we spend much of our early days in learning the symbolic language of practical intercourse... this is not the language with which we begin as children. Words in everyday use are not signs with fixed and invariable usages; they are poetic images. We speak an heroic language of our own invention, not merely because we are incompetent in our handling of symbols, but because we are moved not by the desire to communicate but by the delight of utterance (p. 61)".

It is that final duality I want to take up: I believe it contains the germ of the distinction I want to make, and I believe utterances of both kinds will be found in varying proportions at all stages of development. "The desire to communicate" leads us to employ language as a means to nonlinguistic ends, a way of getting things done in the world. "The delight of utterance" represents language as an end in itself: talk as an end in itself, that is (in some senses), talk for the sake of talking; talk as a pleasurable activity; or perhaps— if we could pin down an illusive idea—talk *as play.* "To play with something" would certainly seem to be the converse of "putting it to a useful purpose." To play with a substance—putty, for example—is to be concerned with the nature of the substance in a way that is open to all its characteristics and possibilities rather than only to *some* of them, those appropriate to a useful purpose in mind. With speech, for example, the desire to communicate may safely ignore the noises we actually make when we speak; yet play with speech seems often to consist largely in deriving pleasure from these noises. Ruth Weir's records of the presleep monologues of her 2½-year-old son show how he rings the changes on particular sounds:

bink
let Bobo bink
bink ben bink
blue kink

Moreover, he seems to play with grammatical substance when he rings the changes within a structural slot,

What colour
what colour blanket
what colour mop
what colour glass

and with ideas themselves. As Weir has pointed out, such ideas as "belongingness and hence love" provide an underlying theme for one of his monologues, and variations on the theme weave in and out of his talk in something that suggests rondo form (Weir, 1962).

When children's play takes the form of make-believe, or *symbolic play,* it establishes itself clearly as activity in the spectator role. The ludic symbols are used to reconstruct remembered experiences or to construct imagined ones; the represented events are not actually taking place, and the players in the game cannot therefore be pariticipants in the technical sense on which the distinction is based. In D. W. Harding's (1962) words,

The imaginary spectatorship of fantasy and make-believe play has the special feature of allowing us to look on at ourselves, ourselves as participants in the imagined events—the hero in the rescue fantasy, the victim of assault, the defendant rebutting unjust accusations, the apparent nonentitiy suddenly called to national responsibility. In spite, however, of seeing himself as a participant in the story, the daydreamer, or the child engaged in make-believe, remains an onlooker, too; in all his waking fantasy he normally fills the dual role of participant and spectator, and as spectator he can when need be turn away from the fantasy events and attend again to the demands of real life. (p. 136)

But what of other kinds of play? In a recent article Bruner refers to Vygotsky's statement that "a child's play must always be interpreted as the imaginary, illusory realization of unrealizable desires" (Vygotsky, 1967) but himself assigns that function to symbolic play and suggests that an earlier form of play has different ends in view, those of "extending to new limits already achieved skills." This he calls "mastery play," and he describes it as double-ended: "In the first case a new object is fitted into as many routines as available; in the second, a newly mastered act is addressed to as many objects as available." On these grounds he characterizes play as a type of activity in which "ends are changed to fit available means, and means and ends become admixed" (Bruner, 1973). Anthony Weir's presleep monologues might be seen as an example of play in this sense: Linguistic ability that would in his daytime activity have furthered whatever enterprises he had on hand are now—because he has been put to bed and left alone to go to sleep—available means with no prescribed ends to serve. It is perhaps enough here to suggest that both forms of play—make-believe and mastery—contribute to the delight of utterance and will tend to characterize nonutilitarian forms of speech and moreover that each prefigures in its own way characteristics of the verbal arts, the developed forms of language in the role of spectator. It is indeed no novel idea to relate the purposes of play in childhood with the purposes of the arts in adult life.[1]

From delighting in one's own utterance to offering it for the entertainment of others is a small step, and many children take it. There is of course a shared delight in playful conversation, but I am thinking here of a more deliberate performance. Given a listener willing to be "entertained," many children will deliver "a spiel," a highly characteristic form of sustained utterance, often accompanied by rhythmic movement (such as walking to and fro), often spoken in a rhythmic, incantatory manner, and sometimes even sung. Here is the performance of a 3-year-old; she had just had her dinner, as her reference shows—and it shows also that she is aware that what she is doing is an "it," a performance:

There was a little girl called May
and she had some dollies—
and the weeds were growing in the ground—
and they made a little nest out of sticks

---

[1] See, for a notable example, Winnicott (1971).

for another little birdie up in the trees
and they climbed up the tree—
and the weeds were growing in the ground
(*I can do it much better if there's some food in my tum!*)
the weeds were growing in the ground—
the ghee (?) was in the sun and it was a Sunday—
Now we all gather at the seaside
and the ghee was in London having dinner in a dinner-shop—
and the weeds were growing in the ground—
and we shall go there again—we shall go there again—
we shall go there again
'cos it's a nice Sunday morning and a fine day....

There is a loose narrative structure to the piece, but what marks it more strongly is its 'celebratory' manner: We are reminded that Auden emphasized the value of poetry *as celebration,* as a way of "paying homage by naming" (Auden, 1956).

In both the speech and the writing of young children, then, we can observe a distinction between, on the one hand, what is strictly "a desire to communicate," a use of language as a means to some end beyond itself, a way of "getting things done," and, on the other, a playful use in which speech or writing constitutes an end in itself, entered into for "the delight of utterance," whether that delight takes the form of a story, a celebratory performance, a jingle to dance to, a pleasing incantation, or a game of "mothers and fathers." It is this second category that we have been at pains to illustrate. We have suggested, further, that when young children first learn to write it is mainly writings in the entertaining and playful category that they produce, since their practical demands—giving information or asking for it, making requests, and so on—are mainly met in speech. That language in the first category should be designated "language in the role of participant" needs no explanation since "participating in the world's affairs" is no more than a ponderous way of saying "getting things done." That the second category should be designated "language in the role of spectator" calls, I think, for further comment.

SPECTATOR AND PARTICIPANT ROLES

When we use language to work on a joint task, to get our own way, to buy or sell, to exchange information, to instruct or persuade people, to argue, to quarrel, to solve a problem, or to work out a theory—that is, when we use language to get things done—this is language in the role of participant. When we use language to recreate past experience or create virtual experience as objects of contemplation, this is language in the role of spectator. Mothers use it in gossiping about their children's exploits, footballers use it when they exchange anecdotes after the match, children use it when they play "mothers and fathers"; we all use it when we read or write stories or tell or listen to travelers' tales. As participants, we draw upon our representation of past experience in order to construe the current situation, and our focus is upon making sense of, and acting upon, that situation. As spectators, our focus is upon maintaining the unity and coherence of our total representation of past experience, and with this end in view we work upon experiences in which we have participated, or might participate, but in which we are not presently participating. Thus, evaluation and the organization of feelings and attitudes are important aspects of activity in this role. As participants, we use language to shape experience in order to handle it; as spectators, we use language to digest experience.[2]

Harding pointed out that the purpose behind our willingness to take up the role of spectator is an evaluative one. As participants we evaluate a situation in order to know how to act in it, but our evaluation is subject to the constraints of prudence and practical self-interest. As spectators we have no irons in the fire, no axes to grind, since we do not stand to gain or lose from the events we contemplate. In effect, as participants we *apply* some part of our value system; it is our concern as spectators to develop and refine the system itself. When we gossip about events we offer an evaluation both in the choice of events to talk about and in the construction we place upon them as we talk; what we ask for in return is corroboration or modification of the values we offer. To have our value systems confirmed by those fellow members of our society with whom we are in sympathy constitutes in Harding's words "a basic social satisfaction" (Harding, 1963).

Corroboration of this important idea has come recently from an unexpected quarter. Labov and Waletzky (1967), in carrying out a linguistic analysis of oral narratives of personal experience, found it essential to distinguish two types of clause: narrative clauses, identified by virtue of the fact that they are undisplaceable in the serial order of clauses, and other clauses which are to some extent displaceable. To these latter clauses they assign the function "evaluative," and where they find narratives which contain no such clauses (and no implicit evaluation in the narrative clauses) they label them "empty or pointless narratives." That is, we ordinarily recount experiences for an essentially evaluative purpose.

SUBJECTIVE AND OBJECTIVE ORDERS

When Susanne Langer distinguishes between discursive and presentational symbols and speculates on the inferences to be drawn from that distinction, she provides the final touches to the view I want to present here. Her thesis is

---

[2]Amplification of this summary statement may be found in Britton (1971) and Britton, Burgess, Martin, McLeod and Rosen (1975).

set out in two weighty volumes under the title *Mind: An Essay on Human Feeling* (Langer, 1967 & 1972); clearly I can offer no more than the barest outline of her main idea. By means of *discursive symbolism,* a rule-governed system for public intercommunication (principally exemplified in discursive language), we analyze, organize, interpret, and communicate our experiences of the perceptible world. To this end, the organizing principles of the system include the screening out of the purely individual cum unique aspects of experience (notably the feelings—those aspects of every human experience that originate within the experiencer). What is achieved is an ordering of a familiar kind, the cognitive order—logical, verifiable, and public—the order in which information is received, handled, and stored in every sphere of operations from the everyday to the scientific or philosophical. The fully developed *presentational symbol* reflects another order, one far less familiar and about which far less is known: the order that inheres in a work of art. The principles governing the organization of a work of art do not demand any distinction between thought and feeling, cognition and affect; that distinction is an artefact of the alternative system, the cognitive. A work of art is not a communication encoded in a symbol system (as is a discursive utterance) but rather is itself a single, unique, and complex symbol. It is complex in structure in order to carry meaning at a variety of levels; private and personal aspects of experience are conveyed by giving them resonance within the unified and intricate structure.

All that is very general: How can we hope to specify the organizational principles by which human experience is projected into a work of art? Langer's speculations are still at an exploratory stage. She suggests, as one example, a parallel with the process of "physiognomic perception" as psychologists have described it (a global, dynamic way of perceiving which responds to expressiveness at the expense of detail) (Langer, 1967); as another example, a parallel with the concept of "symbol" as Freud used it in accounting for dreams (Langer, 1964); and above all a process of representing the tensions and resolutions "which by their very occurrence . . . immediately generate structure" and which relate a work of art to the phases characteristic of every living act, the shape of the elements that make up the continuum of life (Langer 1967). It is by such means, she argues, that the quality of an inner experience is arrested for contemplation and expressed, made communicable to other human beings.

To return briefly to the spectator/participant distinction, we may now add two glosses that relate Langer's ideas to our own. We have illustrated utterance in spectator role by referring to gossip on the one hand and the verbal arts, literature, on the other. Gossip stands at the informal end of the spectrum and literature at the "formal" end. In other words, the farther we move from gossip toward literature, the greater the degree of organization and the more fully Langer's laws governing presentational symbols will be operating. What we have at the extreme is a "verbal object," a unified and self-contained virtual experience, isolated from the rest of life. To speaker, writer, or reader, this will constitute *an experience of order.*

A similar spectrum, applying a different set of organizational laws, the cognitive, will move from the informal use of language for practical purposes to the deliberate use of language adapted to the purpose of carrying out sophisticated verbal transactions. The informal ends of both scales may be characterized as *expressive* language—language that is not projected far from the speaker, the language of everyday face-to-face speech, more or less context bound, loosely structured to reflect a speaker's preoccupations—language that relies on an interest in the speaker as well as in his message. This gives us, in simple diagram form,

Language in the role ___ ___ ___ ___ ___ | ___ ___ ___ ___ Language in the role
  of Participant | of Spectator
TRANSACTIONAL _____ EXPRESSIVE _____ POETIC
                                |

In terms of linguistic competence, an utterance in expressive language is one in which the *rules of use* are at their least demanding; development in either direction will involve the taking on of one or the other of two distinct sets of rules of use.

SOME DEVELOPMENTAL STAGES

Clearly, in the early stages expressive speech will be an all-purpose instrument from which, in the face of particular demands, a range of adapted forms, both of speech and writing, will develop. Three major dimensions in that development will be the move from immature to mature expressive language, that from expressive to transactional, and that from expressive to poetic. Looking first at the development of transactional language, we may note that the greater number of our verbal transactions concern the handling of information. It is surely a sound developmental principle that what we learn about the world should be founded upon a process in which objective knowledge, information, is derived from our own first-hand experience. It is a process which relies heavily upon talking and writing as its means, yet schools in general have made the mistake of outlawing written forms of the process from the teaching/learning dialogue. Here is an exception, a piece of writing by a 10-year-old boy in a Yorkshire primary school:

How I Filtered my Water Specimens

When we were down at Mr. Haris's farm I brought some water from the brook back with me. I took some from a shallow place by the oak tree, and some from a deep place by the walnut tree. I got the specimens by placing a jar in the brook and let the water run into it. Then I brought them back to school to filter. . . . The experiment that I did shows that where the water was deeper and was not running fast there was a lot more silt suspended as little particles in the water. You could see this by looking at the filter paper, where the water was shallow and fast there was less dirt suspended in it.

Mr. Harris, the oak tree, and the walnut tree were a part of the experience as the writer knew it; they are not a part of the objective knowledge—the scientific facts—he is in the process of deriving from that experience. In terms of language, these expressive features in the writing keep the experience alive in the record; as the writer becomes more skillful at deriving facts from experience he will shed the expressive features to move into a transactional mode without losing his grip upon the experience which is the source of his information. In more general terms, we must stress the value of expressive talk and expressive writing as instruments of learning in the elementary school.

A fascinating study of some of the stages by which young children take over the conventions and operational principles of spectator role utterance has been made by Applebee (1978). He found that children as young as 2½ begin to adopt some of the simpler conventions of story form (the consistent past tense, the opening formula "Once upon a time," and the closing formula "happy ever after"). By 6, they show established expectations about the sorts of things that are likely to happen in stories and the kinds of characters that are likely to appear; conventional attributes already work for them—those of the witch, the fairy, the lion, the fox, and so on. He found a systematic development in children from 2 to 5 in the structure of the stories they tell; using two notions of "centering" and "chaining," he plotted a sequence of structures quite closely resembling the stages Vygotsky plotted for concept formation (Vygotsky, 1962). One of the most interesting developmental changes he studied was that of the child's perception of the relationship between events in a story and his own life experiences. For the very young child the two worlds are virtually one: even the 6-year-old will sometimes hotly defend the real existence of his favorite storybook characters. "The progression seems to be from total acceptance of story characters to a stage at which they are real but very far away, to an awareness of insurmountable contradictions between what story characters do and the child's knowledge of the possible. At this last stage, story characters become 'just a story'" (Applebee, 1973).

The 10-year-old from Yorkshire illustrated for us the use of language in the participant role as a means of exploring the external world, a means of making sense of his experiences in it. We have an 8-year-old from Toronto now to illustrate how taking up the role of spectator may be a means of *digesting* experience, of coming to terms inwardly with the events of our lives. Like the other piece, it shows a transitional phase but illustrates it more graphically since the change takes place within the single piece of writing. From a perfunctory beginning—expressive at least in the sense that it is very loosely structured—those organizational principles we cannot yet specify begin to take over and shape his writing. The boy in the story is, of course, the writer himself:

> Once upon a time there was a little boy, and he didn't have a mother or a father. One day he was walking in the forest. He saw a rabbit. It led him to a house. There was a book inside of the house. He looked at the book and saw a pretty animal. It was called a horse. He turned the page and saw a picture of a rabbit, a rabbit just like he had seen in the forest. He turned the page again and saw a cat. He thought of his mother and father and when he was small and they had books for him and animals for him to play with. He thought about this and he started to cry.
> While he was crying a lady said, "What's the matter, boy?"
> He slowly looked round and saw his mother.
> He said, "Is it really you?"
> "Yes my son. I'm your mother."
> "Mother, mother are you alive?"
> "No child. This is the house that I was killed in."
> "Oh mother why are you here?"
> "Because I came back to look for you."
> "Why mother? Why did you come back to look for me?"
> "Because I miss you."
> "Where is father?"
> "He is in the coffin that he was buried in. But don't talk about that now. How are you son? You're bigger and I'm glad to see you."
> "It's been a long time mother."
> While the boy and the mother were talking his father came into the room and said, "Hi son. How are you?"
> "Fine," said the boy, "fine."
> Suddenly the mother and father came to life. The boy was crying, and the mother and father were crying too. God suddenly gave them a miracle to come to life. The boy looked at the mother and father and said, "Oh mother, oh father."

We have suggested that what is afoot when children write stories—autobiographical and fictional—is essentially an evaluative process. In offering their values they offer a part of themselves; the satisfaction they seek is above all that of being accepted.

REFERENCES

Applebee, A. N. *The child's concept of story.* Chicago: Chicago University Press, 1978.
Applebee, A. N. Where does Cinderella live? *The Use Of English,* 1973, *25*(2), 136–141.
Auden, W.H. *Making, knowing and judging.* Oxford: The Clarendon Press, 1956.

Britton, J. N. *The arts in education.* London: Evans Brothers, 1963.

Britton, J. What's the use? A schematic account of language functions. *Educational Review* 1971, *23*(3).

Britton, J., Burgess, T., Martin, N., McLeod, A., & Rosen, H. *The development of writing abilities (11 to 18).* London, Macmillan Education, 1975.

Bruner, J. S. Organisation of early skilled action. *Child Development*, 1973, *44*, 1-11.

Harding, D. W. The role of the onlooker. *Scrutiny*, 1937, *VI*(3), 247-258.

Harding, D. W. Psychological processes in the reading of fiction. *British Journal of Aesthetics*, 1962, *II* (2), 134-147.

Harding, D. W. *Social psychology and individual values* (rev. ed.). London: Hutchinson & Company, 1963.

Labov, W., & Waletzky, J. Narrative analysis: Oral versions of personal experience. In J. Helm (Ed.), *Essays on the verbal and visual arts, Proceedings of the 1966 Annual Spring Meeting of the American Ethnological Society*, 1967.

Langer, S. K. *Philosophical sketches.* Baltimore: The Johns Hopkins University Press, 1964.

Langer, S. K. *Mind: An essay on human feeling* (Vols. I and II). Baltimore: The Johns Hopkins University Press, 1967 & 1972.

Oakeshott, M. *The voice of poetry in the conversation of mankind.* London: Bowes and Bowes, 1959.

Squire, J. R. (Ed.). *Response to literature.* Champaign, Ill.: National Council of Teachers of English, 1968.

Vygotsky, L. S. *Thought and Language.* Cambridge, Mass.: The M. I. T. Press, 1962.

Vygotsky, L. S. Play and its role in the mental development of the Child. *Soviet Psychology*, 1967, *5*(3), 6-18.

Weir, R. H. *Language in the crib.* The Hague: Mouton, 1962.

Winnicott, D. W. *Playing and reality.* London: Tavistock Publications, 1971.

12 Metalinguistic Functioning in Development

Margery B. Franklin
Sarah Lawrence College

In the everyday world, we carry out a wide range of activities in varied contexts and in relation to varied goals, sometimes with conscious intent and a grasp of factors in the situation (as in building a table or giving a lecture) and sometimes in a less thoughtful, more automatic way (as in playing tennis or acknowledging a greeting). A large proportion of *performances-in-context* can be readily conceptualized in pragmatic, means-ends terms. There is another type of performance which seems to rest on taking a markedly different stance toward one's activity. In these *reflective performances* the focus is on the activity itself, the material in use, and/or the relation between means, ends, and context.

Speaking most often occurs as a performance-in-context, an activity geared toward the expression of feeling, transmission of information, formulation of ideas for oneself or others, influencing of other persons, etc. As a performance-in-context, it is modulated and influenced by multiple factors in the situation. Under some circumstances, an act of speaking or a component of the act becomes the focus of attention. An activity (or medium) that ordinarily has the status of instrumentality or means to an end then assumes a different character: It is disembedded from the context of ongoing action and becomes an "object" which can be inspected, operated upon, related to other "objects," and so forth. As indicated earlier, this shift in focus or orientation lies at the center of all reflective performances (here, by definition) and is not limited to the domain of language or speech. While the dividing line between such performances and performances-in-context (or, in other terms, pragmatic-instrumental acts) is not hard and fast, the distinction seems valid on experiential grounds, and it may be central in the analysis of human action.

When Jakobson (1960) identified the metalingual function, he illustrated the kinds of acts that are performed in a speech situation for the purpose of gaining clarification at the moment or acquiring information about the code in some more long-range sense (that is, information about word meanings, syntactic patterns, and perhaps also pronunciation). Cazden (1975) has pointed to the contrast between language-as-instrumentality and language-as-object-of-awareness that is implicit in Jakobson's formulation and has suggested that attending to language forms per se can be regarded as a special type of performance. However, her analysis (discussed further below) elaborates the notion of metalinguistic awareness rather than performance.

I am proposing that metalinguistic functioning be viewed as reflective performance in the sphere of language/speech. In this chapter, the performance metaphor is articulated in terms of *procedures* which are carried out on aspects of speech or language. In the next section, some of these procedures are described and illustrated: I begin with *focusing and disembedding* as the procedures which provide *objects* for further meta-linguistic operations—*differentiating, evaluating, correcting, explicating*, and *relating terms*. The chapter concludes with some further comments on the object in metalinguistic performance, the interpretation of explicating, and the bases of metalinguistic functioning (specifically, the differentiation of speaking from other activity and the emergence of reference).

PROCEDURES IN METALINGUISTIC PERFORMANCE

Focusing and Disembedding

In studying the development of language comprehension and other aspects of cognitive functioning, we often ask children questions or request them to make particular judgments about linguistic items. If they give odd answers or do not respond, we suggest that attention wandered, the instructions were not understood, or the task was not age appropriate.

Alternatively, it could be emphasized that the child did not—perhaps could not—*focus* on a given aspect of language or speech as such, disembedded from the context of discourse. Consider the following (Brown & Bellugi, 1964):

> Another week we noticed that Adam would sometimes pluralize nouns when they should have been pluralized and sometimes would not. We wondered if he could make grammatical judgments about the plural, if he could distinguish a correct form from an incorrect form. "Adam," we asked, "which is right, 'two shoes' or 'two shoe?'" His answer on that occasion, produced with an explosive enthusiasm, was "Pop goes the weasel!" The two-year-old child does not make a perfectly docile experimental subject. (p. 134)

TABLE 12.1

Mother	Child
Chair look	Lemme see .... Chair look. Where look? (Child does not offer judgment; looks around room, perhaps for chair.)
Find cup	Lemme see a cup .... Where a cup? (No judgment offered; looks around; looks up at mother.)
Pull wagon	Dis .... Pull wagon. (No judgment given; goes over and begins to tug a toy wagon.)
Shoes put	O.K.! (Turns, looks down, picks up foot with one hand, and pretends to put on shoe.)

This episode illustrates the difficulty often encountered by psycholinguists attempting to elicit linguistic intuitions (most often, judgments of grammaticality) from young children. By contrast, Gleitman, Gleitman, and Shipley (1972) were remarkably successful. They asked three children, ranging in age from 26 to 30 months, to make judgments of "silly" or "O. K." about sentential utterances which varied in form (normal vs. reversed word order, complete vs. telegraphic). It seems that the children could not only grasp what was being asked of them but were correct in the judgments to a significant extent. Recently, I asked a friend to query her daughter, 25½ months old, about some of the phrases used by Gleitman et al. The mother gave the following instructions and repeated them at intervals.[1] "I'm going to say some words, and you tell me if they're funny or O.K." The first time the instructions were given, the child was asked if she understood and responded in the affirmative. A typical portion of the protocol reads as shown in Table 12.1.

It seems that the young child being queried by her mother does not attend to the phrase *qua* linguistic entity, a delineated unit disembedded from the ordinary context. Quite the contrary, she seems to take the phrases as requests, attempting to make sense of them in terms of a field of action; the utterances are firmly embedded in a pragmatic-action context. This illustrates a failure of *focusing and disembedding*. It is interesting that the same child responded quite differently when asked about the meanings of words. To "orange" she said "peach," to "box" she said "car," and to "milk" she replied "food ... drinking." While her ideas about these word meanings deviate from accepted adult usage, she seems able to focus on the word as unit.

Anecdotal material such as that cited suggests that some parts of the speech flux may be more readily delineated than others, more readily made into "objects," all other things being equal. Thus, words can be taken as entities at an age when phrases are still difficult to disembed from the flow of everyday speech and the context of action.

---

[1] I thank Joyce and Stacey Riegelhaupt for their help.

Focusing and disembedding are the procedures through which aspects of language or speech are circumscribed or delineated. These procedures provide the "objects" upon which further procedures can be carried out. In this sense, they are primary—they are a necessary component of any more complex metalinguistic activity, and sequentially they must come first in any metalinguistic performance.

Differentiating

> (E): "Mama: went: to the shop." How many words? (S): "Three." (E): "The first?" (S): "Mama." (E): "The second?" (S): "Went." (E): "The third?" (S): "To the shop." (Luria & Yudovitch, 1971, p. 101)[2]

> (E): I'm going to say a word and I want you to tell me how many different sounds you hear. O.K.? Let's start with "sheygot."

> (S): sh–ay–got. (Irving, 1975, p. 30)

The first example illustrates a 6-year-old's ability to analyze a sentential utterance into component parts, in this case into word units. The child is one of two twins with delayed speech development studied by Luria and Yudovitch (1971); this twin, Yura, had received speech training and other instruction during the study period. The uninstructed twin, Liosha, was not able to perform the same task successfully. In the second example, a 6½-year-old child succeeds in segmenting a word-like unit into syllables; this child could also segment speech sounds into phonemic units. Some children of the same age have difficulty with these tasks.

Such tasks involve analysis of sound patterns in speech and, more specifically, the segmenting of a whole into appropriate units (i.e., words, syllables, phonemes). The first example illustrates additional procedures of counting the number of units and locating the position of each within the larger pattern. Children's ability to analyze speech into segments has been studied from various vantage points, often in relation to beginning reading. Many would agree with Zhurova (1973) that "The task of sound analysis arises specifically at that moment of transition from the oral, acoustic form of speech to the written" (p. 143). Some argue that ability to segment speech into syllables is important for learning to read, while others (Savin, 1972) suggest that analysis into phonemic units is required. In any case, there is evidence that performance on sound analysis tasks shifts markedly in the period of 5 to 7 years, at least among children in cultures where reading is introduced during that time (cf. Cazden, 1972).[3] It seems likely that sound analysis most often

---

[2]An editor's footnote (Luria & Yudovitch, 1971, p. 101) explains that the colons indicate the three Russian words of the original.

[3]In her exploratory study, Irving (1975) found an extremely high correlation between performance on sound analysis tasks and reading level. Zhurova (1973) indicates that subtle training techniques may be important in helping children to grasp differentiations like these that are not part of the ordinary uses of language.

occurs in a task context, but some of the procedures involved are also called upon in other activities—for example, in playful but purposeful rhyming (Franklin, 1975).

Differentiating involves subdividing a whole or unit into component parts (segmenting), often as preparation for additional subprocedures like counting parts of the whole or locating a part within the whole, e.g., first-second-third or beginning-middle-end in a sequence. For the latter subprocedures, the "wholeness" of the object must be maintained to some extent while parts and relations are identified. Developmentally, one would expect that simple differentiation or segmentation could be accomplished prior to more complex subprocedures involving part-whole relations (e.g., locating in a sequence).

In this discussion, *differentiating* procedures are illustrated in terms of the phonological aspect of language. This is intended as illustrative only. Like other procedures, *differentiating* can be applied to a range of linguistic "objects"—for example, to compound words (cf. Berko, 1958).

Evaluating and Correcting

LG: How about this one: *I am eating dinner.*
CG: Yeah, that's okay.
LG: How about this one: *I am knowing your sister.*
CG: No: *I know your sister.*
LG: Why not I am knowing your sister—you can say *I am eating your dinner.*
CG: It's different! (shouting) You say different sentences in different ways!
    Otherwise it wouldn't make sense! (Gleitman et al., 1972, p. 150)

In this excerpt from an exchange between psycholinguist mother and 7-year-old daughter it is possible to delineate three processes or procedures: *evaluating* (when the child judges the "correctness" of the sentence), *correcting* (when the child changes the sentence, here successfully), and an attempt at *explicating* (when the child is asked to explain the basis for the correction, which she does not accomplish here). *Explicating* is discussed as a distinct procedure in the following section.

Evaluating a linguistic item as correct or incorrect must involve either matching (comparing) the item to a specific item of the language *or* judging whether it is in accordance with general rules of the language. These should not be construed as conscious processes. The difference between them can be seen in the following: A child shown a picture of a fish and asked what is wrong with the description "This is a fiss" responds, "No, you have to say 'fish!'" This is a match-to-sample process which involves knowing the correct pronunciation of a particular word rather than general rules of the language. By contrast, when we recognize that "challah" (as pronounced in Hebrew) could not be an English word, we draw on background knowledge of phonological rules of the English language.

Evaluating can be carried out in relation to a range of linguistic "objects." However, in most studies done to date, the crucial items presented for judgment contain specific syntactic peculiarities. While the primary intent is to gain information about children's knowledge of underlying rules of the language, investigators have sometimes noted the vicissitudes of *evaluating*. For example, Gleitman et al. (1972) note that some children initially tended to accept any sentence as correct ("good") and recognize that skilled probing is required in such cases. Two points should be emphasized. First, judgments about linguistic items cannot be considered meaningful (or interpreted as reflecting underlying knowledge) unless there is basis for assuming prior *focusing and disembedding* and some further grasp of task structure. Second, it is important to distinguish inaccuracies that arise from failure to engage in *evaluating* from those where *evaluating* occurs; when the child gives an appropriate type of response, we can generally infer *evaluating*, even if the answer is wrong from the adult point of view.

By definition, *evaluating* involves judgment of an item in relation to another item (a comparison process, as in match-to-sample) or in terms of some form of background knowledge. On an experiential level, it involves some global sense of "fit" or "non-fit" rather than an explicit judgment. *Correcting* must rest on a more differentiated view of the linguistic entity. It is not sufficient to globally apprehend that something is amiss. Rather, some identification of the location or nature of error is required if there is to be an appropriate change. In studies reported, the request for evaluation is usually followed by a requirement for correction, for example, "How would you say it?"or "What did I say wrong?". The distinction between *evaluating* and *correcting* is seen in the fact that subjects can sometimes carry out the former without completing the latter. Furthermore, here as elsewhere, the procedures may be successfully executed in relation to one type of linguistic "object" and not in relation to another. For example, in a study of 2-year-olds, deVilliers and deVilliers (1972) found that the children who were least advanced in spontaneous speech (measured by mean length of utterance) did not correctly evaluate wrong-word-order sentences but correctly evaluated sematically anomalous sentences, although they could not correct the latter. Somewhat more advanced children could evaluate wrong-word-order sentences but not correct them, while the most advanced children could evaluate *and* correct the range of sentences presented.[4]

When subjects are told that there is an error in the stimulus, they can skip *evaluating* and begin the error detection that presumably preceeds *correcting*, but there is no guarantee of success. Asked to correct an error in a stimulus sentence, children sometimes eradicate the error and then introduce an

---

[4]See deVilliers and deVilliers (1974) for further discussion of relations among production, comprehension, judgment, and correction at various stages in early language development.

additional (extraneous) change which they seem to regard as the correction—often indicated by intonational emphasis. For example, a 5-year-old asked to correct the error in "Why Jane doesn't like that book?" said "Why Jane *doesn't* like that book?", apparently thinking that the sentence needed a shift in emphasis.[5] Spontaneous normalizations (eradications of errors) also occur in imitation tasks (e.g., Smith, 1971); these would not appear to meet the criteria for metalinguistic performance but can be viewed as borderline phenomena.

Explicating

Both anecdotal material and more systematic research indicate that there is a genuine difference between being able to provide appropriate answers on a language task and being able to explain the basis for the answer. In general, it is the attempt to get underneath manifest or surface-level behavior that leads investigators to query children about "reasons." Answers to such probes constitute an important source of data in many developmental studies, not only in language acquisition and performance.

Some research illustrating the discrepancy between giving appropriate answers on language tasks and giving reasons is discussed in this section. My point is that "giving reasons"—explaining one's own performance—should be recognized as a distinctive kind of activity. It occurs only under rather special circumstances such as an explicit request from another person or the self-imposed effort to solve a problem. The term *explicating* refers here to explaining one's own performance or "giving reasons" in the sense indicated; when applied to linguistic performance as "object," it is considered to be a metalinguistic procedure.

In their study of the development of double-function terms, Asch and Nerlove (1960) found a marked discrepancy between the comprehension of such terms (e.g., "sweet" as a description of thing or substance and as a description of a person) and the ability to state the relation between the two meanings, which, in fact, begins to emerge only around 11 or 12 years of age. Recently, Winner, Rosensteil, and Gardner (1976) investigated the development of metaphoric understanding through the use of multiple-choice tasks in which subjects were given a choice of 4 possible interpretations for each of 16 metaphoric statements and an explication task in which a matched group of subjects was asked to provide their own interpretations of the same 16 statements. It was found that between the ages of 6 and 14 there was a marked decrease in the percentage of incomplete answers on the explication task (from 25% to 2%) as well as a dramatic increase in the prevalence of responses

---

[5]This and some other examples were provided by Donna Zalichin.

called "genuine metaphoric" (from 5% to 79%).[6] Furthermore, at each age level, the prevalence of genuine metaphoric responses was lower on the explication task than on the multiple-choice task. As the authors say, these findings suggest that the ability to comprehend metaphoric constructions occurs earlier (developmentally, chronologically) than the "ability to explain the rationale of a metaphor" (p. 296). Further insight into the interrelation of metaphoric comprehension and explanation would be provided by using the same subjects for the two task situations.

Studies of language development that are specifically focused on the acquisition of semantic and syntactic structures often require children to provide explications. Reports indicate that subjects sometimes carry out *evaluating* and *correcting* and fall into silence or difficulty on *explicating*. Earlier, an example was given of a child who could evaluate and correct "I am knowing your sister" but could not engage in explicating the syntactic peculiarity. Interestingly enough, this same child had no difficulty in explaining (in a nonformal way) the semantic peculiarity of "George frightens the color green." Gleitman et al. (1972) point out that the two 5-year-olds they queried provided far fewer explanations of their corrections (both syntactic and semantic) than did the 7- and 8-year-olds. This is one more indication that explaining lags behind other types of performance for given language tasks. Interpretations of this discrepancy are discussed below under Riddles of Explicating.

Relating Terms

The procedures discussed thus far describe some proportion of the performances we would designate as metalinguistic. Other important phenomena include recognition of homonymic relations (on which punning is built), paraphrasing, providing definitions of words, and more specialized performances such as giving antonyms on request. Specific analysis of these phenomena in terms of metalinguistic functioning lies beyond the aims of this chapter, but a few comments on defining and related tasks will help to clarify the approach.

Obviously, word definition tasks ask for word meanings. There seem to be two general approaches to providing such meanings. The first, and perhaps the earliest developmentally, is to link the word directly to something in the external world—to illustrate its application to an object or event, often by pointing to something in the immediate field. While this kind of overt performance cannot tell us how the subject understands the relation between

---

[6]Categories for responses on the comprehension task were magical, metonymic, primitive metaphoric, and genuine metaphoric. For the explication task, two additional categories were used: inappropriate metaphoric and incomplete metaphoric (see Winner et al., 1976, p. 293).

verbal term and object, it could represent the beginnings of understanding that language is a medium used to talk about the world and, more generally, about experience. As part of the primitive "naming game," this kind of performance may prefigure more advanced understandings of the referential aspect of language.

The second approach to definition tasks is to give a verbal response. Research shows that verbal responses range from associations (e.g., "peach" in response to "orange") to the coordinate use of categorizing and essential characterizing (e.g., "A fork is a tool or instrument used for eating"). Most studies of defining not only establish criteria for what counts as a definition but also differentiate types or levels; several developmental sequences have been proposed (cf. Cazden, 1972).

Viewing the range of responses on definition tasks, we can suggest that subjects' responses depend not only on the structure or organization of the relevant semantic fields but also on the "plan of search" that is used in a particular situation. If we assume that the relevant terms and concepts are present as part of the person's semantic/conceptual knowledge, then alternative definitions reflect differing plans of search. There may be developmental changes not only in the structure of the semantic field(s) but in the nature and variety of plans of search that are available.[7]

It is the search in the semantic field that is considered a performance, and more specificaly a performance of *relating terms*—here, words to other words or concepts rather than words to objects. From data available (cf. Roberts, 1965), we can suggest that some plans of search seem to involve "reaching upwards" to a superordinate (dog: an animal), others "reaching downwards" for an example (fruit: banana), and others identifying parts or attributes (sun: hot) or functions (hammer: to pound with); still other plans seem to involve "reaching sideways" for equivalent expressions or true synonyms. To designate strategies in this way one must attribute a certain structure to the child's subjective lexicon. Where this is done without empirical support, it is hazardous, and any specification of strategies is likely to reveal adultopomorphism on our part; for example, we may wrongly suppose that the child's definition of dog as "animal" is a genuine categorizing response.

Studies of word association (cf. Nelson, 1977) and antonym formation should provide clues about developing plans of search as well as about underlying conceptual/semantic organization. In a task explicitly structured as an opposites game, Clark (1972) found that almost 50% of the 4-year-olds provided "adult correct" responses. Other kinds of responses in such tasks include the "negation response" (e.g., old: not old), which Heidenheimer (1975) interprets as a strategy transitional between context responding

---

[7]See Nelson (1977) for a discussion of interpretations of the syntagmatic-paradigmatic shift; parallel distinctions between underlying conceptual organization and task strategies are at issue.

(e.g., full: tummy) and true antonymic responding. Young children may profess understanding of the opposites game and yet give responses which range from clang associations (more: door) to primitive contextual responses (open: out). Their "opposites" responses to terms without conventional antonyms (cf. Pollack, 1976) are an additional source of information about varieties of *relating terms*.

Relating terms has been discussed thus far in terms of searching in semantic fields. However, some of the variations in response on definition tasks, antonym tasks, and so forth may reflect not only the structuring of these fields and the use of varying plans of search but the extent to which the field is differentiated from other fields (the field of action, the field of things). In definition and antonym tasks, procedures of *relating terms* are applied to words supplied by the investigator. But how does the child understand the word? What kind of "object" is it? Clang responses occur when phonetic properties become salient, perhaps as a result of not understanding task instructions; here, the word has not been taken within a semantic field. Context responses (e.g., table: kitchen) may reflect an overlapping of fields or a simplified one-to-one mapping; the stimulus word can only be related to terms referring to other aspects of a real-life situation in which both objects would be found.

This characterization of *relating terms* must be understood as a rough first approximation. Further analyses of task structures and subjects' responses should yield a specification of subtypes.

THE OBJECT IN METALINGUISTIC PERFORMANCE

The term "object" as used here denotes that aspect of language or speech which is at the focus of attention in a given metalinguistic performance. The object can be the sound of a word or nonsense phrase, the meaning of a word or sentence, morphological or syntactic aspects of simple and more complex constructions. One's own utterance or linguistic performance can become the object—as in some cases of *explicating*. Where the performance involves *relating terms*, the original term is the object, and the procedures (e.g., searching the semantic field) do not so much require operating upon it as with it, or in relation to it; this suggests that it may be necessary to differentiate generic types of metalinguistic performance.

In discussing *focusing and disembedding*—the procedures which provide the object initially—I emphasized the activity of the subject and, more specifically, the importance of attentional processes in the delineation of the object. One might say that a piece of the field achieves its status as object by virtue of the person's attitude. However, even in the material provided in this chapter, we see some other determinants in what can be called object formation. As indicated earlier, stimulus factors—such as the natural boundaries provided by pauses in speech—may function analogously to sharp brightness gradients that produce contours in visual figure-ground phenomena. Alternatively, words may be more readily unitized and isolated than sentences not because of physical stimulus factors but because of novelty—most ordinary speech does *not* occur in single-word utterances. It has also been suggested that some kinds of experience with language may be important in preparing the ground for metalinguistic functioning. In this vein, Cazden (1975) hypothesized that practice or play with aspects of language—at a remove from practical communicative uses— could facilitate the development of metalinguistic ability and, in particular, the aspect described here as *focusing and disembedding*.

The interplay of attentional processes and stimulus factors in object formation should be considered developmentally. Only by examining instances of "failure" in relation to cases of "success" (comprehension) will we be able to discern the emergence and development of different aspects of object formation—that is, changes in the ability and/or propensity to focus on various aspects of language. Earlier, there was an example of a 2-year-old girl who seemed able to focus on words and to grasp the general structure of a defining task but who could not disembed phrases from the contex of ongoing speech and action. Evidence suggests that slightly older children can focus on phrases and sentences and so engage in further metalinguistic activity. Clearly, more data will provide a basis for specific hypotheses on developmental sequences.

RIDDLES OF EXPLICATING

Earlier, I noted the widely observed discrepancies between giving an appropriate answer and providing explanations on a language task (i.e., *explicating*). The discrepancies have been interpreted in various ways: in terms of differences in amount or kind of underlying knowledge, differences in accessability of such knowledge, and/or nonspecific interfering factors which make the first kind of performance (giving an appropriate answer) easier than the second (giving reasons for the answer). It is important to recognize the underlying assumptions of such interpretations and to open up the possibility of alternative formulations.

In her paper on metalinguistic functioning, Cazden (1975) points to the theoretical distinction between "having" or possessing a certain kind of knowledge and "availability" or "accessibility" of this knowledge. This formulation seems to accept a now-classic distinction between "competence" and "performance" but adds and gives emphasis to processes of access—or, in terms of the memory literature, "retrieval." As proposed it appears to account for performance variations primarily in terms of accessibility or "levels of awareness" rather than in terms of amount or kind of underlying knowledge. However, it could easily be extended to incorporate the latter and perhaps was intended to do so from the start. Cazden suggests that the first level of awareness consists in being able to detect anomalies and make judgments of correct/incorrect; at the seond and higher level, one can analyze linguistic productions and thus explicate the basis for a particular judgment or choice.

Although Cazden's emphasis on accessibility and related concepts of mobilization would not be considered controversial now, it should be recognized as a distinct point of view. It contrasts—however subtly—with the type of explanation that takes for granted a rather more direct relation between what children say and what they think. In this other (and perhaps more traditional) view, verbalizations are anlayzed as direct indications of underlying thought processes and/or cognitive structures of a more enduring sort. For example, in discussing children's responses to questions about words, Papandropolou and Sinclair (1974) emphasize levels or stages in children's understanding (cognitive structuring)—from what they term a premetalinguistic phase to fully developed metalinguistic comprehension. Winner et al. (1976) (see also Gardner, Kirchner, Winner, and Perkins, 1975) categorize children's explications of metaphor in terms of types regarded as levels, ranging from "magical" to "genuine metaphoric," as mentioned earlier.

As noted, these two approaches differ in that the latter takes children's verbalizations as fairly direct indicators of underlying structures, while the other assumes a less direct relation and gives more weight to factors affecting performance. But both assume that explications, like other verbal perform-ances, can be viewed as products of more or less stable operating structures. This is problematic in two respects. First, there is failure to recognize that giving explanations under task conditions reflects the child's interpretation of the particular situation *as much as* his/her underlying knowledge and relates in a complex way to what he or she might say under other circumstances. Second, these formulations suggest unquestioning acceptance of a typical competence/performance model. Such models characterize knowledge in terms of relatively fixed structures and performances as products to be "read" for the information they supply about underlying state. Alternatively, performances can be considered in their own right, as activities, parts of an ongoing process. Viewed in this way, performances are not merely indices of already-formed knowledge but are acts that contribute to the formation of meaning in situations. This characterization may be particularly apropos with regard to children's explications in task situations.

I am suggesting, then, that we consider children's explanations (including explications) not only as revealing stable underlying knowledge or as reflecting plans and strategies but—more radically—as improvisational acts that often serve meaning formation functions (cf. Sperber, 1975). In the future, this line of thinking may be extended to questions of defining and other forms of *relating terms* where present theorizing is constrained by the metaphor of "semantic field"—with fields conceptualized as more or less stable structures, albeit changing developmentally.[8]

LANGUAGE AND CONTEXT: DISEMBEDDEDNESS AND REFERENCE

To this point, metalinguistic functioning has been described in terms of performance. Relatively little has been said about underlying abilities or orientations. It is clear that the occurrence of metalinguistic performance must depend on more general understandings of language/speech in relation to context. In other words, the child must have some understanding of language as an "autonomous medium" in order to engage in *bona fide* metalinguistic performances. This understanding is not all-or-none but evolves through a series of phases. Here I shall roughly characterize the first three levels of progressive "decontextualization" or disembeddedness of language from context.[9]

At the *first* level, speech occurs as an accompaniment to action and may even be considered part of action. Prelinguistically, the child's vocal activity is often cotemporaneous with overt bodily activity—sometimes seeming to serve not only as accompaniment but as rhythmic support. Many of the child's first words arise in the context of action and reveal their activity embeddedness even in their form. Some names originate in action upon objects. For example, a child of 17 months evolved the term "whew" (slightly aspirated) as a name for lights. The word had developed from his own action: the blowing out of candles, which involved expulsions of breath accompanied by sound. Other early names derive from the sounds made by objects; typically, these occur first as accompaniment to an ongoing event. For example, a 15-month-old child said "gubba gubba" when the water gurgled down the bathtub drain; this subsequently became a name for the bathtub stopper. Conventional terms such as "bye-bye" and "hi" are learned as accompaniments to specific actions and only later are used apart from overt bodily activity. The same appears to be true of many early action terms—for example, "uppy," initially accompanied by reaching upwards, presumably a request to be lifted. More lengthy utterances—nonsentential strings of

---

[8]See Litowitz (1977) for a recent discussion of developmental changes in defining; this analysis draws on notions of semantic field and other underlying structures but also emphasizes that responses reflect strategies adopted in line with specific understandings of task requirements.

[9]Although Werner and Kaplan (1963) do not delineate levels in this way, the presentation here is closely related to their formulations; see, in particular, Chapters 3 and 4.

idiosyncratic forms or words (sometimes a chant)—often occur as accompaniment to ongoing activity. Conceivably, these could be the early analogue of the type of narration that accompanies and perhaps guides organized play at slightly older ages (cf. Franklin, 1977). At this first level, words and sometimes phrases uttered by another are generally taken as signals for action; the specific semantic content may be minimally comprehended (cf. Luria, 1959).

The *second* level is the beginning understanding of the referential nature of language, the "aboutness" of speech. Identifying the transition from terms as accompaniment to action (or, directly expressive of emotion) to names as designators remains problematic (cf. Marshall, 1970). It may be suggested that referential use of terms not only involves indication of something "out there" but a differentiation among alternatives which requires having distinct terms for different kinds of things and/or events (cf. Dore, Franklin, Miller, and Ramer, 1976). Implicit here is the idea that linguistic referring acts require some differentiation of the sphere of language/speech from the sphere of objects and actions. The difference between the utterance of "whew" (aspirated) as accompaniment to blowing out a candle and the subsequent application of this term (now modified, nonaspirated—unaccompanied by action-on-object) not only to lighted candles but to house lights, street lamps, and the full moon serves to exemplify the distinction. First understandings of the referential nature of language can also be inferred from one-word utterances which are more predicate-like than name-like (cf. Dore, 1975). Similarly, children's early combinatorial utterances and their comprehension of speech directed to them often provide evidence of some grasp of the "aboutness" of language. However, at this level, both speaking and understanding are very closely tied to context. Typically the child's utterances concern the here-and-now and gain their meaning only within the situation (cf. Greenfield and Smith, 1976). The speech of others is taken with reference to the immediate field and cannot really be understood apart from such contextual support; the latter would seem to be the case for the 2-year-old cited earlier who understood her mother's utterances only as directives for action, embedded in a pragmatic frame.

At the *third* level, it becomes possibe to carry on conversation about objects and events not in the immediate field and to talk about ideas (however simple) and quasi-hypothetical situations. While there is clearly a differentiation from action and more independence from immediate contextual support, utterances are typically interpreted in terms of their communicative meaning and where possible their concrete reference. For example, a 5-year-old who was asked what is wrong with the sentence "Why the kitten can't stand up?" quickly responded "Because he's too little." The child's attention went immediately to the referential content; the syntactic error was insignificant by comparison and perhaps undetected. While words are not actually confused with things (i.e., taken as equivalent), the differentiation of the sphere of language/speech from the sphere of objects/events is not yet stable. Thus, words or names are sometimes regarded as attributes of their referent objects, properties of words and objects are not well distinguished, and questions about words are typically taken as questions about things. Two studies are particularly relevant here. Papandropolou and Sinclair (1974) asked children ranging in age from 4:5 to 10:10 to say what a word is, to say whether given terms (e.g., happy, take, the) are words, to say long and short words. The following response of a 5-year-old to the question "What is a word?" is typical of answers in this age range (Papandropolou & Sinclair, 1974):

> A word is something true . . . it's something . . . anything at all. . . it can be a chair, or a cupboard, or a book or a leaf or a dog or people or a bottle or to drink or a block. . . . (p. 244)

In general, in the 4-to-5 age group, questions about words were treated as questions about things. For example, "pencil" was said to be a word "because it writes" and "train" is a long word because "there are lots of carriages." Markman (1976) found that even slightly older children (5 to 7 years of age) tend to take questions about words as questions about things and often reject the idea that a word retains its meaning in the absence of concrete exemplars.[10] it thus seems appropriate to say that at this level the spheres of language/speech and objects/events are only tenuously differentiated for the subject. Nonetheless, speaking is clearly disengaged from other action, and talk has meaning in the absence of immediate contextual support. Language is regarded primarily as "what you say" and "what you hear"—that is, *as discourse.* It follows that utterances are generally interpreted within a communicative-meaning context: A word or phrase is part of speaking, and its importance lies in its reference—what it is about.

At more advanced levels, language becomes more and more an "autonomous medium" through which various kinds of meanings can be expressed and elaborated in the absence of immediate, nonverbal contextual support. This progressive differentiation of language and nonverbal context is paralleled by a development *within* the verbal sphere: growth of the ability to disembed aspects of language from the context of discourse. This means that more "discourse-like" units—sentential utterances—can become *objects* in metalinguistic performance. At the same time, the progressive conceptual differentiation of the sphere of language/speech and the sphere of persons, objects, and events makes possible the metalinguistic performances which

---

[10]As Papandropolou and Sinclair (1974) suggest, in the age range of 5 to 7 years, words begin to have some autonomous reality, and the word-referent relationship is increasingly understood- a fact attested to by the kind of play with sound-meaning connections that is evident in punning.

involve finer handling of vehicle-referent relationships—punning, the more complex forms of defining and paraphrasing, production and analysis of figurative language, and so forth. Undoubtedly, these specific evolutions are part of the more widespread development of ability to engage in *reflective performance* as differentiated from *performances-in-context*.

SUMMARY

In the central part of this chapter, metalinguistic functioning is describe in terms of a performance metaphor that pictures a person performing *procedures* on an aspect of language taken as *object*; six types of procedures are described and illustrated. This is followed by a brief discussion of the notion of *object* in metalinguistic performance and further remarks on the interpretation of *explicating*. Finally, it is acknowledged that the occurrence of metalinguistic performances must rest on some general understandings of language in relation to the world, and so the chapter concludes with a rough sketch of early phases in the progressive differentiation of language, discourse, and nonverbal context. The next step is to refine and buttress the conceptualization developed here and to explore its applicability to the domains of nonverbal symbolization.

REFERENCES

Asch, S., & Nerlove, H. The development of double-function terms in children. In B. Kaplan & S. Wapner (Eds.), *Perspectives in psychological theory*. New York: International Universities Press, 1960.

Berko, J. The child's learning of English morphology. *Word*, 1958, *14*, 150–177.

Brown, R., & Bellugi, U. Three processes in the child's acquisition of syntax. In E. Lennenberg (Ed.), *New directions in the study of language*. Cambridge, Mass.: The M.I.T. Press, 1964.

Cazden, C. *Child language and education*. New York: Holt, Rinehart, & Winston, 1972.

Cazden, C. Play with language and metalinguistic awareness: One dimension of language experience. In C. B. Winsor (Ed.), *Dimensions of language experience*. New York: Agathon Press, 1975.

Clark, E. V. On the child's acquisition of antonyms in two semantic fields. *Journal of Verbal Learning and Verbal Behavior*, 1972, *11*, 750–758.

deVilliers, J. G., & deVilliers, P. A. Competence and performance in child language: Are children really competent to judge? *Journal of Child Language*, 1974, *1*, 11–22.

deVilliers, P. A., & deVilliers, J. G. Early judgments of semantic and syntactic acceptability by children. *Journal of Psycholinguistic Research*, 1972, *1*, 299–310.

Dore, J. Holophrases, speech acts and language universals. *Journal of Child Language*, 1975, *2*, 21–40.

Dore, J., Franklin, M. B., Miller, R. T., & Ramer, A. L. H. Transitional phenomena in early language acquistion. *Journal of Child Language*, 1976, *3*, 13–28.

Franklin, M. B. Aspects of symbolic functioning in childhood. In C. B. Winsor (Ed.), *Dimensions of language experience*. New York: Agathon Press, 1975.

Franklin, M. B. *The functions of language in play*. Paper presented at the meetings of the National Association for the Education of Young Children, Chicago, 1977.

Gardner, H., Kirchner, M., Winner, E., & Perkins, D. Children's metaphoric productions and preferences. *Journal of Child Language*, 1975, *2*, 125–141.

Gleitman, L. R., Gleitman, H., & Shipley, E. F. The emergence of the child as grammarian. *Cognition*, 1972, *1*, 137–164.

Greenfield, P., & Smith, J. H. *The structure of communication in early language development*. New York: Academic Press, 1976.

Heidenheimer, P. The strategy of negation and the learning of antonymic relations. *Developmental Psychology*, 1975, *11*, 757–762.

Irving, K. J. *Metalinguistic awareness and how it relates to the beginning reading process*. Unpublished M. A. thesis, Sarah Lawrence College, 1975.

Jakobson, R. Concluding statement: Linguistics and poetics. In T. A. Sebeok (Ed.), *Style in language*. Cambridge, Mass.: The M.I.T. Press, 1960.

Litowitz, B. Learning to make definitions. *Journal of Child Language*, 1977, *4*, 289–304.

Luria, A. R. The directive function of speech in development and dissolution, Part I. *Word*, 1959, *15*, 341–52.

Luria, A. R., & Yudovitch, F. Ia. *Speech and the development of mental processes in the child*. Baltimore, Md.: Penguin, 1971.

Markman, E. M. Children's difficulty with word-referent differentiation. *Child Development*, 1976, *47*, 742–749.

Marshall, J. C. Can humans talk? In J. Morton (Ed.), *Biological and social factors in psycholinguistics*. Urbana, Ill.: University of Illinois Press, 1970.

Nelson, K. The syntagmatic-paradigmatic shift revisited: A review of research and theory. *Psychological Bulletin*, 1977, *84*, 93–116.

Papandropolou, I., & Sinclair, H. What is a word? Experimental study of children's ideas on grammar. *Human Development*, *1974*, *17*, 241–258.

Pollack, D. T. *A study in opposites*. Unpublished M.A. thesis, Bank Street College of Education, 1976.

Roberts, A. *Development in children's understanding of analogies*. Unpublished doctoral dissertation, Clark University, 1965.

Savin, H. B. What the child knows about speech when he starts to learn to read. In J. F. Kavanaugh & I. G. Mattingly, (Eds.), *Language by eye and by ear*. Cambridge, Mass.: The M.I.T. Press, 1972.

Smith, C. S. An experimental approach to children's linguistic competence. In J. R. Hayes, (Ed.), *Cognition and the development of language*. New York: Wiley, 1971.

Sperber, D. *Rethinking symbolism*. New York: Cambridge University Press, 1975.

Werner, H., & Kaplan, B. *Symbol formation*. New York: Wiley, 1963.

Winner, E., Rosensteil, A. K., & Gardner, H. The development of metaphoric understanding. *Developmental Psychology*, 1976, *12*, 289–297.

Zhurova, L. Ye. The development of analysis of words into their sounds by preschool children. In C. A. Ferguson & D. I. Slobin (Eds.), *Studies of child language development*. New York: Holt, Rinehart & Winston, 1973.

IV

SYMBOLISM AND THE MYTHIC WORLD

13 Symbolism: From the Body to the Soul

Bernard Kaplan
Clark University

It is by no means the parochial fancy of a small coterie of emancipated souls that the capacity to symbolize distinguishes human beings from other forms of animal life. Even those who accept the warrant of claims puporting to demonstrate some degree of symbolic functioning among our primate relatives are likely to concede that there are modes of symbolic activity found among human beings that obtain nowhere else in the animal kingdom. Ernst Cassirer's characterization of man as *animal symbolicum* (1944, p. 26) seems to have found widespread acceptance. Yet the eagerness with which people of quite diverse theoretical allegiances have adopted Cassirer's formula should alert us to the likelihood of underlying disagreement concerning the meaning and ramifications of the notion of human beings as symbolic animals. One need only look at the proceedings of any conference dealing with symbols, symbolism, and symbolization to see how far apart on the fundamentals are those who agree on the facades (e.g., Bryson, Finkelstein, Hoagland, and MacIver, 1954, 1955). One need only consult the writings of such giants as Whitehead (1959), Cassirer (1953, 1955, 1957), Urban (1939), and Burke (1966a, 1966b) to realize that we cannot expect to arrive at a universally shared monolithic conception of the symbol or the symbolic process.

There are doubtless several reasons for the prevailing lack of accord concerning the notions of "symbol" and "symbolization." One of the reasons for the discordance is that different scholars consider the role of "symbols" in different world contexts. Those who ask about the nature of symbols and symbolic activity with regard to the scientific sphere are likely to interpret symbols as arbitrary signs and to treat symbolization as mere signification. On the other hand, those who consider symbolization in relation to a mythical being-in-the-world will see symbolization as an act of representation and symbols as more or less "naturally" related to that which they represent. I am saying, then, that answers to the question "What is symbolization?" can be arrived at only through decision, not through discovery. We are dealing with a matter of persuasive definition rather than unbiased observation—a problem of conceptualization that cannot be settled by turning to the "world of fact" or by appeal to enlightened authority. With this in mind, I propose to consider symbolization in a way that deviates from most attempts by psychologists to define and locate the phenomena of symbolic activity. Instead of considering symbolization as a species of signification, as resting on the attachment of verbal signs or pictures to perceptual objects, I would like to urge that we take symbolization as referring principally to the attemtps to use some medium to represent something—some experiential content—that is not tangible or visible to the subject. I am suggesting, then, that the prime form of symbolization occurs when *abstract intangible states of affairs are realized in a concrete medium.*[1]

Rich material for understanding this process is found in Silberer's (1951a, 1951b) investigations of hypnagogic imagery. Using himself as subject, Silberer examined the way in which abstract thoughts are translated into images as one falls asleep. I do not want to review Silberer's work here but simply to adapt some examples to illustrate the process of symbol formation occurring while one is *consciously* intending to represent a state of affairs in some medium. Silberer (1951a) reports the following:

> In a state of drowsiness I contemplate an abstract topic such as the nature of transsubjectively (for all people) valid judgments. . . . The content of my thought presents itself to me in the form of a perceptual (for an instant apparently real) picture: I see a big circle (or transparent sphere) in the air with people around it whose heads reach into the circle. The symbol expresses pratically everything I was thinking of. The transsubjective judgment is valid for all people . . . : the circle includes all the heads. . . . Not all judgments are transsubjective: the body

---

[1]It is not my purpose to define symbolization in such a way as to exclude from consideration— for example, as merely representation—those activities of children (or adults) in which one refers to some ostensibly established states of affairs by way of words or pictures that one draws. I am perfectly content to have as a manifestation of symbolization the drawing of houses, persons, trees, etc. And I do not gainsay the value in some contexts of finding out when the child's drawings approximate those of adults in our society, that is, meet some standard of veridicality of representation. But I would also like to find a place for a notion of symbolization that allows for symbolization in the very organizations of the perceptual manifold, that allows for a symbolization in which an ordinary thing can become god via a hierophany (cf. Eliade, 1963), that allows for symbolization in conditions in which what we would take to be symbol and what we would take to be symbolized are not yet distinguished from each other, and that allows a place for a notion of symbolization akin to the notion of symbolism so dear to the hearts of the romantics and to the aficionados of the creative imagination. It is the latter notion that is my concern in this presentation.

and limbs of the people are outside (below) the sphere as they stand on the ground as independent individuals. . . . (p. 198)

Let us consider another example: One can think about trying to smooth a passage in a written essay and attempt to form an image to represent that state of affairs. Now, in addition, we can specify a domain of representation, for example, carpentry. In this case, the ideas about smoothing out a passage in writing might very well be represented in terms of a person planing a piece of wood (cf. Silberer, 1951a, p. 202). In the hypnagogic state, as in dreams, the ideas are not experienced as taking place "inside"; rather, they are embodied "externally" as objective states of affairs.

These are phenomena of primary symbol formation—situations in which an abstract, intangible content is represented and given shape in a "concrete" medium such as visual imagery. Freud deals with this in his consideration of "regard for representability" in dreams, suggesting that the specific form given to the dream thoughts or latent content is governed not only by requirements for disguise but by the nature of the dream medium itself—a medium which is, in Freud's view, primarily visual.[2] As pointed out above, it is possible not only to specify a generic medium (i.e., the pictorial, gestural, sonic, etc.) but also—or alternatively—to suggest a particular domain as the context or "field" for representation. Thus, we can take the idea of smoothing a difficult passage in writing and imaginatively represent this in the domain of carpentry. In a number of informal investigations, I have asked people to represent feelings (e.g., anger) through the imaginative transformation of objects (e.g., an apple), to name the vegetable or musical instrument or color that best represents a given personage (e.g., Gerald Ford, Einstein, etc.), to represent the meaning of expressions such as "ac-dc" in the political sphere, and so forth. Interestingly enough, most adults find it possible—and often easy—to represent ideas or feelings in terms of specific domains of activity, types of objects, spheres of sensory attributes, etc. In all of these situations, an idea or set of ideas from one domain is represented, incarnated, in another domain—the original idea is realized in the terms or vocabulary of the second domain.[3]

---

[2]Freud views the problem of representability in dreams as related to the more general issue of representing the abstract in a pictorial medium:

Whatever is pictorial is capable of representation in dreams and can be fitted into a situation in which abstract expression would confront the dream representation with difficulties not unlike those which would arise if a leading political artical had to be represented in an illustrated journal. (Freud, as cited in Rapaport, 1951, p. 196)

[3]The "line schematization technique"—which requires subjects to represent meanings through constructing or interpreting nonpictorial line patterns—provides another means of investigating the transformative process in symbol formation (cf. Werner and Kaplan, 1963, 1978).

How is it possible to do this—to conjoin domains that causally and pragmatically have nothing to do with each other, to see relations between orders that are totally disparate? We must recognize that queries such as "If Dostoevski were a musical instrument, what kind of musical instrument would he be?" strike us as bizarre *unless* we adopt a particular stance or attitude, a certain frame of mind. I shall refer to this frame of mind, this state of being-in-the-world, as "mythopoetic." It must be clearly distinguished from the pragmatic-utilitarian state of being-in-the-world that generally prevails among sober adults of the "civilized" world during their waking hours. Here I shall argue that the mythopoetic stance is requisite for genuine symbolizing activity—the kind of imaginative transformation and representation of which I am speaking. It is common to children and adults but is more prevalent among children and, to some degree at least, more "typical" of the child's mentality. However, with some exceptions—primarily in the sphere of play—it is difficult to investigate primary symbolizing processes in children. They have difficulty reporting on their experience and, equally important, in shifting stances *on request*—that is, at the request of an investigator in a task situation. These two considerations lead us to suggest that the exploration of mythopoetic states and symbolizing acitivities *in adults* may facilitate our attempts to understand symbolizing processes in the child. Here, I shall offer a few remarks to supplement what I have already intimated concerning mythopoetic states—beginning with adult experience and moving to a brief consideration of the child. Then I shall return to the question raised earlier: What are the means by which we bridge totally disparate domains in the process of symbolizing?

All of us, as adults, are absorbed into the mythical world on occasion or, indeed, on many occasions. We occupy such a world in our dreams. Typically, however, we are able to distinguish our transitory immersions in a mythical world, where magic reigns, from our ongoing involvement in a complexly structured world of everyday social life, where facts cannot be altered by wishes. Sooner or later, we locate the objects and events of our fantasies in the domain of "appearances," in the sphere of the "subjective," in the realm of the imagination. To be sure, there are some adults who lose, or who have never quite found, the capacity to distinguish and allocate their variegated experiences; they cannot differentiate personal dream from social fact, indiosyncratic desire from public deed, or subjective wishes from objective accomplishments. In such cases, of course, we are dealing with psychotics. But, as I have indicated, this way of organizing experience—the mythical—is not by any means restricted to psychotics. It's a way of being-in-the world that involves magic, omens, a breakdown of the differentiation between the animate and the inanimate, and between self and other, as contrasted with our pragmatic utilitarian well-socialized way of being-in-the-world where this belongs here and that belongs there and never the twain shall meet.

In an ideal-type mythical world—uncontaminated by the empirical-pragmatic—there is a little clear distinction between the I and the not-I, between the subjective and the objective. Correspondingly, there is no clear differentiation between reality and appearance. Experiences, whatever their "real" source, especially experiences of the unfamiliar and the distressing, are quasi-substantialized and objectified, that is, taken as standing against, as outside the control of, as alien to a self not yet aware of itself.

In this world, as Cassirer (1955) puts it, "the nuances of significance and value which [empirical] knowledge creates in its concept of the object, which enable it to distinguish different spheres of objects and to draw a line between the world of truth and the world of appearance, are utterly lacking" (p. 35).

The kind of "thinking" which constitutes the mythical world does not possess the means for relating, comparing, and subordinating particular experiences to other experiences, of assessing current engrossments against engrossments suffered in the past or impressions expected in the future. That is because there is no clear distinction among memory, perception, and anticipation for those fully absorbed in the mythical world. Correlatively, there is no clear distinction among past, present and future. The sovereign criterion of actuality is intensity of feeling. Whatever seizes our interest and attention is real.

Given this way of being-in-the-world, it should be relatively clear that the kinds of phenomena one experiences in the mythical domain will not be the same objects and events one entertains in everyday waking life. In that domain, the objects and events of experience are incarnations of the active-affective-volitional impulses of the subject and are therefore susceptible to the most sudden and radical transformations. As a rough analogy to this kind of feeling-induced transformation, one might consider how personal objects with whom we are intensely involved undergo remarkable changes as they move from gratifying our desires to frustrating our wishes.

What of the child? The young child, by all theoretical accounts, lives in a world where there is little differentiation between subject and object, between the internal and the external. There is ostensibly little differentiation between the literal and the metaphorical, between the physical and the spiritual. Many developmental theorists would accept these presuppositions. Piaget, in both earlier and later work, provides copious examples of the very young child's inability to distinguish self from nonself, to separate dreams from waking reality, to differentiate the properties and relations of objects from one's egocentric connection to and actions upon them. Werner (1978) has gathered materials from a wide variety of sources to illustrate the relative lack of differentiation of self and world, object and action, and fantasy and reality that characterizes the young child's being-in-the-world. Depth psychologists of all persuasions who have worked with young children offer striking illustrations of the kinds of phenomena I mentioned above in describing the mythical world. Nonprofessionals who have paid close attention to their own children have witnessed the objectification of inner states—imaginary playmates, monsters in the dark, the reality of dreams, etc.

It is perhaps paradoxical that the naive onlooker gets the clearest indication that the young child is immersed to a large extent in a mythical world when the child is in the process of coming out of that world—that is, when the child has begun to draw a line between the mythical domain and the domain of the empirical pragmatic. I refer to the symbolic or pretend play of the small child, which is increasingly recognized by the child as "just play." The boundary here is, of course, tenuous, in the sense that the "just play" wall can quite easily crumble. Campbell (1959, p. 22), drawing on Frobenius, provides an excellent illustration of this kind of dissolution. A father gives his 4-year-old daughter three burnt matches and tells her to play. She begins with the matches, transforming them into Hansel, Gretel, and the witch. Suddenly, after a period of time, the little girls shrieks in terror and comes running to her father in great fright: "Daddy, Daddy, take the witch away! I can't touch the witch any more!" Here, clearly, we see how deep feelings can transform the objects established by adaptive intelligence and can turn virtually anything in the environment into an expression of affective-emotional life.

It is not accidental, then, that watching the child in the play sphere—in the mythical world, as it were—provides what may be our clearest veiw of the emergence and early manifestation of symbolic functioning: the embodiment of meanings in objects, the imaginative transformation of objects, the externalization of thoughts and feelings at a remove from the pragmatic-utilitarian world of everyday occurrence.

Before going on, it is necessary to insert a few points of clarification, qualification, and caution. First, I do not mean to suggest an equation between the fantasizing adult and the delusional psychotic or between either of these and the young child. The contents of their mythical worlds differ and so too the manner in which they deal with these contents. The conditions under which they enter, remain in, and leave their mythical worlds differ. The degrees of tension between immersion in the mythical world and involvement in the empirical-pragmatic world differ. Second, I do not mean to suggest that anyone can live alone and solely in a mythical world. To survive, one must live, concurrently or alternately, in the pragmatic-utilitarian world or depend on a caretaker who lives in that world. No matter how one construes instrumental-practical action, one must engage in such action to bring about actual effects in the world. The third point follows immediately. There is no question that the growing child adapts to the exigencies of his/her physical and social environments. This adaptation takes place spontaneously and joyously as well as through the coercive powers of socialization. In other words, the "normal child" progressively subordinates the mythical world to the empirical-pragmatic scientific world. This does not mean, however, that the mythopoetic state of being-in-the-world is lost. I have suggested that it continues to exist in adulthood and, in some individuals, to flourish. As the child matures, there is progressive differentiation of spheres of activity (or spheres of being) and an adaptation of modes of psychological functioning to the specific "requirements" of differing spheres (e.g., the pragmatic everyday sphere, the play sphere, etc.).

At a time when there is considerable emphasis on what is called cognitive development, and when metaphors of information processing are dominant in the study of cognition, it is essential to reiterate that I am talking about symbolizing in its more radical forms and not about symbolization in the more limited sense familiar to contemporary cognitive psychologists. In cognitive psychology, the term "symbolization" is typically used to refer to acts which enable an organism (presumptively human) to use one element of experience to indicate or designate a state of affairs which can be independently ascertained or apprehended. The term "symbolization," as I intend it here, is closer to the notion of symbolism as found in the works of Jung, Eliade, and others. In the case of symbolism, there is no clear indication of a "something else" but rather an embodiment or incarnation of certain intangibilia in material form. I am speaking, then, not of how the child or adult indicates or represents previously articulated cognitions of self and world but of how feelings as well as ideas can be realized (or, more radically, created) in and through the use of material form (cf. Kaplan, 1962).

We can entertain the notion that perception itself—especially for the young child—is a symbolic medium in that perceptual "objects" embody feelings and ideas (meanings) of a more general nature; the objects thus stand as the embodiment of universals in a concrete form. This neo-Kantian thesis is inherent in Arnheim's (1969) notion of visual thinking. However debatable such a view of perception may be, it is generally agreed that imagery—the perceptualization of the nonpresent or intangible—is a symbolic medium. Clearly, perception and imagery cannot be distinguished in terms of the "material"—rather, the distinction comes from the point of view of the subject: Images are perceptions that are experienced as having an external or quasi-external character; they are objects to the subject's consciousness. Consider the difference between the dream experience while sleeping and the dream recalled. It is clear that in Silberer's investigations—discussed earlier— ideas and feelings are being "objectified" in the form of images. Here, as in the line schematization technique, the notion to be symbolized appears or is presented initially in verbal form and then realized or represented in a nonverbal medium. The use of such examples should not obscure the fact that language—in its more developed forms and elaborated uses—is itself a symbolic medium. Poetic language may constitute the apex of symbolization in language.

Whether we are talking about perception, imagery, the use of objects in play, elaborated forms of language, or other symbolic media—and, clearly, there are important differences among them—we come to the question raised earlier: What are the means by which disparate domains are bridged in the process of symbolizing?

The mind is *terra incognita*. We symbolize the mental or spiritual in terms of something that pertains to the sensory-motor domain or the perceptible domain. Once we have selected the universe of discourse (i.e., the field of representation), we search within it for that which seems a fitting embodiment, an appropriate realization, of the feeling or idea. How can we do this? This is the Kantian question. Consider, as an example, the notion of "grasping an idea." How is mental grasping related to the act of actually grasping a physical object? How is it that we can talk intelligibly about something abstract and mental in terms of a physical action? Or, to put the question somewhat more formally, what operations of mind are entailed in order for us to make such leaps—to apply terms from the domain of the body and body action to the domain of mental activity, the social domain, the cultural domain, the "spiritual" domain, and other domains of experience? We cannot hope for a definitive answer to this question. But I would like to suggest that "dynamic schematizing activity" (cf. Werner & Kaplan, 1963) is the process through which disparate domains are spanned in the process of symbolizing. Such activity involves physiognomizing the "objects" of the two domains in similar ways, in terms of dynamic vectors and spatial relations that would seem to be rooted in body movement or mobilization of the body. It should be noted that I am not speaking of overt bodily movement but of "internal gesture."[4]

We find that in the Freudian view the mental and spiritual are generated from—and can be reduced to—the physical. In most classic psychoanalytic interpretations of dreams, for example, ultimate references are to the body, to body parts and body functions. Thus, Freud takes all mental phenomena and reduces them to corporeal phenomena; this is his ontology and his theory of knowledge. It seems to me essential to question this. It can be argued that the symbol is Janus-faced, that it faces in two directions simultaneously. This is the thesis that I am setting forth here—a view also articulated by Eliade (1963) and Jung, among others. In these formulations, the symbol is the mediator between the domains of the spiritual or mental and the physical or corporeal. The basic phenomena or notions that are symbolized are not "objects" or

---

[4]Clearly, I am not speaking about questions of truth or falsity in the empirical sense, that is, of symbolic forms being more or less accurate or veridical representations of some meaning, but rather of how a feeling of "fittingness" across diverse domains is achieved in the process of symbolizing. The emphasis here is on symbolizing *qua* process, not on symbol *qua* product. I would point out that the role of internal gesture in symbolizing may best be understood on a phenomenological level, and inquiry on the phenomenological level may in fact turn out to be crucial theoretically. Additionally, we may examine other formulations concerning the transcendence of disparate domains. Most of these remain rather general; by contrast, the concept of dynamic schematizing activity is less ephemeral, particularly as one considers its exemplification in body movement.

body parts but ideas or feelings that are intangible or, in regard to some phenomena, ineffable (as in the religious-spiritual sphere). One might say, then, that "objects" as apprehended or known are the embodiments of "ideas." We recognize that this notion can be traced back to Plato. In this scheme, the abstract and intangible is manifested in the body and manifested or "objectified" in things in the world.

We may gain clarity by considering the crescendo as an example. The crescendo is something slowly mounting, mounting and then culminating. This is a body rhythm. It is also a phenomenon found in music. So we see that this is a way of organizing the sensory manifold, a patterning of experience or a structure imposed on experience. Freud would argue that the crescendo is invariably a sexual symbol, that any crescendo phenomenon finds its ultimate referent in the sphere of the body. For example, if a person dreams of climbing a staircase, Freud would claim that this had to do with sexual intercourse. Without denying that "referring downwards" may often be appropriate, I can suggest that a form such as a staircase or a ladder embodies some "higher" idea such as the idea of spiritual ascent. Needless to say, if one's ontology does not allow the possibility of "referring upwards," it is not possible to arrive at the latter interpretation. If, on the other hand, one's ontology allows it, then a symbol can be interpreted in both ways, as *referring in both directions simultaneously*. In this sense, the symbol has a fundamental ambiguity, an inherent bivalence or bidirectionality. This is well illustrated in the significance of cockfighting in Balinese culture, as interpreted by Geertz (1971).

Unfortunately, psychology in general still tends to be positivistic. The interpretation of the spiritual or mental in terms of the material and the corporeal prevails, and so too the interpreting of symbols downwards. We have come to think of this as scientific, and it is relatively unquestioned. I am suggesting that it is not necessarily scientific and that it is an approach which requires questioning of the most serious nature. Following Jung, Eliade, and others, we must consider interpreting symbols anagogically, that is, as going from the material to the "spiritual" as well as the reverse. As indicated above, we must understand that just as the symbolizing process involves transcending domains through simultaneous patternings of experience in differing spheres, so symbols can refer "upwards" and "downwards" simultaneously. It is this double reference that allows symbols to function as integrative forms—uniting the material and the spiritual, the literal and the metaphoric, the perceptual and the rational, body and soul.

ACKNOWLEDGMENTS

This chapter is an edited version of my remarks at the Wheelock College conference, infused with some elements of my paper "The Mythical World of the Child," presented at a symposium at the AAAS meetings in Boston, Massachusetts in 1976. I would very much like to thank Margery B. Franklin for her skill in recovering the sense of my comments and for relating them to the AAAS paper.

REFERENCES

Arnheim, R. *Visual thinking*. Berkeley: Univerisity of California Press, 1969.

Bryson, L., Finkelstein, L., Hoagland, L., & MacIver, R. M. (Eds.). *Symbols and values*. New York: Harper & Bros., 1954.

Bryson, L., Finkelstein, L., Hoagland, L., & MacIver, R. M. (Eds.). *Symbols and society*. New York: Harper & Bros., 1955.

Burke, K. *Language as symbolic action*. Berkeley: University of California Press, 1966(a).

Burke, K. *The philosophy of literary form*. Berkeley: University of California Press, 1966 (originally published, 1941). (b)

Campbell, J. *The masks of god: Primitive mythology*. New York: The Viking Press, 1959.

Cassirer, E. *Essay on man*. New Haven, Conn.: Yale University Press, 1944.

Cassirer, E. *Philosophy of symbolic forms* (Vol. I: Language). New Haven, Conn.: Yale University Press, 1953 (original German Ed., 1923).

Cassirer, E. *Philosophy of symbolic forms* (Vol. II: Mythical Thought). New Haven, Conn.: Yale University Press, 1955 (original German ed., 1927).

Cassirer, E. *Philosophy of symbolic forms, Vol. III: Phenomenology of knowledge*. New Haven, Conn.: Yale University Press, 1957 (original German ed., 1929).

Eliade, M. *Myth and reality*. New York: Harper & Row, 1963.

Geertz, C. Deep play: Notes on the Balinese cockfight. In C. Geertz (Ed.), *Myth, symbol and culture*. New York: Norton, 1971.

Kaplan, B. Radical metaphor, aesthetic and the origin of language. *Review of Existential Psychology and Psychiatry*, 1962, *2*, 75–84.

Rapaport, D. *Organization and pathology of thought*. New York: Columbia University Press, 1951.

Silberer, H. Report on a method of eliciting and observing certain symbolic hallucination phenomena. In D. Rapaport (Ed.), *Organization and pathology of thought*. New York: Columbia University Press, 1951. (a)

Silberer, H. On symbol-formation. In D. Rapaport (Ed.), *Organization and pathology of thought*. New York: Columbia University Press, 1951. (b)

Urban, W. *Language and reality*. New York: Macmillan, 1939.

Werner, H. *Comparative psychology of mental development*. New York: International Universities Press, 1957 (original German ed., 1926).

Werner, H., & Kaplan, B. *Symbol formation*. New York: Wiley, 1963.

Werner, H., & Kaplan, B. Symbolic mediation and the organization of thought. *Journal of Psychology*, 1957, *43*, 3–25. Reprinted in H. Werner, *Developmental Processes: Heinz Werner's Selected Writings* (S. S. Barten and M. B. Franklin, Eds.) New York: International Universities Press, 1978.

Whitehead, A. N. *Symbolism*. New York: Capricorn, 1959 (originally published, 1927).

Author Index

Subject Index